ANDREW
JOHNSON

ANDREW JOHNSON

THE RENAISSANCE OF AN AMERICAN POLITICIAN

GARRY BOULARD

ANDREW JOHNSON
THE RENAISSANCE OF AN AMERICAN POLITICIAN

iUniverse books may be ordered through booksellers or by contacting:

iUniverse
1663 Liberty Drive
Bloomington, IN 47403
www.iuniverse.com
844-349-9409

ISBN: 978-1-6632-2029-5 (sc)
ISBN: 978-1-6632-2030-1 (e)

Print information available on the last page.

iUniverse rev. date: 04/05/2021

ACKNOWLEDGEMENTS

I am indebted to the following for their timely and helpful assistance: David Albert, Main Serials Paraprofessional, Albuquerque Bernalillo County Library; Aaron Blecha, Library Information Specialist, Zimmerman Library, University of New Mexico; Robert J. Coomer, Director, Illinois Historic Preservation Agency; Nancy Dennis, Assistant Dean, University of New Mexico Libraries; John DeLooper, Special Collections Assistant, Seeley G. Mudd Manuscript Library, Princeton Library; Christine Goch, Head of Reference, Cambria County Library System; William Gilbert Gonzales, Library Assistant, Fine Arts and Design Library, University of New Mexico; Owen Gregory, Archivist, Chicago Board of Trade; Demaris Hill, Circulation Services Senior Manager, Alachua Cuonty Library District; April Hines, Librarian, George A. Smathers Libraries, University of Florida; Ervin L. Jordan, Jr., Research Archivist, Harrison/Small Library, University of Virginia Library; Carl Katafiasz, Head of Ellis Reference, Monroe County Library System; Curtis Mann, Director, Sangamon Valley Collection, Springfield Public Library; Ida Mazzoni, Assistant Director, Albuquerque Bernalillo County Library; John McClure, Reference Department Manager, Virginia Historical Society, Center for Virginia History; Meg McDonald, Interlibrary Loan Specialist, Albuquerque Bernalillo County Library; Mark Patrick, Special Collections Coordinator, Detroit Public Library; Judith Russell, Dean, University Libraries, George A. Smathers Libraries, University of Florida; Karen Schmiege, Main Serials Librarian, Albuquerque Bernalillo County Library; David Schneider, Researcher, Special Collections Library, Albuquerque Bernalillo County Library; Cheryl Schnirring, Manuscripts Curator, Abraham Lincoln Presidential Library; and Charmaine Wawrzyniec, Reference Assistant, Ellis Reference and Information Center, Monroe County Library System.

Also, my thanks to Virendra Chudasama, Changhwa Hong, Seyi Oluwaleimu, Nickolas Porraro, Andres Vergara and Ethan White for their continued friendship, support, and good fellowship during the writing of this book.

For Chris Philip

CONTENTS

CHAPTER ONE

AN AIR OF CHRONIC ANXIETY

Around 8 o'clock on the wintry cold rainy evening of February 24, 1868, a Washington correspondent for the *New York Herald* arrived at the White House and amiably tried to push his way through a crowd made up of "women gaily chattering and laughing, policemen shouting, orderlies rushing hither and thither, hackmen roaring, sometimes cursing—Senators, Congressmen, generals, colonels, officials of all kinds and plain citizens of all sorts hurrying to the grand point of attraction." [1]

For the hundreds of well-dressed men and women removing their heavy overcoats in the White House cloakroom as they moved in a boisterous herd towards the Red Room, the "grand point of attraction" was the final official Executive Mansion reception of the season, so described by the *Daily National Intelligencer* as "the most brilliant of the season." [2]

It was a gathering devoted to food, drink, laughter and gossip made all the more fun by the simple fact that the event was coming one week before the onset of Lent.

But for the *Herald* reporter, much more interesting was what was going on in the oval-shaped Blue Room, where he caught sight of a preternaturally grim man, neatly dressed and quietly talking with a small group of visitors.

"Strange that with the Damocles sword of impeachment and destruction suspended over his head he can converse so affably with his hosts of guests," the reporter marveled as he stared at Andrew Johnson, the 17th president of the United States, and first president, as of around 5 p.m., to be impeached by Congress.

This was exciting stuff: presidents had come and gone before. Some were defeated for re-election. One died of natural causes. Abraham Lincoln was assassinated. But no president had ever been forcibly removed from office, and to make it all the more nerve-wracking, that removal would not be by the people, but members of Congress, exercising a power that was always their prerogative, but one few imagined would ever actually be used.

The House of Representatives vote to impeach the president, with his fate now soon to be decided by the Senate, left everyone a little giddy. The members voting on impeachment had been worked up for days, composing and subsequently delivering marvelously complicated speeches for and against the action. To many, it seemed like the most important vote they would ever make and a certain nervousness accompanied their actions.

Meanwhile, reporters ran through the corridors of the Capitol as though they had lost their heads, frantically recording the members' votes and trying to jot down their remarks, while telegraphing news flash alerts on the action to their newspaper offices in New York, Boston, Detroit, Chicago, New Orleans, and dozens of other places in between.

Carriage drivers, soldiers, government clerks, bartenders and the lubricated people they served, everyone, could talk of nothing else: a president was about to be brought down. It all seemed so revolutionary. It was so unprecedented.

But now in the middle of the storm sat Johnson, looking "wonderfully like a man whose mind was at ease, and whose conscience did not torture him for the heinous high crimes charged against him," observed the reporter. [3]

Finally getting the chance to shake Johnson's hand, the reporter asked him about the overwhelming 126 to 47 House impeachment vote, coming after four hours of largely one-sided debate during which Indiana Representative Morton Hunter described the President as a "usurper of power, a supporter of treason, and a disturber of the public peace of the nation." [4]

Kansas Representative Sidney Clarke had charged Johnson with "afflicting the land with disorder, unsettling all business, and making the hearts and homes of the patriotic heavier with suspicion and darker with dread than resulted from all the sorrows of the war," while the slender and bearded John Peter Cleaver Shanks, also of Indiana, got right to the point: "I am in favor of the official death of Andrew Johnson without debate. I am not surprised that one who began his presidential career in drunkenness should end it in crime." [5]

Shanks' drinking reference was a cheap shot. Like many politicians of his day, Johnson drank, but only sporadically, at best. He was not, as Abraham Lincoln once made sure to point out, a drunk.

But during the 1865 inaugural ceremonies officially swearing in Lincoln for a second term as president and Johnson for his first term as vice-president, Johnson was splendidly and entirely drunk, having downed several shots of whiskey moments before the ceremony, compounding a hangover from a party he had attended the previous night.

His physical response may have been more an example of what happens when a man who doesn't usually drink, suddenly does, rather than, as was charged at the time, a man who was a regular drunk.

In either case, reporters, dignitaries, Congressional wives, and others watched Johnson walk uncertainly into the Senate chamber on the arm of outgoing Vice-President Hannibal Hamlin, before delivering a meandering speech defensively recalling his modest roots in a manner that made some listeners think he was not only drunk but deranged.

Michigan Senator Zachariah Chandler, no stranger to getting drunk, claimed that he had "never been so mortified" as when he heard Johnson's remarks, adding "Had I been able to find a hole I would have dropped through it out of sight." [6]

One observer remarked loudly "There's a gas bag." Attorney General James Speed whispered to Navy Secretary Gideon Welles "the man is certainly deranged," while Secretary of State William Seward wondered if Johnson was simply overcome by being back in the Senate where he had once served. [7]

Like Seward, Chief Justice Salmon Chase tried to find an explanation for Johnson's behavior, later saying he was "grieved by the sad conduct of Andy Johnson." But Chase also noted that Johnson was in Washington after three years of Civil War service as the Military Governor of Tennessee, years in which Johnson's life was in daily danger.

"I honor him greatly as one who risked everything for his convictions. There are few who do," Chase continued, before perceptively adding of those convictions: "He has, I think, the martyr spirit and would die for his." [8]

Now, almost exactly four years later, visitors in the packed House gallery could laugh at Shanks' reference to Johnson as a drunk, but his additional use of the word "crime" was anything but funny.

Johnson was officially being accused of "high crimes and misdemeanors," a phrase written in Article Two of the U.S. Constitution designed to cover a broad range of offenses. The specific charges would soon be formally submitted to the Senate, but the spirit of the House vote was animated by Johnson's decision to dismiss Edwin Stanton from his post as Secretary of War.

In so doing, Johnson's Radical Republican foes charged, he had violated the spirit and intent of the Tenure of Office Act, a constitutionally dubious law forbidding the President from getting rid of any of his cabinet secretaries without the prior approval of Congress.

This was a serious charge to be compounded as the impeachment managers presented their case in the Senate, and delivered in an atmosphere portending not only the removal of a sitting U.S. president, but also, as Pennsylvania Representative Thaddeus Stevens put it, the possibility of imprisonment "in the penitentiary afterward under criminal proceedings." [9]

Johnson, to a growing rank of detractors, was entirely a criminal, a man who had gone out of his way to illegally frustrate the will of Congress.

It wasn't that he had vetoed a series of Radical Republican acts designed to reconstruct the South along more humane racial lines. Those vetoes were reluctantly acknowledged as perfectly legal actions that were nevertheless also seen as personal affronts to an unprecedentedly aggressive Congress. And besides, the vetoes were all easily overridden.

It was in getting rid of the prickly Stanton, after being warned that such a move would lead to his impeachment, that Johnson engaged in what was seen as a clearly illegal action, daring, in the process, Congress to do something about it.

"I rejoice in the madness of this last act of his brazen defiance of the Constitution and the laws," declared Indiana Representative George Julian in noting that the sacking of Stanton had given to Johnson's foes the weapon they needed to at last end his presidency. "The devil has come to our rescue just at the point where the courage and virtue of men give way."

Continued Julian, whose contempt for Johnson was steeped in themes of personal betrayal, having early on hoped for so much more from him, "We are indebted to the stupid rebel malignity of Andrew Johnson for the courage which at last shall hurl him from the White House and consign him once more to the fond embrace of his rebel confederates in the South and their faithful allies in the North." [10]

The impeachment vote was front page news in papers and a galvanizing call to arms for voters across the country who had come to despise the President. "Congressional Republicans received bagfuls of mail congratulating them on a deed long overdue," historian Brenda Wineapple has noted of the immediate anti-Johnson response to the impeachment vote. [11]

James Sheppard Pike in the *New York Tribune,* one-time ambassador to the Netherlands who had returned to the U.S. and his former occupation as a reporter in 1866, was, like Julian, animated by a sense that the President had turned on the very people who had voted for the Lincoln-Johnson ticket in 1864. "He has gone over to the enemy, and turns all his guns upon those who gave him command of their citadels."

"These facts admit of no dispute, whatever may be the pretenses offered in excuse," continued Pike. "With or without apology, he thus stands before the world an apostate and a traitor in every essential feature of his conduct." [12]

But while it may have seemed that forces larger than he was capable of battling were now conspiring against him, Johnson was not without support. He, too, was receiving bagfuls of mail; letters and cards both elegantly and crudely written, attesting to a grass roots backing of a President who was viewed as the only thing standing between the Constitution and legislative anarchy.

"The bone and sinew of the Republic are with you," wrote O.W. Gardner of Boston on the day of the impeachment vote. "We appreciate and admire the noble stance you have taken and are pursuing for upholding the Constitution and civil liberty." [13]

In a country not quite three years removed from the bloodiest war in the nation's history, Johnson enthusiasts did not see their support for him as the stuff of idle café chatter, but a summons to action.

"Permit me on behalf of one hundred well-disciplined men to say that I am at your service at a moment's notice to aid you in sustaining your cause," policeman James Mc Laughlin wrote to Johnson from New York. [14]

"I offer you my humble service & life in any capacity which you may see fit to use them," declared Joseph Leigh of Petersburg, Virginia. [15]

From Omaha, James Hammond emphatically told Johnson: "I take this opportunity to offer you the service of 75 good men as a personal guard, all of whom are ready to give their lives in the cause of liberty and the protection of the respected Chief Magistrate of the nation." [16]

The Congressional anarchy most feared by the President's supporters was suddenly inspiring an anarchy all of itself in response: "Offers of armed support swamped the president," notes impeachment historian David Stewart. "He could have 1,000 men from New Jersey and a regiment of Kentuckians, or 30,000 Virginians, 2,000 from Louisiana, and 100,000 from Missouri."[17]

The reports, the rumors, the whispers of an angry, inchoate armed response from the hills and farmlands and tough working class districts of the cities, only naturally unnerved Johnson's congressional foes, many of whom began to imagine unwashed mobs rushing up the steps of the Capitol, smashing their way through the ornate polished wooden doors of the House chamber, and putting to use the business ends of their rifles.

Noting the prospect of "tumult and bloodshed," Congressman Julian presented a brave front, trying to reassure his anxious colleagues that if an assault was in the making, "ten thousand swords will leap from their scabbards, a million bayonets, at the first bugle call, will glisten in the sun."

Julian, perhaps also trying to convince himself, additionally promised: "Brave heroes will fill up the ranks: the honor of the old flag will be maintained; peace and quiet will be restored, and the nations of the earth will again learn that ours is a government of law." [18]

Julian was most likely greatly reassured when he learned that Illinois Republican Senator John Alexander Logan, who had helped organize the massive veterans group known as the Grand Army of the Republic, an organization with more than 300,000 members, would soon move into the War Department where he would sleep on a cot, ready at a moment's notice to command any number of armed veterans tasked with crushing a Johnson-inspired guerilla attack on Washington.

In the middle of this whirlwind, with threats flying in every direction, and the specter of violence growing seemingly by the hour, stood Johnson himself, calm and, if possible, contemplative.

Reporters in Washington, members of Congress, even some in his own cabinet, regularly missed an essential feature of Johnson's makeup. Coming from the most modest roots imaginable, and associating throughout his lifetime with people disenfranchised, disillusioned and one paycheck away from desperation, Johnson sincerely believed himself a tribune of the people. He knew them all: the blacksmiths, carpenters, farmers, mechanics and others who actually worked for a living. He knew their struggles, he knew their dreams, he knew their disappointments. He knew them, because for so long he had shared those same struggles, dreams, and disappointments.

And the laborers of the country felt they knew him, too. Crudely-composed letters to Johnson marked with misspellings from men and women not at all comfortable writing letters, attested to their belief that he cared about them, that he was, in the end, one of them.

That idea, that support that Johnson had seen and heard and read of so many times in his career, provided him with a confidence and even arrogance that he was at all times doing the right thing. He had never been a part of the Southern plantation aristocracy, nor was he a Boston or New York blueblood with a sterling family lineage.

He was instead a man of the people, and certain that in this role, he was always doing the right thing. It was, in fact, impossible for him to imagine that he could do anything different.

Johnson had hosted a glittering state dinner for the diplomatic corps two nights earlier, an affair thick with the ministers and their wives from

England, France, Greece, Italy, Portugal and a dozen other countries, and seemed entirely indifferent to the question of Congress impeaching him. "I know they are capable of anything," he responded with an air of resignation.

Did he then actually think an impeachment resolution would be voted out of Congress? "I don't know, indeed," he answered. "Nor do I care." [19]

On the day of that impeachment vote, Johnson was pacific, telling a correspondent "God and the American people would make all right and save our institutions." [20]

Now the *New York Herald* reporter, at last getting a chance to talk with the President in the Blue Room, expressed surprise that Johnson seemed so tranquil in the midst of such chaos. Responded Johnson: "I have no doubt that it will all come out right yet." [21]

Johnson, in fact, had two reasons to be tranquil. The first was his sense that his opponents could never really muster the two-thirds vote needed in the Senate to oust him. There would be a lot of noise and fury, but at the end of the day it would finally come to nothing.

But he also secretly *wanted* to be convicted, thought reporter Joseph McCullagh, who enjoyed a long conversation with the President on the matter, noting that "he rather courted the martyrdom of it."

"He said if they convicted him, he would start out through the country with a view of convicting them before the people," continued McCullagh, who imagined Johnson railing from city to city and village to village, castigating the Radical Republicans who stole the presidency from him.

"Nothing would have suited him better," remarked McCullagh. [22]

For now, Johnson's even-keeled response, soon to be reported in newspapers across the country, made the President seem not just sublime, but above it all, unbothered by the petty machinations of a petty Congress.

But the impression was illusory and at odds with a man who, in private encounters, declined to engage in the amiable kind of "kicking it around the table" exercises that Lincoln enjoyed when discussing a particular issue with members of his cabinet.

Colleagues had remarked upon it for years. In Cabinet meetings, in the caucus gatherings of fellow party members when he was a Senator, in meetings with state lawmakers when he was the governor of Tennessee: Johnson was very often the quietest man in the room.

In fact, he sometimes seemed downright indifferent to whatever discussion was going on around him, sitting upright, with his hands folded on his lap, nodding in the direction of the last person speaking in a way that seemed to signal agreement, but usually signaled nothing at all.

But then he might suddenly become argumentative, sometimes absurdly so, especially when a colleague or visitor dared to voice an opinion different from his own.

Serving with Johnson in the Senate in the late 1850s, Jefferson Davis many times witnessed a pattern: "Some casual word dropped in debate, though uttered without a thought of his existence, would seem to wound him to the quick," Davis recalled. After such an explosion, Davis noted, Johnson would "shrink back into the self-imposed isolation of his earlier and humbler life."

Davis, in these remarks, was playing too much the innocent. He knew, as a blueblood, exactly the words and phrases and inferences that aroused Johnson's fury. Anything that seemed to remind Johnson of his imagined social inferiority would set him off. So would arcane discussions about the Constitution, a topic upon which Johnson was sure he possessed a superior knowledge.

Even so, Davis, rather cruelly, attributed much of Johnson's explosiveness to his pride, or as he put it, "the pride of having no pride." [23]

Similarly, Ulysses S. Grant on many occasions observed a strangely quiet Johnson in cabinet meetings suddenly launching into an insulting interrogation of a department head, administrative bureaucrat, or military official who may have said stated an opinion different from his own.

Once offering his ideas on the course he thought Johnson should take in the aftermath of the disastrous 1866 mid-term elections, Grant tellingly reported to a colleague: "It elicited nothing satisfactory from him, but did not bring out the strong opposition he sometimes shows to views not agreeing with his own." [24]

General William Tecumseh Sherman noted the same pattern. Initially hoping for Johnson's success, he soon found himself disenchanted with the way the President went about making decisions. "He never heeds any advice," Sherman had written several days before the impeachment vote.

"He is like a General fighting without an army," Sherman continued. "He is like Lear roaring at the wild storm, bareheaded and helpless." [25]

Even Johnson's admirers admitted these things were so. "The President was doomed to conflict," said his aide William Crook, who, after first distrusting Johnson in the early days of his presidency, soon grew to respect his work habits and ethics.

"He was a man who found it impossible to conciliate or temporize," continued Crook. "As uncompromising as the terms of his speech, as straight as the challenge of his eye, Andrew Johnson's opinions and policies did not change. His goal being ahead of him, and seen in a clear light, he neither saw nor considered possible an indirect path to that goal."

"It was inevitable," added Crook, "when other men were going in opposite ways, that there should be a collision." [26]

Gideon Welles, habitually annoyed by almost everyone and everything, seemed to feel a kinship with the President that was perhaps forged by their shared sourness: "Few men have stronger feeling; still fewer have the power of restraining themselves when evidently excited," he said of Johnson. [27]

In the early weeks after Lincoln's assassination, when almost everyone wished Johnson well, a reporter for the *St. Louis Republican* seemed to suggest, despite the initial romanticization of Johnson and his storied past, that all was not as it seemed with the new President. Studying Johnson's face, the reporter noted: "He has an apparent frown on his countenance, even in repose. He is of the cold-blooded order, no blood in the face, and understands the sardonic grin to perfection." [28]

When Charles Dickens visited Johnson in the White House, the great novelist was taken by two things. A sign on the wall in the President's outer office instructing guests to "kindly use the spittoons," and Johnson's chilly presence.

Johnson's face, thought Dickens, was "not imaginative, but very powerful in its firmness (or perhaps obstinacy), strength of will, and steadiness of purpose."

The President was "not a man to be turned or trifled with," continued Dickens. "A man, I should say, who must be killed to be got out of the way. His manner is perfectly composed. We looked at one another pretty hard. There was an air of chronic anxiety about him; but not a crease or ruffle in his dress, and his papers were as composed as himself." [29]

Despite these varied accounts of Johnson's private behavior, the full of his personality had for years been easily seen in public when he made a speech, particularly of the off-the-cuff variety that had served him so well back in the rural town squares of Tennessee. These long harangues, punctuated by attacks of a most personal nature on his opponents and sometimes inaccurate quotations from the Bible, Constitution, or great works of literature, were splenetic events obviously cathartic to an explosive personality, and always regarded as lively entertainment to listeners sitting on wooden benches in the summer heat who were willing to take in a performance that could last for up to four hours.

But the harangues would prove spectacularly less successful once Johnson became president, especially in the fall of 1866 when he travelled around the country with a trainload of administration officials, including an entirely embarrassed Grant, engaging in increasingly vituperative exchanges with ordinary citizens, and sometimes, admittedly, thugs hired by Johnson's foes who turned out to harass him.

Johnson paid a steep political price for his outbursts on what became popularly known as the "swing around the circle," losing the support of major metropolitan newspapers as well as moderate members of Congress who had been, until then, willing to give him the benefit of the doubt.

"He is perverse, distempered, ignorant & thoroughly wrong," Massachusetts Senator Charles Sumner, who had long ago given up on the notion that Johnson could ever do anything right, wrote in the aftermath of the trip, as those moderate lawmakers joined his ranks. [30]

"Was there ever such a braying Ass as Johnson?" asked the poet Lydia Maria Child who had once numbered herself among his admirers. [31]

Said the *Chicago Tribune*: "The national interest in the disgraceful conduct of the man is that he is the President, and to that extent the country is involved in the disgrace." [32]

The opposition to Johnson not only became substantially larger after the conclusion of the swing around the circle, in many ways it also became more irrational, with prominent Radical Republicans in Washington soon fantasizing about ways to lay low his administration, and launching several premature and clearly ill-thought-out moves to impeach him more than a year before that action became a fact.

Those moves alarmed Benjamin Brown French, long-time federal Commissioner of Public Buildings, who said he had heard of a particular Radical Republican bid to purchase for $50,000 one or several letters that Johnson was said to have written to John Wilkes Booth, Lincoln's assassin.

French thought the idea of a Johnson-Booth correspondence was ridiculous, but nevertheless felt comfortable enough one day to ask Johnson point blank: "Did you ever write a letter to Booth?"

Johnson, who had gotten wind of the same rumors of a correspondence with the infamous actor, responded immediately: "Never!" adding "I never saw the man, to my knowledge." [33]

French, who had personally known every president going back to Andrew Jackson, subsequently said of Johnson: "I sincerely believe him to be the most unjustly persecuted man I ever knew, and have an abiding faith that he will come out of the furnace pure gold, undefiled by the wicked and malicious attempts that demagogues and villains are making to ruin him." [34]

But despite the fact of loyalists like French, Johnson knew he could never again let loose in public the way he did during the swing around the circle. After 1866 his public addresses were for the most part stiffly formal affairs, restrained entirely by notes he had written out beforehand.

Yet Andrew Johnson would not be muzzled. There were still available to him places and times when he could let his feelings be known.

One venue was through the device of the open public letter, a practice he had most controversially put to use in early 1868 when he sent a tendentious more than 3,000-word communication to Grant that made all of the newspapers and enraged Congress, arguing over whether or not the General had ever agreed to permanently replace the dismissed Stanton.

That letter provided Johnson's foes with only the latest proof that he was needlessly combative, and perhaps mentally unbalanced, while Johnson supporters saw the document as evidence that he was a strong president, on top of his job, and much too smart to be done in by the vicissitudes of bureaucratic betrayal.

More effectively, Johnson additionally got a chance to air his grievances whenever a citizen's group visited the White House, often to lobby for a particular issue or to simply present Johnson with a petition or plaque of appreciation.

Dreadfully boring events in practice, such encounters, with the visitors uncomfortably grouped together, awed by the ornate surroundings of the White House, were a regular part of the Washington press corps' beat, and for that reason Johnson astutely perceived that they could be exploited for a larger purpose.

Two days after the House impeachment vote, in fact, a group of prominent Baltimore leaders called upon the president, asking for his help in protecting the rights of Americans living in foreign countries.

Johnson showed interest, promising to do all he could to satisfy the pleas of the delegation. Then he quickly transitioned into his first official extended remarks since the impeachment vote.

"I beg you to believe that in an honest effort to faithfully discharge the high and responsible duties imposed upon me by the Constitution and the laws, I will consider no personal sacrifice too great for me to bear," Johnson said.

"From my advent into public life, now some years ago, until the present time, I have passed through many ordeals in the struggle for the interest of the people," he continued.

Never, not for a moment, he said, had he "swerved from the straight line of duty."

On the contrary, he could honestly say that "as of yet there has been no occasion when having been assigned to the duty, I have abandoned my post."

Perhaps referencing those many who would, indeed, pick up arms to defend him, Johnson continued: "I rely now, as in the past, upon the intelligence, the patriotism, and the virtue of the American people, who I believe will come in all their might and strength to the rescue of their country and save it from the distraction which now seems to threaten its ruin."

Johnson did not, of course, actually want to issue a physical call to arms. He averred chaos as much as the next person, and had seen enough of it in wartime Tennessee to last a lifetime.

But he did imagine and was greatly sustained by the idea that untold millions were at his back, representing the true American idea that seemed to so elude his Congressional critics. To this end, Johnson told the Baltimoreans, "I will perform my duty, let the consequences be what they may." [35]

His Baltimore visitors may have wondered what any of this had to do with the rights of Americans overseas. But for anyone else who knew Johnson, the reporters, friends, foes, and family members who comprised so much of his daily life, the inference was clear: on the matter of his being forcibly removed from the White House, he was going to fight.

In the end, it was the one sure thing that Andrew Johnson knew to do.

CHAPTER TWO

"The Union Has Found a Gallant Defender"

Andrew Johnson never forgot what it was like to want; to crave food and shelter and clothing. "I have grappled with the gaunt and haggard monster called hunger," Johnson evenly remarked in his later years, personifying the belief that a hungry childhood always makes for a lifelong appetite. [1]

At a deeper level, Johnson additionally craved the stability that he assumed belonged to those who were wealthy and didn't have to endure the ordeal for essential survival that he and everyone else he knew suffered on a daily basis. Wanting what an imagined elite had, he early on also felt an unbridled contempt for that same elite.

Born on December 29, 1808 in Raleigh, North Carolina, Johnson's hopelessness seemed especially foreordained three years later when his father, Jacob Johnson, died from a heart attack most likely caused by pneumonia, several days after saving two men from drowning in the icy waters of Hunter's Mill Pond.

The Raleigh death of one more poor person in what was then a place of less than 1,000 people was of little notice to the world, and it wasn't until 1867, when Johnson was president, that a citizen's group erected a monument to Jacob's memory. "He was my father, and of him I am proud," Johnson remarked at the monument's unveiling.

Johnson added that his father was "an honest man and faithful friend, a character I prize higher than all the world fortune which could have been left me." [2]

While his mother, Mary "Polly" McDonough Johnson, 29 years old at the time of Jacob Johnson's death, tried to provide for Andrew and his older brother William for the most part of the next decade, she eventually agreed to sign over an adolescent Andrew, along with his brother, as indentured servants to a Raleigh tailor named James J. Selby, who pledged to train the two boys as tailors.

This was a promising development offering Andrew and William the chance to learn a trade singular in small town and urban America. "The tailor was a familiar and essential figure in the life of the community," note Leroy Graf and Rudolph Haskins, the editors of Andrew Johnson's papers.

"Not only did he fashion the usual articles of masculine apparel—coats, vests, pants and greatcoats—but he also mended clothing and cut out garments for others," the editors add. [3]

As was typical of many tailor shops across the country, Selby's business was additionally a place where men congregated, talking about this and that, but sometimes, of particular fascination to the young Johnson, the issues of the day.

One such man was a colorful British radical named Hugh Wolstenholme, who must have been treasured by the other habitues of Shelby's shop for his entertainment value, reading aloud from a proletarian protest newspaper called the *Sheffield Iris*. [4]

It must have been difficult for the young Johnson to entirely pay attention to the trimming of a vest while listening to Wolstenholme, who also enjoyed reading from the Bible and works of Shakespeare. Not only did these performances excite in Johnson an appreciation for the written word, but just as vitally, the written word as spoken.

Johnson's association with Wolstenholme, who would eventually find solace in a remote one-room cabin in the woods outside Raleigh, came to an abrupt end when he and bother William in the early summer of 1824 decided to run away, thereby illegally breaking their contract with Selby.

Exactly why the boys fled from Selby would never be known, but if Johnson's personality as an adult provides a clue, it may well have had something to do with Selby pushing too hard.

Selby shortly ran an ad in the *Raleigh Gazette* that would one day be reproduced in dozens of national newspapers and Johnson biographies, undoubtedly because it was so suggestive of similar listings for escaped slaves: "Ran away from the Subscriber, on the night of the 15th instant, two apprentice boys, legally bound, named William and Andrew Johnson," Selby wrote, offering a reward of $10 for anyone who could "deliver said apprentices to me in Raleigh, or I will give the above reward for Andrew Johnson alone."

Although Selby inadvertently reversed descriptions of the boys, what he wrote of Johnson's appearance was the first documented account of him physically, making note of his "dark complexion, black hair, eyes and habits." The notion of a young boy with "dark habits" may have seemed peculiar to readers of the *Gazette*, but undoubtedly served to underline what was even then a sort of brooding, forlorn presence powerful enough for Selby to think worth mentioning.

That Selby also made a point of declaring that he would settle for just "Andrew Johnson alone," also indicated that he regarded Andrew as the more talented of the two brothers. [5]

In the months to come Johnson, later acknowledging that he left Raleigh a "penniless and inexperienced boy, to make my way in the world," took several detours and adroitly avoided anyone who may have been pursuing him. At some point he wandered about on his own, with William going off in a different direction. [6]

It was a dizzying, nerve-wracking journey into the unknown that Johnson would repeat nearly four decades later, on the run in Tennessee and Kentucky, during the early months of the Civil war when Confederates, angered by Johnson's pro-Union stance, had vowed to kill him on sight.

Johnson eventually ended up nearly 300 miles to the east in Greeneville, Tennessee, a town of just a few hundred people hugging the Appalachian Mountain range. Reunited with brother William and his mother and step-father, Johnson defiantly rented out a small shop, hanging a wooden sign above the building's front door reading simply "A. Johnson. Tailor."

It was in Greeneville that Johnson's fortunes took a decided turn for the better. He met Elizabeth McCardle, a shoemaker's daughter, who encouraged his interests in writing and reading by teaching him composition.

Married in the spring of 1827, the couple would eventually have three sons: Charles, Robert and Andrew, Jr., with two daughters, Martha and Mary.

At some point during this time Johnson, in his endless pursuit to read everything he could get his hands on, got hold of a copy of the U.S. Constitution and from the opening words "We the People," couldn't stop reading it, transfixed by the grace, flow and meaning of the language, responding to it with what would become an almost religious fervor.

For him, the Constitution was proof not only of America's superiority as a country, but that its system of government was designed to protect democracy, and with it the interests of even the poorest person (excepting, of course, slaves). His reading and, through the years, constant re-reading of the document inspired both an expansive and limited view of the world. Expansive in the sense of the states possessing the supreme power in the country. Limited, in that almost any program coming out of Washington was one that had to be viewed with inordinate suspicion, a view that, as president, would greatly circumscribe his dealings with Congress.

For better or worse, his reverence for the Constitution, and his own personal interpretation of it, would prove a daily constant for the rest of his life, providing a stability in a country that sometimes seemed unstable, and order during times of great disorder.

Stability and order. As though he was trying to put forever behind him the chaos and dirt of his youth, Johnson by his early 20s would always be impeccably dressed, his nails cut, boots shined, hair coiffed, habits he embraced for the rest of his life. Cleanliness was an obsession.

Even more, papers on his office desk were invariably stacked in a neat pile, systematically read and acted upon, and then put in another neat pile before being neatly stored away. As president, Johnson's quest for order would see him implement the first comprehensive White House filing and storage system, with his secretaries and aides depositing all correspondence and documents in clearly-marked folders for convenient access.

In Greeneville, Johnson's tailor shop prospered. He knew his trade, was good at what he did, and delivered his product promptly. "My work never ripped or gave away," he would one day recall, eventually hiring several journeymen tailors to keep up with the demand. [7]

An example of the shop's vitality was seen in a letter he some years later wrote to friend and lawyer Robert Reynold, remarking "Please pardon this incoherent scrawl, there has been seven or ten men in my shop since I commenced writing this letter. I have been expecting the mail every minute." [8]

As with Selby in Raleigh, the Johnson shop was a place attracting men who wanted to shoot the breeze, occasionally or sometimes very often discussing political affairs. Johnson, it was soon noted, rarely held back when it came to the issues of the day, expressing opinions on any number of topics noted for the confident, if sometimes didactic, manner in which they were delivered.

In a small county and even smaller town, a young man with energy and imagination can go far, and Johnson had both. At the age of 27 he was elected to the first of eight one-year terms to the local board of aldermen, serving as mayor in both 1834 and 1837.

From a run-away apprentice to chief executive of a small town in just eight years was an impressive advance by anyone's measure, but not really that unusual in a time when the nation was young and the vast majority of the adult generation uneducated, unlettered men of the frontier happy to turn over the complicated work of local governance to anyone who exhibited ability.

Not surprisingly, having made a name for himself locally, Johnson by 1834 was an obvious candidate for the state legislature, winning the first of two terms in both the House and later Senate, advocating for the rights of the working man and eventually angering powerful interests when he unsuccessfully proposed doing away with a law that gave slaveholders more representation in the legislature than non-slave holders.

His reputation would soon be established: he enjoyed and was effective at public speaking, was a hard-working public servant, and nearly always preoccupied with winning one for the workingman against the aristocratic interests.

As Johnson moved up the political ladder, he additionally enjoyed a measurable amount of material success. He purchased at auction the two-room building on Main Street that served as his tailor shop, and later built a handsome two-story brick house across the street for his family. From there he eventually bought a much more splendid eight-room structure, also with two stories, known locally as the Homestead, a building that he would also add onto.

His increasing wealth allowed Johnson to additionally purchase several slaves, although none were used for traditional plantation work, all confining their labors to working as his servants. How many slaves Johnson would actually own remains unknown, although it was certainly never more than ten, and may have been less than five. One particular slave named Sam proved demanding and, according to Johnson's daughter Martha, may have been more Johnson's master than the other way around. [9]

By 1840, Johnson as a state legislator had developed very definite ideas on how public campaigns at any level of government should be conducted, preferring to speak for hours on end in public squares, eviscerating opponents, but at the same time giving a serious airing to the issues of hand.

For that reason, he was offended by the successful 1840 presidential campaign of General and Whig Party nominee William Henry Harrison who, after being attacked by one newspaper for secretly wanting nothing more than to retire to his log cabin where he could drink hard cider, was promoted in endless rallies, posters, and pamphlets as the log cabin and hard cider candidate.

This effort, said Johnson with no small amount of disdain, "was not conducted on principle. The people were addressed with bacchanalian songs, and the arguments presented to them were log cabins, baboons, coons, gourds, foxes, and a thousand other things too tedious to mention." [10]

Just three years later Johnson won the first of five terms in the U.S. House representing East Tennessee. The move to Washington, which he made without his wife, although daughter Martha came along with him, would have been life-altering for anyone else leaving rural Tennessee, even though Johnson had already served for eight years in Nashville, a growing city of 7,000 people in the early 1840s.

Washington's population was nearly five times larger with just under 34,000 people, and as the nation's capital was also a hub of political, cultural, and business activity. There is no evidence that Johnson partook in the social swirl of Washington that was so dominated by wealthy Southern plantation owners, preferring instead to spend his free hours wandering through the stacks of the Library of Congress, constantly trying to satisfy an appetite to read and learn.

Early on, Johnson admitted, the job of being a Congressman threatened to overwhelm him, a situation greatly at variance with the control he normally exerted over everything he did. "I have to attend to the business of 11,000 freemen, and a letter here and one there." Eventually, Johnson continued, such correspondence "amounts to an immense quantity of business."

"I must confess I had but a poor conception of it myself till placed in my present position," Johnson added. [11]

But he soon enough got used to the demands of the job and, increasingly confident as a legislator, often criticized his own Democrat party for what he regarded as its lack of leadership, supported the Mexican-American War, backed bringing Texas into the Union, and promoted religious tolerance during a time of rising resentment in America due to the increased immigration of people from Ireland and Germany, the majority of whom were Catholics.

"The Catholics of this country had the right secured to them by the constitution of worshipping the God of their fathers in the manner dictated to them by their own consciences," Johnson declared, warning that any move to punish or ostracize them "would find a majority of the people" opposed. [12]

The election of fellow Tennessean James Knox Polk to the White House in 1844 should have been a moment of triumph for Johnson, providing him with the kind of access and influence other Congressmen could only hope for. But Polk, angry that Johnson had not supported him prior to the Democratic convention, ignored most of Johnson's requests for federal jobs and other favors. By the summer of 1846, Johnson told long-time friend Blackston McDannel, "In relation to the appointments made by the President, I have but little to say, having signally failed in everyone I desired." [13]

Johnson would eventually accuse Polk of "low cunning." [14]

The feeling was mutual: combining Johnson with fellow Tennessee Congressman George Jones, Polk confided to his diary "I would almost prefer to have two Whigs here in their stead, unless they act better than they have done in the present session of Congress." [15]

While Johnson, by 1847, had every reason to feel satisfied with his life and career, he remained edgy and remote. He had friends, but most felt they never truly knew him, a feeling that didn't abate even after he became a member of the Masonic Order of Freemasonry, following the examples of George Washington, James Monroe, Andrew Jackson and James K. Polk. He remained loyal for the rest of his life to a secret society that he made no secret of being a part of, one that only required, at best, twice-monthly attendance and good fellowship.

Yet for all of his career success and social station, Johnson remained edgy and remote. He had friends, but most felt that they never truly knew him. And the many more who admired him did so from a distance. In essence, even in the best of times, Johnson was very often sullen and unable to shake off the shadows of his boyhood and his resentments of those who had more.

"The refined and cultivated he apparently disliked," noted Oliver P. Temple, who would run against Johnson for Congress in 1847 and remained a lifelong Johnson observer. "These reminded him of his own deficiencies, and in the depths of his heart he detested them."

"In fact," added Temple, "he hated everything superior to himself." [16]

One Sunday in early 1847 Johnson wrote to McDannel complaining about a property transaction in Greeneville that had not worked out to his satisfaction and announcing that he was sick of the town: "If I should happen to die among the dam spirits that infest Greeneville, my last request before death would be for some friend (if I had no friend, which is highly probable), I would bequeath the last dollar to some Negro to pay to take my dirty, stinky carcass after death out on some mountain peak and there leave it to be devoured by vultures and wolves, or make a fire sufficiently large to consume the smallest particle, that it might pass off in smoke and ride upon the wind in triumph over the god-forsaken and Hell-deserving, money-loving, hypocritical, back-biting, Sunday praying scoundrels of the town of Greeneville."

This missive, extraordinary even by Johnson's normally gloomy standards, suggested that in the end there was no one in life he could rely upon, not even members of his own family, and that upon his death it would be a stranger, not a loved one, who would see to his remains. His reference additionally to paying "some Negro" to do the job showed obviously that he didn't think any of his slaves would do the deed, in particular the always-complaining Sam.

The vultures and wolves that would devour his remains cannot be too far removed from the real and imagined enemies Johnson had in life, foes, some of them more powerful and wealthy than he, who would be only too happy to see him decimated, or so he always thought.

Yet the ultimate imagery of smoke from his burned body floating over Greeneville allows this vision of a personal dystopia to conclude on a high note: he would "ride upon the wind in triumph" far above and over the petty malcontents who had tried to grind him down.

What McDannel must have thought upon receiving this explosion can only be imagined. Perhaps he knew Johnson well enough to realize that he was capable of violent bursts of anger that were often followed by an eerie calm, which was on display in the same letter only several sentences later when Johnson signed off: "Please accept my assurances of a sincere friendship." [17]

The fury expressed by Johnson in his correspondence with McDannel was for the most part rooted in his ongoing fear of being marginalized either socially, politically, or financially. But its possible that the blackness that persistently visited him was at least somewhat animated by any number of physical ailments of which he regularly complained.

He would soon become an enthusiast of a commercial nostrum called Arnold's Great Union Pills, advertised as being good for "complaints of the head and breast, stomach and bowels, liver and spleen, kidneys and urinary organs." [18]

The product was in everyway medically worthless, its only function being one as a placebo. But Johnson was convinced the pills were a "sovereign remedy with me for all complaints." [19]

Johnson may have also addressed what ailed him with liquor, although the evidence was scant that he was in any way an alcoholic. In the fall of 1848, Johnson regaled McDannel with an account of his going to Baltimore with several friends for a night of dining, the theater, and much drinking. The imbibing went on throughout the evening and well into the early morning, with Johnson back at his desk in Washington by 11 a.m., "neither sick, drunk nor groggy." [20]

The hours-long drinking bout could be seen as evidence of a man with a substance abuse issue, but everything about the evening was out of character for Johnson, including his viewing a troupe of pubescent Viennese girls dancing on the stage of Baltimore's Front Street Theater, "all dressed up in the richest and most gaudy manner, performing every imaginable evolution." [21]

The fact that Johnson felt compelled to give McDannel a detailed account of his adventures in Baltimore was more proof than anything else that the evening, including his alcohol consumption, was out of ordinary for a man who rarely allowed himself the pleasures of a night on the town and the comradery of carousing companions, let alone a bout of serious drinking.

During the fall of 1848, the 40 year-old Johnson made the acquaintance of Abraham Lincoln, who was then serving his only term in Congress as a Whig representing central Illinois. While the 6'4" Lincoln was half a foot taller than the 5'10" inch Johnson, Johnson was nearly a month and a half older.

The two men on several occasions conversed informally, at one point speculating on members of the far-flung Lincoln family tree who may have been residing in East Tennessee, the possibility always open in a much smaller nation that the relatives of one future president could well be known by the relatives of another. [22]

Neither man in the late 1840s could have possibly imagined how their lives would someday so profoundly and even tragically intersect.

Because, by 1849, he was fairly entrenched in his East Tennessee district, a position that was enhanced by tireless labors for his constituents, Johnson was able to focus on issues far beyond the borders of that district, and no issue engaged his talents, energy and passions more than his move to pass what came to be simply known as the Homestead Act, a strikingly visionary bill designed to substantially strengthen the economic and social stability of poor farmers and laborers.

The idea was simple: a low-income resident without property would be eligible to secure ownership of unoccupied public land as long as he committed to working the land, planting crops, and even building a house and barn on it.

No legislation meant more to Johnson in the course of his nearly 50-year public career than the Homestead Act, which over a span of nearly two decades he introduced in Congress in several different forms, with its basic premise always kept intact.

Johnson was willing to talk for hours on first the House floor and later in the Senate, detailing the intricacies of his legislation, most often against the derisive comments of plantation-owning Southern legislators who regarded the measure as nothing short of socialistic. His devotion to the topic was a tribute not only to his perseverance, but something else: to Thomas Ritchie, the editor of the *Washington Union,* Johnson ascribed his motivation from one who "has a heart to feel and a head capable of understanding their [the working poor] greatest interests and dearest rights."

He added, with no sense of embarrassment, although the likes of Jefferson Davis thought the less said on this subject, the better, that his own "experiences and habits in early life with the industrious producing portion of society" had made it possible for him to "duly appreciate the real wants and sympathies of the laboring thousands." [23]

He knew the people the legislation would most help: they were farmers, mechanics and laborers who no matter how hard they tried couldn't seem to get ahead. He talked to them personally, listen to their problems, read the letters they sent him. Those who said Johnson was a man only interested in his own advancement, indifferent to the travails of everyone else, would always be found wanting in these appraisals by Johnson's devotion to the homestead cause.

Although the opposition proved stubbornly implacable in the years to come, leading to the repeated defeat of the legislation, Johnson never gave up, introducing and fighting for the act repeatedly between 1846 and 1860. Not until the spring of 1862 would the idea finally become law, several months after Johnson had left the Senate.

As Johnson, winning one last term in Congress in 1851, contemplated the next step in his political career, he also kept an eye on national politics, astutely remarking of 38 year-old Illinois Senator Stephen Douglas who hoped to get the Democratic presidential nomination the next year: he is "altogether of the hot lead order," whose nascent campaign was "going down as fast as it went up." [24]

Johnson was equally unimpressed with 60 year-old former Secretary of State and U.S. Senator James Buchanan, regarding the Pennsylvanian as remote and uninteresting. "It will require much talent and labor to make Mr. Buchanan popular with the great mass of people." [25]

Johnson seemed to additionally harbor a distrust of Buchanan because the aging man had always been a bachelor, although he never uttered a word regarding Buchanan's sexuality. Later historians have argued that Buchanan was almost undoubtedly gay. Johnson only said that he wondered about the "brain of one whose bosom has never yet swelled with emotions for wife or children." [26]

When the Democrats instead eventually nominated dark horse Franklin Pierce of New Hampshire, Johnson, while wondering if the 48 year-old former Senator was really prepared for the presidency, nevertheless gamely took to the field to campaign for him, at one point nicely defending Pierce against charges that he had fainted while serving as a general in the Mexican American War by noting that in "nine cases out of ten, the accusers of Pierce had not the courage to volunteer in the Mexican War so as to give themselves an opportunity of fainting." [27]

Although Johnson during the 1852 campaign had rather melodramatically declared "I have no political future," he jumped into the race early the following year to become the next governor of Tennessee. [28]

The contest made perfect sense for the 45 year-old Johnson, offering him a wider statewide audience and, if elected, the chance to implement changes which many would soon regard as entirely class conscious.

The Democrats and Whigs had been fiercely competitive in the last seven Tennessee gubernatorial elections going back to 1839, with the Democrats winning three times for an average overall 49.7 percent of the vote, and the Whigs triumphant four times, with an average 50.1 percent.

In the end, Johnson marginally improved his party's average, defeating Whig Party candidate Gustavus Henry with 50.9 percent of the vote in August of 1853. Two months later he was sworn into office at the stately McKendree Church in downtown Nashville.

Once again attacking those who were privileged, Johnson now aired a new beef: the young wealthy male students who, once they attended college, seemed to become almost anarchistic, and certainly anti-democratic, in their views. It was a criticism that would be through the years echoed for generations of elders responding in bewilderment as their offspring studied at a university and returned home with political views suddenly in direct opposition to their parents.

Johnson blamed both the students as well as their professors for the phenomenon, calling them "bigoted and supercilious on account of their literary attainments and assumed superiority, mixed with a superabundance of self-esteem."

To this class, said Johnson, was needed a basic lecture on democracy, which he proceeded to give, describing it as a system of government providing man with "that which enables him to reason correctly and to lift him above all animal creation."

In a reference that later inspired derision, Johnson also claimed that democracy was like the Biblical tale of Jacob's ladder in which men, "in proportion to their merit, may ascend." [29]

What any of this had to do with state government went unsaid. The programs Johnson ultimately advanced were traditionalist in the framework of a mid-19th century Southern governor, calling for a reduction of bureaucratic waste and the state debt. But he broke with the accepted pattern of inactive governance by pushing for prison reform, a tax to pay for infrastructure projects, and the creation of a state library and geological survey.

Johnson's record at the end of his two terms was marginally strong enough to merit re-election, although he uncharacteristically claimed to loathe the idea of having to wage another statewide campaign, telling William Lowry, a friend and supporter in Greeneville: "The intense excitement, the misrepresentations and slanders which will be heaped on the candidates, besides the physical and mental labors that will have to be performed, and that too, in the dust and heat of summer, at a heavy expense, with all this before me, and the uncertainty of success, is almost enough to deter me from the undertaking." [30]

Despite these protestations, Johnson made the race, but barely won re-election with 50.8 percent of the vote, indicating that the Whig opposition to him on display in 1853 had only hardened.

Despite this lackluster performance, Johnson was viewed by some portions of the national press as a potential candidate for president in 1856 and admitted to being interested in the proposition. When the Democrats instead selected James Buchanan, Johnson once again expressed his lack of enthusiasm for the aging Pennsylvanian, describing him as "my last choice and harder to defend and fewer elements of popularity than the other men [President Pierce, Stephen Douglas, and Lewis Cass]." [31]

Ultimately he loyally campaigned for the standard-bearer, while privately and presciently predicting a stronger-than-anticipated turnout for John Charles Fremont, the dashing explorer and Republican nominee who expressed his opposition to the continued expansion of slavery. "I am well satisfied that the strength of the Black Republican will astound everyone when it is polled," Johnson confided to his son Robert. [32]

In fact, Fremont confounded analysts, winning 11 states and 114 electoral votes to Buchanan's 19 states and 174 electoral votes. Carrying the electoral rich states of New York, Massachusetts, New Jersey, Ohio, and Illinois, Fremont paved the way for Abraham Lincoln's victory four years later, a result that even the sagacious Johnson could not have foreseen.

In the weeks after the 1856 election Johnson once again took stock of his fortunes. He could run for re-election to the statehouse, but decided that a seat in the U.S. Senate was more in keeping with what by now were his firm national ambitions, telling Sam Mulligan that it was essential in politics to forever keep moving "onward & upward and not to pause any place until the people become tired and restless."

"It is better to get of their way a little too soon," Johnson added, "than to be in their way a little too long." [33]

Elected to the U.S. Senate in November 1857 by a vote of the state legislature, Johnson returned to Washington where he rented out a room at the modest three-story St. Charles Hotel. He had entered a city split by an angry battle currently being waged by President Buchanan and

Stephen Douglas over the issue of expanding slavery. Buchanan was more than willing to sign off on a fraudulently engineered constitution in the Kansas Territory that would force slavery on what would become the new state of Kansas.

Douglas, hardly a friend of the abolitionists, thought Buchanan's stand was rotten and promised to wage war against the President in Congress. The conflict between the two men threatened to rip to pieces the party's sectional coalition, and thus chances of future Democratic national success.

Once again Johnson revealed his lack of confidence in Buchanan, reporting to his son Robert that the President "has but few friends in either house of Congress who are willing to stand firmly and closely by him." [34]

When the issue was finally settled by a new anti-slavery constitutional vote in Kansas, it was clear that Douglas had represented the future, while Buchanan was mired in the past.

Also once again Johnson introduced homestead legislation, finally realizing a dream come true with its passage in both houses of Congress in the spring of 1860. But the victory proved exceedingly short-lived after Buchanan vetoed the legislation, questioning whether "Congress under the constitution, has the power to give away the public lands either to States or individuals." [35]

Throughout the winter and early spring of that year Johnson's name was repeatedly mentioned as a possible candidate for president. The *Lincoln Journal* of Fayetteville, Arkansas put his name on its masthead as it's preferred nominee. The *New York Herald* listed him as a likely choice should Douglas falter, while the *Nashville Union and American,* calling him "one of the nation's jewels," advocated his nomination. [36]

The good press also included praise from the *Washington Evening Star* for his homestead legislation, lauding Johnson as a man who "conquering early difficulties and disadvantages of social position, has attained high and honorable public stations, the duties connected with which he has in all respects faithfully discharged." [37]

Johnson, for his part, was intrigued by the possibility of a movement in his favor at the coming Democratic convention, telling his son Robert, who was travelling with the Tennessee delegation to advance his father's interests at the Charleston meeting, to not do anything to annoy the Douglas forces on the off chance that if the Illinois Senator failed, his supporters might transfer their loyalty to Johnson. It was important, Johnson advised, to occupy "an acceptable position to him and friends." [38]

Johnson's moment at the convention never arrived. The implosion of the Democratic party that he had long anticipated instead saw the Charleston meeting disbanding in early May without selecting a presidential nominee. Disheartened delegates gathering again in Baltimore during the third week of June finally, if unenthusiastically, selected Douglas.

A breakaway group of Southern dissidents, meanwhile, stormed out of the Baltimore meeting to form their own convention, nominating John Breckinridge, Buchanan's 39 year-old vice president. Douglas was now officially the nominee of the Democratic National Party, while Breckinridge was the nominee of the National Democratic Party.

Johnson deplored the party's state of affairs, telling one correspondent that he was "more than willing to do all in my power, mental or physical, to restore peace and harmony in our ranks in the state and out of it." [39]

But a divided party facing off against a united Republican party now headed by Lincoln, Johnson knew, was doomed. "The Democratic party is in ruins," Johnson told George Jones in mid-August, adding "and the Government [is] tending to disunion and revolution." [40]

Reluctantly, Johnson decided to back Breckinridge, whom he knew personally and liked. He returned to Tennessee to do his part for the campaign even though John Bell, former senator from the Volunteer

State, was running as the presidential nominee for the Constitution Union Party.

Johnson's efforts left some unimpressed, with the *Republican Banner* of Nashville charging "Andrew Johnson is exclusively and particularly for Andrew Johnson in this canvas." [41]

In the end the four-party split allowed Lincoln to win the White House with 39.6 percent of the vote, while in Tennessee, where Lincoln wasn't even on the ballot, Bell bested Breckinridge, 47.7 percent to 44.6 percent, a result that embarrassed Johnson.

He was glumly back in Washington in early December. The long talked-of move on the part of Southern leaders to finally secede from the Union was now taking real shape in the wake of Lincoln's election. "I see no possibility of preserving the Union, nor indeed do I consider it desirable," Louisiana Senator John Slidell candidly told Buchanan several days after the election, happily anticipating the coming divide. [42]

"Times, monetary and political, look gloomy," Johnson wrote to son Robert on December 6, "everything seems to portend evil." [43]

On December 18, just days after the first session of the 36th Congress convened, Johnson rose to deliver an extraordinary address. Although he was rightly looked upon by his Southern colleagues, including especially Jefferson Davis, as a maverick, especially for his endless support of homestead legislation, Johnson was nevertheless from and of the South and undoubtedly aware that this was a time of convulsive agitation requiring all Southerners to stand as one.

As Johnson began his remarks he did not disappoint the Southern fire-eaters, many of whom now pressed into the galleries. Proposing three amendments to the Constitution that he thought could provide a legal solution to a growing national chasm, Johnson called for the direct popular election of the president and vice-president, an idea he had talked of for years, only this time with the stipulation that presidential tickets must always be composed of a northerner and southerner, in either position.

The federal judiciary, too, would have a membership reflecting a balance between the two sections.

Finally, Johnson suggested bringing an end to the many and tiring debates about slavery with the creation of a special boundary that would run across the belly of the country as more states were added in the west, allowing slavery to exist everywhere to the south, while prohibiting it everywhere to the north.

So far, so good, at least from the Southern point of view, although the thread of Johnson's remarks up to this pointed indicated remedies designed to keep the South in the Union.

But then he dropped his bombshell: "I am opposed to secession," he declared bluntly. The remark set off an instant stir among his colleagues as well as those in the gallery. Johnson pushed on: "If the doctrine of secession is to be carried out upon the mere whim of a state, this government is not stronger than a rope of sand; it's own weight will tumble it to pieces."

Johnson went on to explain his theory of perpetual participation in return for perpetual inclusion by asking: "If a state can secede at will and pleasure," does not a majority of the states, "under the compact they have made with each other," have the "right to combine and reject any one of those states from the confederacy?"

He quickly answered his own question. The states, Johnson said, "have no such rights; the compact is reciprocal." [44]

Johnson's speech put him in immediate peril. Returning to his hotel room, he was cursed and yelled at on the streets by Southerners outraged by his apostacy.

But in a substantially larger context, his remarks, coupled with more extensive remarks he delivered on the Senate floor on between December 18 and 20, transformed him into a truly national figure beyond anything he had experienced before, with comments from the North offering praise, while those in the South eviscerated him.

The *Washington Evening Star* characterized his remarks as an "amble and emphatic speech," delivered from a man who was "emphatically the representative of the laboring classes of the South." Journalist and Clerk of the House John Forney declared: "The cloud that has been hanging over the Capitol and the country has lifted. The Union has found a gallant defender in the American Congress in the person of the living Andrew Jackson of the South, namely Andrew Johnson of Tennessee." [45]

The *Chicago Tribune* said the address had produced the "greatest excitement and indignation among extreme Southern men, who denounce him as a traitor and even propose to hang him when they can get a chance." [46]

The praise continued with the *New York Times* describing Johnson's remarks as a "strong vindication of the supremacy of the Constitution," and the *New York Herald* saying it was the "talk of every circle in Washington." [47]

Equally satisfying for Johnson was the hundreds of letters he received from admirers around the country who praised both his comments and his bravery for making them. Joshua Bell of Danville, Kentucky, saluted Johnson's "bold, earnest & manly words," hoping the Senate would continue to "speak for the Union, for peace & against treason North & South." [48]

From Chambersburg, Pennsylvania, William Crook reported to Johnson that he had read the entirely of his remarks as published in a local paper, noting that they confirmed "the estimate I have always held as to your patriotism and devotion to your whole country." [49]

In Washington, T.W. Linder, describing himself as a "rough frontiersman," thought Johnson's remarks "rang out like the blare of a trumpet," and perhaps said more than he intended when he added: "From this day forth you are a marked man in this republic." [50]

More than 36,000 people requested copies of the speech from the offices of the *Congressional Globe*. Johnson himself paid $225 to have up to 15,000 copies run off by a Washington printer.

Only naturally, Johnson's remarks provoked widespread condemnation throughout the South. The *Montgomery Confederation* newspaper guessed that Johnson's speech "does not reflect the sentiments of one-forth of the people of his state," before adding: "Shame on such a man." [51]

The *Louisville Daily Courier* condemned Johnson for toadying to Northern Republicans, remarking "We do not envy him praise from such a quarter." [52]

From Alabama, a supporter of secession named Hiram Smith wrote to tell Johnson that he considered him a "traitor to your country and that you should receive your just deserts." Smith added: "no man having a drop of Southern blood in his veins would openly proclaim such doctrines." [53]

A man identifying himself as a slave owner in Grand Junction, Tennessee told Johnson that he was ordering one of his slaves to bring a whip with him to Washington with orders to "give your back & shoulders some marks of his attention." [54]

Blackston McDannel on December 29 wrote to warn Johnson that he was being denounced "by a little clique calling themselves democrats. They have been trying for several days to get up a meeting to pass condemnatory resolutions in regard to your course and to burn you in effigy." [55]

A citizen's protest meeting in Friars Point, Mississippi actually did succeed in hanging Johnson in effigy, then for good measure adding the quaint touch of stuffing the cloth figure of him into a barrel, and writing a message to go along with it that read: "Andrew Johnson, the traitor to the South, barreled up and rolled into the river at Friars Point, January 5, 1861." [56]

When reports were circulated that either Jefferson Davis or Texas Senator Louis Wigfall, or both, had engaged in duels with Johnson, the explosive climate of Washington, and the more explosive vituperation of the Tennessee Senator, made the story seem at the very least plausible. Joseph Davis wrote to his brother Jefferson from his plantation near Vicksburg of a rumor "that you had been severely wounded in conflict with A Johnson of Tennessee. Although I disbelieved the report, yet felt much anxiety to know if anything had occurred to justify the rumor." [57]

The rumor, of course, was just that. And it was undoubtedly lucky for Johnson that there was nothing more to it: Davis, a veteran of the Black Hawk and Mexican-American wars, was in every way a skilled marksman. [58]

Johnson spent the early weeks of 1861 watching with dismay, if from a distance, as Mississippi, Florida, Alabama, Louisiana, and Texas followed South Carolina's lead in voting to exit the Union.

On February 5 and 6, Johnson delivered yet one more epic defense of the Union, reciting in exhausting detail all the reasons why secession was foolish. He was now bolstered by a crowd of admirers who packed the Senate galleries and broke the rules of the chamber by repeatedly applauding and laughing at his every joke.

Ominously, at the end of these remarks late on February 6, Johnson declared that for the Union, "I have stood; for it I will continue to stand. I care not where the blows come from, and some will find before this thing is over that while there are blows to be given, there will be blows to receive, and what while others can thrust, there are some who can parry. They will find that it is a game that two can play at." [59]

When Lincoln, after a much-publicized more than 1,200-mile journey from Springfield, Illinois arrived in Washington on February 23 and visited the Capitol two days later, it was noted that Johnson was among only a handful of Democrat senators, including Stephen Douglas, willing to be introduced to the president-elect and speak to him. How both men, in the quick passing of a handshake, sized each other up, is not known. They were, at this moment, just weeks away from entering into a partnership that would forever shape both of their careers as well as a substantial portion of the South.

On the evening of March 4 a group of admirers from New York and Pennsylvania marched in the cold weather to the St. Charles Hotel and loudly called for Johnson to speak to them. He soon appeared, looking happy for the visitation, and delivered brief remarks suggesting that it was the leadership of the South, not the people themselves, who were the true secession enthusiasts.

This was a theme that he had been entertaining for weeks, one undoubtedly bolstered by the many anti-secession letters he was receiving from regular working people back in Tennessee.

The people, Johnson declared, "had been hurried and dragged into secession by disappointed politicians who were aspiring after office and the emoluments of place."

He pitied the people of the South for now having to endure this madness, adding that he would "rather be a subject to the autocrat of Russia than a citizen of the Southern Confederacy." [60]

The Russian remark particularly annoyed the *New Orleans Daily Crescent*, arguing: "The repugnance, we take pleasure in saying, is mutual." The paper added that anonymous sources in Tennessee were hoping Johnson would never return. The state without him, the paper said, "they would welcome. With him, the infliction would be too grievous to be borne." [61]

The Confederate shelling of Fort Sumter on April 12, prompting the Union force there to abdicate, and Lincoln's subsequent April 15 call to the states asking for 75,000 troops to recapture the fort and protect

Washington, among other tasks, made it official: the two sections were now at war.

Lincoln's announcement greatly animated Tennessee's secessionists who now launched their most vigorous effort yet to take the state out of the Union.

Johnson was determined to defeat the secessionists in a manner that no other senator from the North could: face-to-face.

He left Washington for Tennessee on April 21, pensively unsure of the reception that awaited him.

CHAPTER THREE

THE SMOTHERED
FIRES OF VESUVIUS

B efore Johnson left for his native East Tennessee, he stopped for a moment to write a quick note to the President recommending a friend for a federal job in North Carolina.

Pointedly, he added that it was his hope that Lincoln "will find it consistent with the public interest and sound policy to distribute, as near as may be, a fair proportion of the patronage of the government among the Southern states." [1]

This communication was significant for two reasons, the first being that it was the beginning of what would prove to be dozens of letters and messages sent between Johnson and Lincoln during the course of the next four years, tangible evidence of a productive relationship between the two men, often in the midst of the most challenging circumstances.

But the communication also gave evidence of a demand placed upon Johnson at the beginning of the Civil War greater than that of any fellow U.S. Senator: the need to secure paying federal jobs as a stabilizing force in a Southern state on the precipice of anarchy.

The jobs the residents of Tennessee requested ran the gamut from local postmaster to federal marshal to Indian agent, endless pleas from people desperate for work and station, hoping that a word from the increasingly influential senator would turn the trick.

Increasingly, Tennesseans unimpressed with the secession movement also turned to Johnson not just for help, but for guidance and reassurance that somehow everything was going to work out. The idea that Johnson could solve any problem sometimes took on curious proportions, as when Kinson McVay, a farmer in Henderson County, talked about Confederate soldiers seizing his slaves, including one characterized as "scarcely worth his victuals and clothing."

What law would allow for the stealing of "Negroes or money by a parcel of drunken rowdies without showing any authority for their acts," McVay wondered. "I say it is equal to highway robbery." [2]

Johnson's more than 400-mile trip from Washington to Greeneville would take him through the gently sloping hills of southwest Virginia, vibrant with Confederate sentiment. It is not certain if advance notice of his coming was telegraphed to various stations along the way. But what is known is that as the train pulled into Lynchburg, Johnson could look out the window at a crowd of several hundred people, and perhaps as many as a thousand, massed to the front and sides of the town's teeming depot.

With three railroads making it a vital terminus for the movement of Confederate troops and goods, Lynchburg was a hotbed of secession enthusiasm, and for that reason a dangerous waystation for Johnson on his return home.

The waiting crowd was hardly a welcoming committee. Stirred up by local secession movement leaders, including William Hardwicke, the editor of the *Lynchburg Republican* newspaper, the massed gathering was more in the way of a mob intent on acting out their displeasure with Johnson.

Hardwicke was a man given to violence who had, the year before, been involved in a street shooting either directly or indirectly resulting in the death of an editor from a rival newspaper.

Now, as the train stopped, Hardwicke jumped onboard with the notion of wanting to physically pull Johnson's nose, a contemptuous form of assault frequently used in the South of the 19th century between white men with an emphasis on humiliation. How far Hardwicke succeeded in this effort is not known, although some altercation between the two men did occur, with Johnson at one point reaching inside his breast pocket for a pistol he frequently carried with him.

The Senator gave every appearance of being perfectly willing to use the weapon on Hardwicke or anyone else threatening him.

Instead, cooler heads prevailed, including, it was reported, several railroad officials who implored Hardwicke and others to let Johnson go on his way unmolested. [3]

It was later reported that a similar gathering of malcontents in Bristol, hugging the Tennessee border, only allowed Johnson to safely proceed upon the order of Jefferson Davis, wisely worried that an assaulted or even murdered Johnson would only make a martyr out of the Tennessee senator.

Johnson received a far more gracious reception when his train pulled into Knoxville on April 27. Cheered by a waiting group of Union enthusiasts, Johnson stepped off the passenger car and up onto a wooden platform erected just hours before for his visit.

After the travails of Lynchburg, he may have emotionally needed the support and warmth of admirers who cheered his course. Responding, Johnson spoke for around two hours, with a reporter for the local *Knoxville Whig* jotting down: "Whilst he avoided personalities, he dealt out a full measure of justice to the disappointed politicians, designing demagogues, and actual traitors seeking to break up the country and to destroy the country." [4]

Johnson could rarely, if ever, speak for a short while on any occasion, but in this instance, he would have been wise to cut his speech in half. After an hour had passed, with Johnson still holding forth, and word of his performance spreading among the locals, a group of newly sworn-in Confederate soldiers, led by a brass band, stopped just short of the stand.

"The interruption was calculated to bring on a collision," thought William Brownlow, who was sitting on the speaker's stand. Long-time Johnson critic Oliver Temple later he said he was certain that the soldiers' sole purpose was to "break up the meeting, and probably wreck vengeance on Johnson and others." [5]

With the young soldiers obviously possessing weapons and stirred up by the spirit of their mission on a warm spring day, it was obvious that anything could happen. But as with the near misses in Lynchburg and Bristol, catastrophe was averted when two local Confederate leaders stepped in to silence the band and calm the soldiers down.

The moment was poignant for Brownlow, who in more ways than one represented the chaos and confusion of Civil War Tennessee. A deeply passionate, if sometimes vituperative preacher, Brownlow had entered politics in the 1830s and ran in opposition to Johnson for Congress in 1845. There was nothing about Johnson that Brownlow liked, openly declaring his steadfast opposition throughout the entirety of Johnson's two terms as governor.

But now Brownlow, who regarded secession as a moral blunder, manfully rallied to Johnson's side, telling Joseph McDannel, the brother of Blackston McDannel, "Johnson is right."

Johnson's valiant pro-Unionism was as courageous and steadfast as anything that that Tennessee icon named Andrew Jackson had ever done, thought Brownlow, adding: "I will defend him to the last." [6]

Johnson finally arrived in Greeneville on April 29, which like the rest of Tennessee, was violently divided by the politics of secession. Confederates, some perhaps animated by a resentment of Johnson as the most prominent person in town, openly declared their opposition to the Union in general and Johnson in particular.

In a few months Confederate troops would be in firm control of the town to the point of even seizing Johnson's Main Street residence for use as a hospital and forcing Johnson's wife Eliza, already in bad health, to flee. A report that the soldiers had also flogged Mrs. Johnson was entirely without foundation.

Acknowledging that Union army excesses frequently resulted in the same sort of coerced diasporas, Oliver Temple nevertheless wondered about the Confederal action forcing Mrs. Johnson and the wives of several other Greeneville Unionists to leave, recalling that the women were "noted for their mildness and peaceable dispositions." [7]

Johnson's son Robert, like his father, solidly pro-Union and serving in the Tennessee State Legislature, also fled. Son Charles joined the Union's 10th Regiment of the Tennessee, before dying, in 1863, when he fell violently from his horse. Andrew Johnson, Jr., relocated with his mother to Carter County where they both stayed with daughter Mary Stover. Mary's husband, Daniel Stover, spearheaded the Union's 4th Tennessee Volunteer Infantry Regiment, heavily populated with displaced pro-Union east Tennesseans.

Johnson's most astute and socially graceful child, Martha Johnson Patterson, who had attended an elite boarding school in Georgetown while her father served in Congress, remained in Greenville with her lawyer husband David Patterson. But while Patterson would serve as a circuit judge for the Confederate government, he later explained that he only did so in an effort to mitigate the excesses of Confederate prosecutors subjecting local Unionists to a questionable rule of law.

How secession and the Civil War played out in Tennessee, where everything, Johnson quickly perceived upon his return, had become personal, was seen with Governor Isham Harris, who early on declared his fealty to the Confederate government. Harris served as the point man beginning in early 1861 for the movement to take Tennessee out of the Union via a referendum ultimately rejected by voters. Harris tried again, this time through the more successful mechanism of the state legislature, which approved a secession ordinance.

Johnson had never had much use for Harris, whom he sarcastically described as "King Harris," before breezily adding: "So far from being my king, I would not have him for my slave." [8]

After the Governor had again asked voters to approve a secession referendum, Johnson dared to speak out. But to his dismay he saw that a shift had occurred on June 8 when state voters did, indeed, now signal their support of the referendum, the change in sentiment due almost entirely to Lincoln's calling up of troops to wage war against the Confederacy.

It was clear that Johnson would have to leave Tennessee. His political base was now uncertain, his enemies were about to be in full or partial control throughout the state, including most gallingly in east Tennessee where any resistance would be ruthlessly repulsed. Most important, Johnson's life was now more at risk than ever before. While Jefferson Davis may have doubted the wisdom of seeing Johnson killed, that sentiment clearly was not shared by Governor Harris nor the thousands of Confederate soldiers and sympathizers in the state who would love to see nothing more than a shackled, struggling Johnson carried by a mob to a sturdy tree where he would meet his destiny at the end of a rope.

What thoughts ran through Johnson's mind as he contemplated these very real threats can only be imagined. Suddenly, he was a nomad. He had fled from real or imagined pursuers before when he and brother William in 1824 had broken their apprenticeship contracts with the tailor James Selby and disappeared into the woods.

But this was different. Johnson then was an almost invisible boy, seen by few, known by even less. Now he was one of the most visible men in the South, his face printed in newspapers, a platform presence who by this time in his career had spoken before and been seen by thousands of people.

A normal person might have taken to a disguise, or travelled by the darkness of night as he endeavored to leave Tennessee. Johnson, instead, very visibly departed his home state in the middle of the day by carriage, traveling along a public dirt road via the Cumberland Gap.

Was he hoping for a confrontation? Did he want to be killed? Did he nourish the thought of the same martyrdom that Jefferson Davis, for one, was determined to deny him? At any point he could have been stopped by gun-toting Confederate sympathizers determined to do away with him. As it was, at several points, his carriage was fired upon.

The explanations for Johnson's behavior were simple: he could not shrink from a fight. True, he was leaving Tennessee, but the state was for the moment in the possession of enemy powers, giving him little choice.

Even so, he would leave of his own accord and at his own pace, arriving in Covington, Kentucky, at the nexus of the Ohio and Licking rivers, where he was received as nothing less than a courageous fighter for freedom.

The Covington reception, made lively by a military band playing a sprightly welcome, caught Johnson by surprise. But what pleased him even more was the unbridled excitement awaiting him up ahead on the other side of the Ohio River in Cincinnati where thousands of people lined the streets to cheer him.

Checking into the modern downtown Burnet House, Johnson soon addressed a crowd that had assembled outside the building. Always ready to provide yet one more indictment of the secession movement, Johnson told his Cincinnati admirers that that movement was entropic, "making war upon everything that has a tendency to promote and ameliorate the condition of the mass of mankind."

Noting the warrant for his arrest, Johnson calmly replied that he was "no fugitive, especially no fugitive from justice," a remark that sparked laughter. Instead, he said, if he was anything, he was a "fugitive from tyranny, a fugitive from the reign of terror." [9]

Johnson, by train, pushed back into Washington, arriving on June 21 for the remaining weeks of the first session of the 37th Congress. Checking into the St. Charles Hotel, he was soon greeted by former New York Democrat Congressman John B. Haskin, who informed him that a band belonging to the 25th Pennsylvania Infantry Regiment and led by a group of admirers from the North was out front, hoping he would appear before them.

Johnson consented, prompting cheers when he declared that in calling up soldiers in the wake of the Confederate shelling of Fort Sumter, Lincoln had "done no more than his duty, and that if he had done less, he would have deserved the halter himself."

Long accused of making personal the most mundane political point, Johnson's reference to his own life and his own struggles in the present context for once seemed entirely appropriate, proclaiming that the Confederates "may confiscate my little property I own in Tennessee. My life may be required to lay upon the alter of my country. But let my country be saved. She is right and justice must prevail while the stars and stripes continue to float over us." [10]

Within days of his return to Washington, Johnson met with Lincoln, who yet one more time recognized in him a serious man entirely serious about actively battling the Confederates in Tennessee.

The President subsequently gave his approval to an imaginative plan to support with federal dollars the smuggling of arms into East Tennessee for battle with the Confederates.

Johnson, for better or worse, now one of the most publicly known men in Washington, was being watched. On June 29, Treasury Secretary Salmon Chase wrote him a quick note, jokingly referring to Lincoln as our "great and good friend," and adding that the President had "expressed the strongest wish to gratify" Johnson by agreeing to the arms shipment expenditure. [11]

But the transaction did not go unreported. A Federal employee and secret Confederate enthusiast named D.L Dalton sent a communication to Jefferson Davis noting that Johnson "has been at [the] War Department frequently and has accomplished goals for ordering the arming and raising of troops for East Tenn." [12]

Davis must have been gratified and perhaps even a little amused to learn of the activities of his long-time nemesis, information that was bolstered on July 1 from a pro-Confederate merchant in Rogersville, Tennessee who said that the arms secured by Johnson were shortly expected to travel to the Volunteer State by a route slicing through the Cumberland Mountains.

Johnson's efforts at raising arms hardly ended there. On July 6 he sent a message to War Secretary Simon Cameron informing him that some thirty boxes of minie rifles currently in storage at the federal Washington Arsenal should be sent to the Union resistance in east Tennessee rather than muskets: "These are the kind of gun above all others needed by our people," he said, adding "They are accustomed to the use of rifles." [13]

Three weeks later Johnson rose in the Senate for what arguably could be described as his most important address regarding the disunion of the country since his highly publicized anti-secession comments of the previous December.

The difference this time was that an imagined secession had become a reality with eleven states, including Tennessee, now out of the Union and a threatened war now an actual war, with the Union in the early going reeling, having disastrously lost to Confederate forces in the humiliating Battle of Bull Run, 25 miles southwest of Washington, just days earlier.

Before he began his remarks, Johnson gazed around the chamber, lit from above by detailed stained-glass and iron skylights, and saw a membership that had been greatly reduced by the more than twenty Southerners who had left the Senate when their states seceded.

The Southern members who had just months before sat at their wooden desks to the right, left, and front of him were all gone, members who often proved to be his most persistent foes. Louis Wigfall of Texas was gone. So was frequent antagonist Robert Toombs of Georgia, who owned almost fifty slaves and a nearly 4,000-acre plantation. But best of all from Johnson's perspective was the absence of Jefferson Davis of Mississippi, a man who just by his very presence, let alone his frequent argumentative interruptions, endlessly annoyed Johnson.

The silence replacing the noise of Davis' perfectly-made and perfectly-nuanced arguments was, from Johnson's perspective, probably the only truly positive thing to come out of the secession movement.

Always a realist, Johnson began his remarks by asserting that the war was currently "without much hope or prospect of a speedy termination." He noted that because of the present ordeal of the Union, there were those who thought the government should become more centralized and even more authoritarian if need be in pursuing its war aims.

He referenced Lincoln, who had wrestled with the same question, noting that the country was, in fact, in a struggle central to "whether the people shall rule; whether the people shall have a government based upon their intelligence, upon their integrity, upon their purity of character, sufficient to govern themselves."

Stating the proposition, Johnson then proceeded to seemingly confuse the issue by noting that he supported Lincoln's suspension of habeas corpus as it applied to suspected and arrested traitors, and also had no problem with the President expanding the military, arguing "I say in these two instances, he is justified by the great law of necessity."

He chronicled the many attempts to placate the South through legislation leading up to the war, charging that Southern lawmakers during the months of endless debates had never been sincere about finding solutions, and that any new attempts now to reach out to the South would prove as fruitless as earlier attempts had been in the past.

"Traitors and rebels are standing with arms in their hands, and it is said that we must go forward and compromise with them," said Johnson.

But they were the ones in the wrong, he asserted. "They are making war upon the Government; they are trying to upturn and destroy our free institutions."

Noting that Southerners had for decades thrived under the Constitution, he offered an indictment of the region's leaders: "You lived under it until you got to be a great and prosperous people. It was made by our fathers and cemented by their blood."

Johnson devoted the rest of his remarks to a valiant defense of his fellow east Tennesseans who continued to resist the Confederates, declaring "We will triumph. We must triumph. Right is with us. A great and fundamental principle of right that lies at the foundation of all things is with us."

Doing all he could to embolden the Union cause after the defeat at Bull Run and in the face of the habeas corpus debate, Johnson soon concluded: "This government must not, cannot, fail. Though your flag may have trailed in the dust, though a retrograde movement may have been made, though the banner of our country may have been sullied, let it be borne onward." [14]

The response to Johnson's speech was effusive, with the *Chicago Tribune* calling it "the fervent and earnest reply of a plain spoken Southern man," and the *New York Tribune* headlining the address as the "Voice of a True Democrat." [15]

Philosopher and Columbia University professor Francis Lieber asked Johnson for a copy of the speech, remarking "May God prosper you and all who struggle, by word or sword, to save the integrity of our country." [16]

On the day that Congress wrapped up its business on August 6, Johnson sent a heart-felt communication to Lincoln, co-signed by East Tennessee Unionist William Carter who was visiting him in Washington, that was partly an epistle of determination, but also a note of encouragement to a besieged President.

"In the midst of the general gloom which hangs over our people, we are happy to give your Excellency every assurance that their loyalty is not diminished, but increased, as their dangers become more threatening." [17]

Johnson politely put off invitations in the following weeks to speak in New York, among other places, preferring instead to travel to Ohio and Kentucky. Departing from Washington by train, he arrived in Cincinnati on August 30.

Once again checking into the Burnet House, Johnson shortly addressed an outside crowd just hours after it was learned that Tennessee Congressman Thomas Nelson, up to now a staunch Unionist, had written out a statement advising the residents of east Tennessee to give up all future resistance to Confederate authorities.

Nelson had composed this statement after his arrest and confinement by the Confederates, making the document one clearly written under duress.

Johnson had regarded Nelson as a valuable ally in the struggle and was saddened to learn of his imprisonment. But he bluntly said he regretted even more Nelson's statement, declaring that if cajoled to write something similar himself, "I would rather be screwed down in my coffin and buried in the earth." [18]

Johnson candidly admitted that the Union cause in recent weeks had been more hard-pressed than previously imagined. He additionally admitted that the Confederates had, for the present, gone far in stifling all dissent in Tennessee.

But that suppressed opinion, asserted Johnson, was not unlike the "smothered fires of Vesuvius which only fall to gather more lava and more heat," before the time comes when "they may burst forth with more destructive fury."

He then made one of his most emotional remarks regarding the struggle in Tennessee, recalling that the "people there are a brave people—I love them."

He uncharacteristically remarked that everything he had accomplished in his long career was due entirely to the people of Tennessee, and lamented his exodus and the exodus of so many unionists forced by threat of death to leave the state.

"What have I done? What has my son done? What have these, my friends, done?"

He would forever stand by "these loyal people."

"They never deceived, they never betrayed me," Johnson declared. "They were never false to their pledges, and I will never be false to mine." [19]

Over the course of the next two months, Johnson would travel throughout Ohio and Kentucky, at loose ends with no place to call home, but exhilarated with the cause of emboldening Unionists in those two states, while also trying to provide emotional support for and comfort to the many Tennessee expatriates he encountered during his travels.

Despite the formidable odds of the moment, Johnson remained steadfastly optimistic, convinced that the Confederates would eventually be pushed out of Tennessee, before they were pushed out of the country and into the sea.

In his many addresses during these weeks, he enjoyed a popularity never before experienced, with border and Northern audiences constantly cheering him; New York, Philadelphia, and Chicago papers proclaimed him as the man of the hour; and the Republicans he had once gone to battle against saluted him as not just one of the stalwart defenders of the Union in the South, but a national figure of unlimited national potential.

It was clear, although Johnson perhaps did not perceive it this way in the fall of 1861, that he could have a rewarding future in Lincoln's Republican party. But Johnson remained devoted to the Southern Democrat party, although it, for the present, was nearly entirely dominated by determined Confederates who regarded Jefferson Davis, not Johnson, as their hero.

In talks several weeks later with Lincoln and the War Department leadership, Johnson had shown enthusiasm for a plan to frustrate Confederate ambitions in east Tennessee that was both daring, and if not supported by Union forces, reckless.

The idea was simple: Union sympathizers in the region would destroy by setting on fire nine railroad bridges used by the Confederates for transporting materials and men into the region.

As this clandestine, late night activity was taking place, Union soldiers would sweep into East Tennessee providing support not just for this guerilla expedition, but acting as the first wave of an invasion that would finally secure the entire region for the Federals.

The only problem was that by the night of the planned attack the Union command on the ground in Kentucky had become wary of the idea, failing to provide any support whatsoever,

As it was, the East Tennessee volunteers did manage to attack nine bridges, and succeeded in destroying five.

Confederate reprisals proved bloodthirsty. As recorded by historian Bruce Catton, there were "raids, innumerable arrests, quick military trials with the head of a drum for the presiding officer's desk and a running noose for the unlucky." [20]

Confederate Secretary of War Judah P. Benjamin recommended that those convicted of the bridge burning should be hung with their bodies "hanging in the vicinity of the burned bridges." As it was, four men were executed in the manner suggested by Benjamin. [21]

"They are redoubling their diligence," Union first lieutenant and East Tennessee resident Leonidas Houk would soon report to Johnson of the Confederates, noting "arrests and punishments upon the slightest suspicion have become common." [22]

Another correspondent, Robert Stanford, a surgeon and occasional contributor to the *Cincinnati Commercial,* told Johnson that the Confederates had produced "a state of suffering altogether too shocking to be described," mentioning that at least three hundred residents, and probably as many as four hundred, had been arrested, shackled, hauled off to trains at the point of a rifle and sent to a Confederate prison camp in Tuscaloosa. [23]

During the very hours that the ill-fated bridge burning was being carried out, Johnson was pushing George Thomas, currently serving in Kentucky as a brigadier general in charge of volunteers, to move into East Tennessee.

Thomas somewhat resentfully responded by noting "I can only say I am doing the best I can. Our Commanding General is doing the same, and using all his influence to equip a force for the rescue of Tennessee." [24]

Thomas was actually entirely put out that Johnson dared to suggest *anything* to him, writing to Brigadier General Albin Schoepf on the same day that it was high time that "discontented persons should be silenced both in and out of the service." Thomas added that while he sympathized "most deeply with the Tennesseans on account of their natural anxiety to relieve their friends and families from the terrible oppression which they are now suffering," any attempt to move the Union army into East Tennessee before it was fully prepared could only lead to disaster. [25]

Schoepf proved a receptive audience: "The outside pressure has become intolerable and must be met with firmness, or the Army will be disbanded," he replied the following day. [26]

As for Johnson's specific plan to invade East Tennessee as soon as possible, Schoepf maintained: "I have never urged it, do not now urge it;

but on the contrary believe that in the present condition of my command (having a large sick list) it would be most decidedly imprudent." [27]

Prospects for action seemed instantly more promising when the 43 year-old Don Carlos Buell was appointed by Commanding General George McClellan in November to replace a thoroughly exhausted William T. Sherman as commander of the newly-organized Department of the Ohio.

A West Point graduate who, according to biographer Stephen Engle, possessed a "rigid belief that war was something that was recorded in the books and that was fought in conformity to a fixed pattern," Buell gave every evidence, or so it seemed, of wanting to take the battle to the enemy, particularly in East Tennessee. [28]

McClellan had high hopes for Buell, although perhaps referencing both Lincoln and Johnson, he warned: "The military problem would be a simple one could it be entirely separated from the political influence." [29]

So warned, after meeting with Johnson in Louisville in late November, Buell told McClellan, "I have talked freely with him, and I think thus far satisfied him. I believe I shall do so entirely as far as our purposes are concerned, but whether the execution will realize all our hopes is a matter for the future to dispose of." [30]

For his part, trying to establish a productive relationship with Buell, Johnson told him of the results of a meeting he had with Lincoln and McClellan once he had returned to Washington for the second session of the 37th Congress.

He reported that both Lincoln and McClellan supported the idea of an East Tennessee excursion out of Kentucky, adding that the people in that section of the Volunteer State remained "oppressed & pursued as beasts in the forests."

"The government must come to their relief," Johnson continued, pointedly adding: "We are looking to you with anxious solicitude to move in that direction." [31]

But Buell soon proved to be in no mood to be rushed, writing back the next day "I assure you I recognize no more imperative duty and crave no higher honor than rescuing our loyal friends in Tennessee whose sufferings and heroism I think I can appreciate." [32]

Johnson must have relished these words. But he was ready for action, more action than Buell at this point was prepared to offer. Two days later Johnson wired Buell: "Ten thousand stands of arms as you requested have been forwarded to be used in East Tennessee."

Clothing for up to 10,000 soldiers would also soon be stored and ready for use in Cincinnati, Johnson continued, adding: "God give you success and to the oppressed people of East Tennessee a speedy deliverance." [33]

Buell spent the next three weeks meticulously planning for Tennessee, but where exactly he would strike he declined to disclose. On December 29, Buell admitted to McClellan that matters were taking longer than anticipated. "It startles me to think how much time has elapsed since my arrival and to find myself still in Louisville."

"I certainly have had a good deal to do and have been very busy about it, but I am satisfied that very few men accomplish as much as is possible, and I cannot assume to be an exception," Buell continued, before telling McClellan that it was his intention to send at least 12,000 troops, in three batteries, into east Tennessee as soon as possible. [34]

Five days later an increasingly impatient Lincoln, already endlessly exasperated by McClellan's failure to aggressively move upon Virginia, wired Buell: "Have arms gone forward for East Tennessee? Please tell me the progress and condition of the movement in that direction." [35]

Responding, Buell protested that "arms can only go forward for East Tennessee under the protection of an army." He then, rather incredibly, said the only reason he was organizing for east Tennessee was because Lincoln, McClellan, and undoubtedly Johnson, although he did not name him specifically, were pushing him to.

"As earnestly as I wish to accomplish it, my judgement has been from the start decided against it," he added of the East Tennessee incursion. [36]

As the delays continued, Lincoln wired Buell, pleading for action and noting "Our friends in East Tennessee are being hanged and driven to despair, and even now I fear, are thinking of taking rebel arms for the sake of personal protection."

Tellingly, Lincoln wondered how he could explain the continuing delay to both Johnson and Tennessee Congressman Horace Maynard, who by now had met with the President several times on the matter. Lincoln was convinced the protracted action was going to lead both men to despair, possibly seeing them resign their federal offices "to go and save their families somehow, or die with them." [37]

It said a lot about Lincoln that he had come to regard Johnson as more determined and certainly more likely to act than some of his own commanders, in particular Buell and McClellan.

He could read this determination in Johnson's face, in Johnson's endless entreaties to help the East Tennesseans, and in Johnson's desire to take to the field himself if something wasn't done soon.

Johnson wanted to fight. So did Lincoln. Recognizing this quality in the senator, Lincoln categorized him in a way that he could not with much of the brass he was daily doing business with, as a man who clearly had the heart of a warrior.

The East Tennessee delay, coupled with the Union disaster at Bull Run and McClellan's Virginia hesitations, created an atmosphere of recrimination in Washington.

Sitting restlessly in the Senate, Johnson appeared a tragic yet brave figure to many who realized his stake in the conflict was larger than that of any other senator: his life was continually under threat in Tennessee, his family dispersed, his property seized.

For those reasons, but also because he was so clearly committed to the Union cause, Johnson found himself appointed to the Joint Committee on the Conduct of the War, a body created during the third week of December and composed of three other senators and four members of the House.

The committee, weighed as it was with Radical Republicans, put Johnson in odd company. The leading lights of the committee, chairman Benjamin Wade of Ohio and Zachariah Chandler of Michigan, had aims beyond Johnson's cherished goal of simply trying to preserve the Union. These men were devoted to the absolute abolition of slavery, and indeed regarded that goal as the preeminent purpose of the war.

Johnson was not an abolitionist and had never been. He had long regarded slavery as a distasteful institution with his only real reservations centering on the fact that it was the province of the South's landed gentry.

But he agreed to serve on what would prove, for Lincoln, to be a nettlesome committee because it might increase his leverage with the Union Army leadership, and in so doing hasten the action in Tennessee.

Johnson's committee membership was, ironically, a lucky happenstance for Lincoln, who would be subject to endless blistering criticism from Wade and Chandler. As the months wore on, Wade and Chandler developed an almost irrational contempt for the President. Johnson never shared in their convictions. It's hard to imagine that in his many continuing conversations with the President that he didn't now and then tip him off on the committee's actions and thinking.

As it was, Johnson's service with the committee was, at roughly two months, short-lived. But as historian T. Harry Williams has pointed out, Johnson "engaged actively with the Radicals." [38]

In his questioning of various commanders, Johnson pushed them in the direction of taking to the field sooner, not later. He wanted more troops in Washington, up to 50,000, to protect the nation's capital, and proposed a Union assault on the Confederacy that would come from many directions simultaneously. He additionally emphasized the importance of disrupting the railroad stretching from Richmond to Chattanooga, arguing "that would be like taking two or three joints out of a backbone." [39]

As the committee hearings continued, Johnson found himself increasingly agreeing with Wade and Chandler that McClellan was not just a slow commander, but perhaps a treasonable one, too. How could McClellan not move, Johnson wondered. It was a question that he would very soon ask of Buell.

Only naturally, the continued delay of any kind of East Tennessee action whatsoever left Johnson in a sullen mood. On January 31, in a speech discussing a resolution to expel Indiana Senator Jesse Bright from the upper chamber for having communicated with Jefferson Davis, Johnson exploded: "Let us go on; let us encourage the Army and the Navy; let us vote the men and the means necessary to vitalize and to bring into requisition the enforcing and coercive power of the Government; let us crush out the rebellion." [40]

Two weeks later Johnson heard from son Robert who was now at a Union camp in Kentucky having fled from Confederate pursuers in Tennessee. "If they had arrested me, I have no doubt, but what they would have hung me," Robert reported in a message that also let Johnson know his wife, daughter, and son-in-law Daniel Stover were still in Tennessee, but for the moment safe. [41]

Before Buell finally moved into Tennessee, Brigadier General Ulysses S. Grant led two divisions up the Tennessee River in a swift attack upon the Confederate garrison of Fort Henry just south of the Kentucky/Tennessee border.

With 17,000 soldiers, Grant opened fire on the fort on the evening of February 5, beginning a general advance the following morning. After about three hours of shelling, what was left of the Confederate force at the fort surrendered.

This signal victory prompted the 39 year-old Grant to make immediate plans for the capture of Fort Donelson some 11 miles to the east. Just three days later Grant's men captured this second installation after Grant, in one of the most memorable lines of the Civil War, responded to a proposed armistice from Confederate General Simon Buckner by declaring "No terms except an unconditional and immediate surrender can be accepted."

Grant added: "I propose to move immediately upon your works." [42]

Roughly 15,000 Confederate soldiers surrendered at Fort Donelson. The fall of the fort, along with reports of Grant's "unconditional" statement, galvanized the North and resulted in Grant's promotion to major general. [43]

What Johnson must have thought of this modest but absolutely determined commander at this point in both of their careers is unknown. That he would someday despise Grant with a kind of all-consuming ferocity that exceeded even his long-standing contempt of Jefferson Davis was obviously in early 1862 unimaginable.

What was certain was that Grant's Fort Donelson victory opened the door to the Union capture of Nashville just over 80 miles to the southeast, with Buell at last showing some action by sending in 18,000 men for the cause.

With Buell moving his Army of the Ohio from the northeast and Grant coming in from the northwest, Confederate General Albert Sidney Johnson made the decision to abandon the Tennessee capital without a fight on February 23.

Although Jefferson Davis greatly admired Johnston, he nevertheless would soon wire: "You have been held responsible for the fall of Donelson and the capture of Nashville. T's charged that no effort was made to save the stores at Nashville and that the panic of the people was caused by the army." [44]

Buell was now put in the, for him, uncomfortable position of trying to manage an entirely chaotic Nashville, with Grant, some six weeks later, leading his men in the massive, swampy, and successful battle at Shiloh in southwestern Tennessee.

For his part, Lincoln immediately recognized an opportunity to restore order both in Nashville and larger Tennessee, returning the state to its natural relationship with the Union. But he needed a man he could trust to manage that arduous task.

On March 3, Secretary of War Edwin Stanton, upon Lincoln's order, sent to Johnson a one-sentence notice informing him that he had been appointed as the new and first military governor of Tennessee, with all the "powers, duties, and functions pertaining to the office." [45]

Johnson was also swiftly commissioned a brigadier general, as approved by Congress. The commission made it possible for Johnson, whose entire career had been on the civil side, to take on any number of military tasks, commanding soldiers of his own choosing.

Johnson's appointment as military governor was both extraordinary and constitutionally vague, the latter ingredient being something that would have normally given this most constitution-obsessed politician pause.

But Johnson was eager to see life returned to normal in Tennessee, even though, as Johnson biographer Lately Thomas would note, the appointment made him the "virtual dictator of Tennessee until a civil government should be established." [46]

This meant he would be in control of both the local and state governments, could organize the courts, censor newspapers, seize property, schedule elections, and arrest anyone he felt like arresting. It was an entirely unique positon for which there was no precedence in American history.

In response, Johnson began packing his bags for Tennessee.

CHAPTER FOUR

An Olive Branch in One Hand and the Constitution in the Other

The appointment of Andrew Johnson as military governor was, at the least, unevenly received.

General William Nelson, commander of the Fourth Division of the Army of the Ohio, and now in Nashville under Don Carlos Buell's command, was appalled by the idea of Johnson being in control of everything.

"*Do not send* Andy Johnson here in any official capacity," Nelson wrote to Treasury Secretary Salmon P. Chase, assuming that Chase might be able to get Lincoln to withdraw Johnson's name.

"He presents a party!" Nelson exclaimed. "Let him come here as a Senator if he wants to. He is too much embittered to entrust with a mission as delicate as the direction of a people under the present circumstances. It would be better if the people here chose a Governor." [1]

From Nashville, an unenthused Buell would soon warn Johnson of his upcoming arrival in the capital city: "You must not expect to be received with enthusiasm, but rather the reverse, and I would suggest to you to enter without any display." [2]

Press response was less tentative with the *Washington Evening Star* remarking "His presence, influence and labors in Tennessee are absolutely necessary for a prompt restoration of the State to the Union." The *New York Tribune* called Johnson's selection "eminently proper, both in view of his peculiar fitness for the office and his great popularity among all loyal people." [3]

Undoubtedly reflecting aristocratic Confederate opinion, the *Charleston Mercury* condemned the announcement, describing Johnson as a man with a "strong native intellect, rude and uncultivated. He is yet a deep schemer, his vaulting ambition never baulked by consideration of honest and good faith." [4]

In fact, in a manner generally unappreciated at the time, Lincoln's choice of Johnson was in many ways brilliant not only because it was putting on the ground a tenacious Unionist determined to stamp out every vestige of Confederate support in Tennessee, but also because Johnson was so superbly knowledgeable when it came to the terrain he was to govern.

His understanding of the inner workings of Nashville was a case in point. He had spent, on and off, ten of the last 27 years in the state's capital city in his cumulative service as a member of the Tennessee House of Representatives, State Senate, and Governor.

He knew every street and alleyway in the metropolis of nearly 17,000 people, he knew the hotels, the restaurants, the private gentlemen's clubs, the theaters, and the churches. He knew the local political and financial powers; and most importantly who was a Confederate and who was a Unionist, as well as those likely leaning in either direction.

Johnson even knew every room, chamber, cubby hole, and hallway of the magnificent stone Greek Revival state capitol, distinguished by it's twenty-eight Greek columns and porticoes on every side of the building. He had for four years held fourth in the handsome, high-ceiling, multi-room governor's office back when he was the state's chief executive, and would only be too happy, if not delighted, to return to a space so hastily vacated, with papers flying in the air, by Isham Harris.

With little fanfare, Johnson departed from the downtown Washington railroad on the afternoon of March 7. Accompanying him was his son Robert, who had moved in with his father in Washington several weeks earlier. Also along for the ride: Tennessee Congressman Horace Maynard; Emerson Ethridge, former Tennessee Congressman; and William Browning, since the summer of 1861, Johnson's private secretary.

Anticipating the command confusion that might be a product of his governorship, Johnson made certain when his train made a stop in Cincinnati to wire Buell, sending a brief entreaty: "Any suggestion that General Buell may think proper to make in regard to the time or manner of my reaching Nashville will be thankfully received." [5]

Once in Louisville the following day, Johnson also sent a message to the new Secretary of War, Edwin Stanton. Just days before, Stanton had informed Johnson that his salary as military governor would be $3,000 a year and that he was allowed to tap into a $10,000 fund to organize a Union home guard in Tennessee. Now Johnson told Stanton that he thought a "judicious & prudent interposition of the pardoning power, in behalf of young men introduced into the rebel armies by force or artifice" would prove a good tool after his arrival in Tennessee. [6]

This message underlined several conceits, the first being that fears Johnson was about to impose a tyrannical control over Tennessee, most particularly persecuting real and suspected Confederates, were displaced. On the contrary, Johnson had already embraced an approach to his new job putting an emphasis on trying to make things work, and reaching out to as many politically diverse factions as possible.

Wiping the slate clean, especially for young Confederates, thought Johnson somewhat optimistically, "will have a happy effect upon the popular mind in our state." [7]

But Johnson's communication with Stanton also provided only the latest evidence of his theory that tens of thousands of working class Southerners, and, again, particularly young boys, had been coerced into joining the Confederate cause by wealthy, older, and more powerful aristocratic forces, the Jefferson Davis types that Johnson blamed for the secession movement in the first place.

The Johnson party arrived in Nashville late on the evening of March 12, checking into the downtown St. Cloud Hotel. Not until the following evening, when he was greeted outside the hotel by a large group of supporters, accompanied by a military band, did he offer his first public comments.

Nashville was clearly a place whose residents were rattled by a succession of events in the last year that had seen the Confederates take over the city by force before abandoning it in the face of the joint Union advance under Grant and Buell.

Stores, restaurants, and bars were closed, with residents pulling out their last savings from local banks and holing up in their homes anxiously awaiting assaults they feared would come from either the occupying Union forces, or a renewed Confederate effort to take the city back.

In brief remarks, Johnson immediately sought to calm matters by noting that he had come to the city "with the olive branch in one hand and the Constitution in the other."

His sole purpose in returning to Nashville, Johnson said, was to "render you whatever aid may be in my power" in ultimately returning Tennessee to the Union fold. [8]

Residing in a small room at the St. Cloud Hotel, and taking his meals in the hotel's dining room, Johnson would several weeks later move to a large, 8,100 square-foot brick house off of Cedar Street, just one block from the capitol.

The handsome residence, seized by Union forces, had belonged to Lizinka Campbell Brown, wealthy Nashville property owner who had left the city for Virginia and would subsequently marry a Confederate general.

The day following his arrival in Nashville, Johnson also set up shop in the familiar surroundings of the statehouse and made quick work of trying to organize his administration, appointing Nashville attorney Edward East as the new government's secretary of state; Joseph Fowler, president of the Howard Female College in Gallatin, as comptroller; and Congressman Maynard as attorney general.

"Johnson's speedy appointment of state officers, though they possessed little authority at first, suggested that he sought to fulfill Lincoln's wishes for an early restoration of civil government in Tennessee," historian William Harris has since observed. [9]

Several days later he brought onboard Edmund Cooper, a Shelbyville lawyer and former member of the state legislature, to serve as a staff assistant; and followed that up by giving a job to Benjamin Truman as an aide. The appointment of the 27 year-old Truman, a reporter who wrote regularly for the *Philadelphia Press* and the *New York Times*, would prove of particular value to Johnson primarily because Truman continued to contribute to those papers, providing stories slanted in Johnson's favor.

All the while the state capitol, which would soon come to be known as "Fort Andrew Johnson," was fortified with cotton bales, earthworks, and palisade fencing, while large cannons were eventually stationed at the base of the building.

On March 18, Johnson issued a carefully crafted roughly 1,200-word appeal to the people of Tennessee explaining the nature of his role as military governor and what he hoped to accomplish.

After briefly chronicling the extraordinary political events of the past year, Johnson noted that in the wake of the Union takeover of Nashville and Confederate Governor Isham Harris's decision to head for Memphis, "the State government has disappeared."

"The Executive has abdicated, the Legislature has dissolved; the Judiciary is in abeyance," Johnson noted.

"The great ship of state, freighted with its precious cargo of human interests and human hopes, it's sails all set, and its glorious flag unfurled, has suddenly been abandoned by its officers and mutinous crew, and left to float at the mercy of the winds and to be plundered by every rover upon the deep," Johnson recorded.

Under such conditions, the federal government, honoring its historic constitutional compact with the states, had no choice but to step in and restore civil rule in Tennessee.

"I have been appointed, in the absence of the regular and established State authorities, as Military Governor for the time being, to preserve the public property of the State, to give the protection of law actively enforced to her citizens, and, as speedily as may be, to restore her government to the same condition as before the existing rebellion," Johnson wrote.

Johnson then invited every citizen of Tennessee, regardless of "party affiliations or past political opinion or action," to join him in the effort to restore order and law in the state.

He promised that those appointed to the top state positions were only going to serve until an election could be held, and equally important, that the people's rights "will be duly respected, and their wrongs redressed when made known."

The duration of the message was spirited by the kind of conciliation fostered by Lincoln, an emphasis surprising to Johnson detractors who expected nothing less than a declaration of dictatorship.

Those who had given voice to the Confederate cause, promised Johnson, would be welcome to return to the Union fold. And while those who did more than just voice an opinion, but openly agitated for the Confederacy, may have to come to terms with the error of their ways, "no merely retaliatory or vindictive policy will be adopted."

On the contrary, "a full and complete amnesty for all past acts and declarations is offered, upon the one condition of their again yielding themselves peaceful citizens to the just supremacy of the laws."

He advised all such would-be expatriates to declare their fealty to the restored Union, "for their own good," before signing off by pointing to his long public record as a predicate to "the performance of my present and future duties." [10]

The appeal was printed on posters and fliers and distributed throughout Tennessee, while also being published in newspapers both across the state and region.

But despite its pacific tone, Johnson knew the appeal's rhetorical power would almost instantly be challenged by real-life events: the tough and inevitably controversial decisions and actions he would feel compelled to take to return Tennessee to civil rule.

The spirit of the document, in fact, was already found wanting in some quarters by Johnson's decision to take control of the Nashville offices of the large Bank of Tennessee, ordering a lieutenant colonel of the Army of the Ohio to "take immediate possession of the building fixtures and appurtenances" of the bank, "and hold it and its controls securely until further orders." [11]

He knew because, once again, he knew everybody in Nashville, that the bank's leadership was made up of Confederate loyalists, and was even more determined to punish the institution for continuing to honor Confederacy currency, even after Union soldiers had moved into the city.

The major assets of the bank had, in fact, been removed to a branch office in Chattanooga, where Johnson, following the money, had Joseph Rye, a top officer there, arrested, while the president of the bank, Francis Dunnington, fled the city. [11]

In short order, some of the office space in the bank's downtown Nashville building was soon set aside for use by the Paymaster of the U.S. Army.

Meanwhile, in trying to find his footing with Buell, Johnson asked the General on March 19 to what extent he could rely upon the military to carry out his various orders, prompting Buell on the same day to courteously respond: "The troops under my command will be instructed to comply with the requisitions which you may in my absence make upon them for the enforcement of your authority as Military Governor within their respective limits." [12]

But Buell added that any such orders to the military, or "requisitions," as the General made a point of saying, "must be dependent on the plan of military operations against the enemy." [13]

This was an exceedingly circumscribed response that essentially told Johnson that Buell would help him when he felt like it, but retained the right at any time to not help at all.

Johnson, instead, quickly decided to go over Buell's head, writing to Stanton on March 21: "I desire to be informed upon whom & to what extent I can rely for the military forces necessary to execute such orders as in the discharge of my official duties I may deem expedient, prudent & proper to make." [14]

Within a day Stanton, adroitly avoiding a direct conflict with the recalcitrant Buell, informed Johnson that he had just sent instructions to Henry Halleck, major general in charge of the Department of the Mississippi, to "place an adequate military force under your command and to communicate with you in respect to military aid." [15]

Stanton's response solved one immediate challenge for Johnson, but he could tell by Buell's non-response response that he was nevertheless going to have trouble with the General in the future. The simple truth was that Buell resented civil authority in general and Johnson in particular, and had determined from the start not to cooperate with the Military Governor simply because he didn't feel like cooperating.

Sure enough, on April 4 Johnson suggested to Buell that a small force of cavalry should be sent to the Kentucky border where, he had been told, the Confederates were especially active, only to receive the almost inevitable response a full seven days later: "With the pressing demand for troops in other quarters, it will not be possible to spare troops for the service you suggest." [16]

Johnson probably shook his head in dismay reading Buell's response, but for the moment he had other pressing matters to attend to.

Looking at the remnants of Nashville's city council as an ashbin of Confederate support, Johnson sent an official notice to the members of that body requiring each to take an oath declaring their loyalty to the Union.

The Mayor of Nashville and leader of the council, Richard Cheathem, had been a particularly enthusiastic Confederate, joining in the 1861 campaign to separate Tennessee from the Union, and raising funds for Confederate soldiers once the war was fully underway. Johnson's move to suspend the council and his subsequent decision to arrest Cheatham after the mayor made a conspicuous point of not taking the oath, could have proven yet one more irritant to Buell who had met with the Mayor not long after he initially entered Nashville, assuring him of the Union's peaceful intentions.

Debating Johnson's request, members of the council shortly issued an official response claiming that as city officials they were "not properly subject to such requirement." [17]

Johnson contemplated what to do next. The idea that he, as Military Governor, frequently flew off the handle, was seen as wide of the mark by the simple fact that it took him nearly two weeks to respond, time undoubtedly spent studying the matter and consulting with lawyers, before issuing a proclamation dismissing the entire council from their offices for having "manifested such disloyalty and enmity to the Government of the United States." [18]

Only by the lights of the most implacable Johnson foe could this action be seen as precipitate. It wasn't just that Mayor Cheatham and the council members had, after due consideration, decided to stick a collective thumb in Johnson's eye, it was also that the council continued to give their support to a rebellion at war with the country they lived in. The council members at this point were clearly trading in treason and were lucky that Johnson didn't round up the whole lot of them.

Simultaneously, Johnson went after the Nashville press, or at least that part of it that had also, like the members of the city council, cheered the Confederates on.

The offenders were several, but most prominently the *Nashville Republican Banner,* which had not only toed the Confederate line, but had also in some ways rather mindlessly promoted the Confederate war cause, implausibly asserting that Grant's takeover of Fort Donelson was actually a Rebel victory and predicting that a Union advance into Nashville was "entirely out of the question." [19]

Johnson ordered the arrest of the *Banner's* editor, George Barber, who shortly announced his conversion to the Union cause, remarking that he had had "an entirely satisfactory conversation" with Johnson and regarded restrictions to be placed upon his publication by the Military Governor as "wholly proper under the circumstances." [20]

Even so, Johnson shortly became an enthusiast of the new *Nashville Daily Union*, which was launched on April 10 with the goal of providing the Federal point of view. Fully appreciating how newspapers survived, Johnson shortly sent a note to Secretary of State William Seward describing the publication as "zealous in its labors for the restoration of the Union," and suggesting that the federal government should select the paper for its advertising and official notices. Johnson himself also soon began to send funds to the paper, months before Washington provided up to $800 in patronage support for it. [21]

With revenue also coming in from bookstore, theater, clothing store, and hotel advertising, the *Nashville Daily Union* could soon boast that it had the "largest circulation of any other daily newspaper that has been published here for years," and that not only was it the official publication of the federal and state governments, it also had "immediate communication with the Military Headquarters, which no other paper here has." [22]

Johnson shortly also got wind of a handful of ministers in the city continuing to uphold the Confederate cause from their pulpits on Sundays. Perhaps the worst of the bunch was Robert Howell, pastor of the First Baptist Church, who in a sermon just months earlier had remarked of the Confederate Army: "Our defenders are impelled no less by their religion than by their patriotism. Can they fail? I do not believe it. It is, I know, possible, but not at all probable. Fail? No, never!" [23]

Pro-Confederate ministers also included Edmund Sehon, pastor of the Methodist Episcopal Church; Reuben Ford, pastor of Cherry Street Baptist; and William Sawrie, pastor of the Andrew Church.

Meeting with the church leaders in his office, with *New York Herald* reporter Samuel Glenn sitting to the side and taking notes, Johnson was blunt: unless the men were willing to sign a loyalty oath, he would be forced to place them under arrest. When the men blandly declined, Johnson not only issued an order for them to be imprisoned, but made a point of remarking that once confined, they should not be regarded as "objects of especial attention," but rather as nothing more than "enemies of our Government, and as such are entitled and should receive such consideration only as attaches to a person guilty of so infamous a crime." [24]

Two of the men were sent to the Camp Mortan prison in Indianapolis, with the rest deposited beyond Confederate lines, where Johnson assumed they could preach to their own kind.

During these same weeks Johnson was tasked by an endless stream of visitors who came to his office asking for help. Men looking for work; women left destitute due to their husbands, fathers, or sons being gone and serving in the war; family members pleading with him to use his influence to secure the release of young Confederate soldiers now being held in Union prisons.

On this final question, Johnson tried a number of approaches, hoping in the process that the release of Southern prisoners could facilitate, in turn, the release of Union prisoners in Alabama where, Johnson informed Lincoln, "they are treated with more cruelly than wild beats of the forest." [25]

Ultimately, Johnson, despite getting the bureaucratic support he needed for such an effort from Washington, was successful in fostering only a small number of prisoner exchanges in the immediate months to come. But the problem would remain to frustrate and haunt him throughout the duration of the war.

His anguish was genuine: he felt badly for all Southern boys locked away up North, convinced that they were victims of the times. But the idea of loyal soldiers and residents from Tennessee, in particular those who had been rounded up in East Tennessee, being deprived and tortured behind bars in the South, maddened him.

Rumors. Johnson was hearing everywhere he went in Nashville that it was only a matter of time until the Confederates tried to retake the city. It was a proposition made all the more discomfiting after Buell moved the vast majority of his troops out of the city to join Grant at Shiloh. "This place as I conceive it has been left almost defenseless by Gen'l Buell," Johnson complained to Stanton. [26]

Stanton, like Lincoln, determined to see that Johnson's government endured, responded within hours: "Immediate steps will be taken to correct the evil." [27]

In the vast majority of his communications with Washington, Johnson during these days repeatedly expressed an optimism that belied his prickly, negative reputation. On March 21, he told Stanton, "I am putting the state machinery in action as fast as possible," adding "All is working well. A great reaction is going on." On April 9, he reported to Lincoln: "All is working well beyond my most sanguine expectations." Three days after that, Johnson, in promising to soon send to Lincoln a full account of matters since his arrival in Nashville, said of general conditions in the state: "They are working better than anyone could have expected." [28]

How to explain this buoyancy? An easy answer is that in taking over the city, organizing his administration, seizing control of such studied institutions as a bank and city council, and changing by force the editorial direction of several newspapers, Johnson had every reason to feel good about what he was doing. Progress was indeed being made, and every act, every move he had made since taking power had only solidified the Union position in Nashville and the state.

But its also possible that these declarations of hope and promise were nothing more than Johnson's attempt to reassure himself. He knew that his position was singularly precarious. Confederate sympathizers still populated the city and state, their presence made all the more threatening now because so many of them had gone underground, their movements increasingly difficult for Johnson to monitor.

Asking Buell on April 24 to not remove a remaining regiment in the city, Johnson received another response from the General who seemed determined to never state anything clearly to the Military Governor: "It will not do to let the Enemy close around your city before we begin to drive him away," agreed Buell, before vaguely promising that any regiment yanked from the city would be replaced soon enough by another. [29]

Johnson thought this was all not just extraordinarily inept, but running at a cross purpose in his effort to convince the people of Nashville that the Union was once again in firm command of the city. The effect, he told Horace Maynard on April 24, "is visible in the face of every secessionist. Secession was cooling down & great reaction in favor of the Union was taking place." [30]

This latter communication sparked a series of agitated messages from Maynard to Stanton to Halleck to Buell, concluding with the Buell's acid observation that his need to send troops south was a "matter of far greater moment than the gratification of Governor Johnson, whose views upon the matter are absurd." [31]

So now it was out: Buell not only had no intention of doing anything that Johnson requested of him, but he regarded the Military Governor as a prattling idiot whose knowledge of military strategy was less than zero.

On the very same day that Buell offered up to Halleck his true view of Johnson, he also sent a quick message to Johnson himself stating "I am anxious to gratify you but you will see the propriety of making all considerations yield to that disposition of the troops which is necessary for the security of Nashville." [32]

Johnson saw Buell's disingenuous message for what it was and exploded. "Petty jealousies and contests between Generals wholly incompetent to discharge duties assigned to them have contributed more to the defeat and embarrassment of the Government than all other causes combined," Johnson bluntly wired Lincoln. [33]

Sympathizing with Johnson's predicament, the President nevertheless said he was inclined for the moment to leave all decisions regarding the movement of troops in Tennessee in the hands of Halleck, arguing that Halleck "understands better than we can here and he must be allowed to control in that quarter." [34]

But, obviously appreciating Johnson's need, at the very least, for straight answers, Lincoln additionally suggested: "If you are not in communication with Halleck, telegraph him at once, freely and frankly." [35]

As Confederate raids throughout Tennessee increased into early May, Johnson could not get over Buell's decision to leave Nashville so exposed, commenting to Stanton: "The very fact of the forces being withdrawn from this locality has inspired secession with insolence and confidence and Union men with distrust as to the power and intention of the Government to protect and defend them."

Eloquently, Johnson said of the flagging Unionists in his midst: "They have not arms, secessionists have."

"The whole moral power has been lost, and, in fact, we are here now almost in a helpless condition." [36]

The day after this message, Johnson stopped into a crowded pro-Union gathering of lawmakers and other local political leaders held in the airy marble House chamber of the state capitol. In what turned out to be a three-hour address, Johnson, still presenting an optimistic face to the public, said the coming violent resistance to the Confederacy was not unlike the "roaring and moaning in the trees [to] indicate the approaching storm."

He then attacked Confederate leaders for the carnage they had wrought. "Look around your streets and see the habiliments of woe, mothers and sisters draped in black," Johnson said. "Who is responsible for this?"

"There is a fearful responsibility somewhere, and let us ask who hurried off husbands and brothers and sons to acts of treachery, and involved them in riot and strife, plunder and contention," he continued. [37]

Interlaced in these remarks was Johnson's increasing conviction that the vast majority of Southern whites were not the enemies of the Union, but the victims of the Confederacy. This conceit was all but lost on a national audience that continued to interpret Johnson's actions and remarks as emblematic of one man standing up against an entire region.

In fact, Johnson, by the day, was harboring an evolving view of the mass of his fellow Southern whites that would eventually entirely dismay his Northern admirers, a view that over time would equate the excesses of Radical Republicanism with the excesses of the Confederate government: they were both powerful, malevolent forces exploiting an unprotected people.

Favorable response to Johnson's House of Representatives address prompted him to decide to travel to other parts of the state and make the case for his administration. With *New York Herald* reporter Samuel Glenn, Johnson made a short 34-mile journey to Murfreesboro on May 24 to give a brief speech in front of the city's courthouse.

The 42 year-old Glenn was an amiable traveling companion. Beginning his career as a compositor, Glenn had started to write for the *Herald* in the late 1830s and was genuinely admired by publisher James Gordon Bennett, who admired few people, for his tenacity and intelligence. A fellow journalist would later say that Glenn was "fond of his toddy, never declining and often tendering the hospitality of the bar and table." He was also a reporter who knew a good story, and just being with Johnson anywhere these days guaranteed that. [38]

When the men arrived in Murfreesboro, they noticed that a rudimentary platform had been set up from which Johnson was expected to speak: two boards placed over the tops of a couple of wooden barrels. Gamely, Johnson stepped up and delivered brief remarks to a crowd that received him tepidly.

In a part of the state that produced a strong vote for John Breckinridge in the presidential election of 1860, Johnson made a point of recalling that he, too, had been a Breckinridge man in the contest. But now that Breckinridge had left the U.S. Senate and become a brigadier general for the Confederate Army, posing a threat to invade Murfreesboro, Johnson had no more use for him. He admittedly found it difficult to despise the gallant Kentuckian the way he did Jefferson Davis. Even so, said Johnson, Breckinridge had deceived him once. This was not his fault, Johnson averred. Were he to be deceived again, "it would be." [39]

Once again, Johnson declared a general amnesty for any young man who had joined the Confederate cause under duress.

During the first week of June, Johnson celebrated the Union advance into and Confederate retreat from Memphis, a victory that only partially alleviated his fears that eventually the Confederate Army was going to launch a new assault at some other point in Tennessee. Just four weeks later came news of Murfreesboro's swift capture by Confederates under the leadership of the intrepid General Nathan Bedford Forrest, a Union defeat that Johnson partially blamed on the "inexcusable negligence and difference between [regimental] commanders." [40]

Despairing that Buell would ever adequately re-enforce Nashville, let alone finally launching an East Tennessee incursion, Johnson told Lincoln on July 10: "General Buell is not the man to redeem East Tennessee." He additionally asked for a change in the leadership of Buell's command, wondering if, as Military Governor, he himself didn't have the power to replace officers and appoint their successors.

"I must have the means to execute my orders or abandon the undertaking," Johnson told the President frankly. [41]

No less candid, Lincoln somewhat jocularly responded: "Do you not, my good friend, perceive that what you ask is simply to put you in command in the West. I do not suppose that you desire this." [42]

Hoping to get a better picture of what was going in in Tennessee, while facilitating a more efficient communication between Johnson and the Union command, Lincoln suggested that Johnson should confer with Halleck as soon as possible. "Telegraph him and meet him at such places as he and you can agree upon." [43]

At the same time, Lincoln sent a short wire to Halleck describing Johnson as "a true, and a valuable man—indispensable to us in Tennessee," and asking that he meet with the Military Governor as soon as possible. [44]

Because of a conflict in schedules, the Johnson-Halleck meeting never took place. Still, Johnson won one bureaucratic victory when Secretary Stanton, upon Lincoln's order, bestowed upon the Military Governor the authority to appoint anyone he desired as provost marshal in charge of Nashville, pointedly adding: "The President hopes this will be satisfying to you and that you will use efforts to prevent any disputes or collision between your subordinates and those of Genl Buell." [45]

While Johnson remained convinced that Buell was hampering Union efforts throughout Tennessee, Brigadier General William Nelson, never a Johnson fan, thought it was the Military Governor himself who was the biggest problem. "The hostility to the United States Government and the troops has increased 1,000 percent," Nelson told Buell in late July.

"It seems settled into a fierce hatred to Governor Johnson, to him personally more than officially," Nelson continued, noting that in conversations with residents no one could point to a single act that Johnson had taken that they opposed. Rather they were against his manner of doing things, a resentment that had become "fierce and vindictive." [46]

For his part, reporter Glenn perfectly understood Johnson's point of view as it applied to the state's vulnerability. In mid-July, Glenn rode out in the countryside, noting of the few Federal soldiers posted in the state: "The Union forces are stationed in small squads along the lines of railroads, at long intervals, and occupy villages in small numbers. The enemy makes a dash into those places, commit their depredations, and then fly upon fleet horses far beyond the reach of the Union soldiery, whose only means of locomotion are their own legs." [47]

With Murfreesboro now under Confederate control, Johnson was convinced an invasion of Nashville was just hours away. His anxieties were shared by residents of the city who stayed indoors, with many of the same stores, taverns, and restaurants that had opened up when the Union took control, once again closed.

The city was hot, humid, and uneasily quiet.

The crisis would pass when the Confederates pulled back from the front of Nashville during the final week of July. But just four weeks later, Buell informed Johnson that he was heading up to Louisville, 195 miles to the north, to block a Confederate takeover of the Kentucky city.

One again, Nashville was left nearly entirely unprotected. Once again, a siege mentality gripped the city. Sleeping at night in the capitol, and spending most of his days with Johnson, Samuel Glenn couldn't help but admire the Military Governor's resolve. "The coolness and calmness of the Governor amid these trying scenes are beyond all praise," the journalist marveled. [48]

"I hope that you will not think it out of place when I state that there must be more efficiency imparted to the Army in this part of Tennessee, or we are doomed to meet with reverses that will retard and protract the War, if not in the end to result in the loss of Tennessee," Johnson told Buell on August 22. [49]

A short time later Buell wired Johnson a justification for both failing to invade East Tennessee as well as fully protect Nashville. He told Johnson of the many other challenges confronting his men in recent weeks, including the need to build railroad bridges destroyed by the Confederates, let alone trying to do anything in a countryside constantly menaced by "an immense force of irregular cavalry." [50]

Buell's need to put on paper the reason for his army's delays most likely had nothing to do with Johnson. He clearly cared not a whit what the Military Governor thought of him. But he was also aware that, given the increasing delays of doing anything in Tennessee, a case was most likely being built in the War Department bureaucracy against him, and wanted to have his side of the story put on the record.

This latest exchange simply and painfully reaffirmed for Johnson that Buell needed to go. In what historian Clifton Hall has described as an "almost despairing letter to Lincoln," Johnson said he was now convinced as he had never been before that Buell would never take the fight to the Confederates, and that he had never intended to in the first place. [51]

Daringly, Johnson exclaimed: "It seems to me that Genl Buell fears his own personal safety and has concluded to gather the whole army at this point as a kind of body guard to protect him." [52]

The last charge was unfair. There was no evidence that Buell was afraid of anyone, but it did seem more apparent that, sympathetic to the South, the General's heart just wasn't in the battle.

"May God save my country from some of the Generals who have been conducting this war," Johnson signed off, expressing a sentiment undoubtedly shared by Lincoln, who had frustratingly been trying at this very time to get George McClellan to move in Virginia. [53]

Johnson did not say as much, but the truth was that by mid-September Nashville had never been more vulnerable. Confederate soldiers outside the city had severed telegraph lines and destroyed a railroad tunnel, leading to yet another sense of impending doom on the part of Nashville's residents.

Hunkered down again with Johnson and a handful of military and administrative aides, Glenn wrote: "We are surrounded by the enemy. Things look gloomy."

"Days, weeks, nay, months roll around and there seems to be no change for the better," declared Glenn. [55]

When Buell at last entered the city in early September, he responded positively to a request from Johnson for a meeting. The encounter could not have been pleasant for either man. Both were war-weary in different ways. Both were also tired and desperate and angry. After some desultory conversation, Johnson asked Buell directly: was Nashville to be "given up or evacuated without resistance?"

As Johnson recalled several months later, Buell responded with "some little warmth that he was indifferent to the criticism that might be made in regard to his policy or manner of conducting the campaign."

Buell additionally told Johnson, or so Johnson said, that the holding of Nashville from a "military point of view was of no great importance." On the contrary, continued Buell, the city should have been "abandoned or evacuated three months ago." [55]

That Buell finally said as much to Johnson in person must have enraged the Military Governor. Soon there were reports that the meeting between the two men had resulted in fisticuffs. The reports were wrong, but undoubtedly reflected what had now become common knowledge: the two men had no use for each other. Rather than assaulting Buell, Johnson probably at this point just wanted him to leave the premises, realizing that there was nothing more to be done with him.

A brief break from the endless tedium of the siege was provided on October 12 when members of the Johnson family arrived in the city. "Even the Governor's Roman sternness was overcome," noted Glenn when he saw him embrace Eliza Johnson. Also arriving: Johnson's son Charles, daughter Mary Stover and her husband Daniel Stover. [56]

But even in the midst of what was obviously a joyous family reunion, Johnson remained pensive. It may have been the silence that bothered him the most. There was no cannon fire. No gun shots. No sounds of troops and wagons and horses clomping into town.

"Nashville is surrounded by rebels committing depredations," noted a dispatch appearing in the *Chicago Tribune* on October 13. "The federals are on half rations. Provisions are at fabulous prices." [57]

"Cut off from communications from the outer world, our supplies becoming exhausted, deprived of almost all articles of luxury, and even comfort, and subject to the ill-disguised sneers and taunts of the Union haters, our lot is a hard one," wrote Glenn in his diary. [58]

Promising news of a different sort finally came from an unexpected source during the final days of October: the national press was reporting that Buell had been sacked by Halleck. The problems were many, but a tipping point was undoubtedly reached after Confederate General

Braxton Bragg was able to successfully withdraw his troops from Kentucky, eluding and essentially outmaneuvering Buell. That, and Buell's attempt to explain to Washington his failure to move into East Tennessee as being due entirely to the Confederacy's larger numbers in the region, determined and doomed his future.

Lincoln, Stanton, and Halleck all now came to the same conclusion that Johnson had reached weeks earlier: Buell had to go. [59]

Almost indifferently, Buell gathered his army for one last meeting to announce he was leaving them. "He laced his words with as much emotion as he could muster," records Buell's biographer, Stephen Engle, "saying it was difficult to leave the army he had shaped and that he alone was responsible for not meeting the desires of the administration." [60]

Johnson felt no sense of triumph over Buell's fall. He was never the sort of man who enjoyed Machiavellian politics. On the contrary, he had hoped from the start that Buell would prove an effective commander and that both of them would by now be celebrating together the liberation of East Tennessee as well as a general routing of the Confederates throughout the state.

Just hours before Buell's dismissal was publicly known, Johnson had sent by courier a quick message to Lincoln declaring that federal troops under a different leadership should now come and "redeem East Tennessee before Christmas."

For the President's information only, Johnson mentioned that he would have "much to say upon this subject at the proper time," adding in an aside that said much about the current state of affairs in Nashville: "I will communicate fully all that has transpired as soon as mail facilities are restored." [61]

CHAPTER FIVE

COME WEAL AND WOE

Just days before General William Rosecrans, assigned to replace Buell, arrived in Nashville, young Johnson aide Benjamin Truman detrained in Washington carrying a note of introduction to be delivered to Lincoln.

The letter, written by Johnson, was to the point: Truman, Johnson informed Lincoln, was a "gentleman of intelligence and character who has been in Nashville since my arrival."

Continued Johnson: Truman was "perfectly familiar with the condition of things here." Anything he might have to say about conditions in Nashville and larger Tennessee, Johnson assured the President, "can be implicitly relied upon." [1]

Truman was in Washington for two reasons: he hoped to re-establish ties with the influential John Forney, publisher of the *Philadelphia Press* and secretary of the U.S. Senate. At the same time, in sitting down with Lincoln, Truman wanted to give him Johnson's perspective on matters in Tennessee.

Whether Johnson or Truman spurred the latter's Washington trip is unknown. Certainly Truman, keeping a foot in both the journalistic and political worlds, had every reason to want to speak with Forney, whose *Philadelphia Press* he would continue to report for sporadically for the duration of the war. But Johnson may have also wanted Truman in Washington because he was concerned about Lincoln's reaction to his latest controversy with yet another Union commander.

General James Negley, who had remained in Nashville after Buell's departure, was soon seen by Johnson as being both unresponsive to the Military Governor's initiatives as well as lacking the ardor needed for his job. On November 8, Johnson told Lincoln that Negley "has done us more harm than all the others & is wholly unfitted for the place." [2]

Several days after he made the rounds in Washington, Truman was able to tell Johnson by letter that he had met with Forney and explained to him Johnson's disenchantment with Negley. More important, Truman accompanied Forney when he subsequently visited the White House. Once there, the influential Forney argued strenuously that Johnson "should have the full control of everything." [3]

Everything in this case meant having actual command control of troop strategy and movements throughout Tennessee. Lincoln, by all reports, appeared amenable, although he declined to comment on Johnson's move to build the Nashville & Northwestern Railroad, connecting Nashville to the town of Johnsonville on the banks of the Tennessee river.

Truman's Washington journey also paid off journalistically, with Forney telling Truman that he regarded him as one of his most valued correspondents. He added that he could write for his newspaper from any number of Southern locales but, Truman emphasized to Johnson, "desires me to go to East Tennessee."

"Therefore, I accepted the latter," Truman said, reflecting a hunch shared by other reporters in late 1862 that something big was finally about to happen in the region of Tennessee that Johnson admittedly cared about the most. [4]

By the time Forney returned to Tennessee, Rosecrans had already established himself in the state, entirely impressing Johnson in the process.

"I feel in strong hope that things will go well in a few days," Johnson informed Lincoln on November 18, pointedly adding that the General was "a man at the head of this army who will fight." [5]

Rosecrans' entrance into Nashville effectively ended, at least for the present, the siege of the city. Even more, his successful move to check Braxton Bragg at Murfreesboro in the early days of 1863 confirmed Johnson's confidence in the General.

The Murfreesboro battle, a happy Johnson informed a relieved Lincoln, "has inspired much confidence with Union men of the ultimate success of the Government, and has greatly discouraged rebels, but increased their bitterness." [6]

Yet, even with this signal victory, Johnson continued to worry about the length and depth of Confederate support throughout the state.

Sitting down in his state capitol office with Rosecrans, Johnson constructed what came to be known as a "Guarantee of Protection," an official state document promising that his administration would protect all "true and steadfast citizens of the United States" willing to state their fealty to the country.

The offer was muddied by a requirement that anyone signing on to the agreement must also come up with a bond which would be forfeited if the signer in anyway provided aid to the Confederate government or travelled "beyond the lines of the Federal Armies." [7]

Johnson and Rosecrans' collaboration on the Guarantee document gave early evidence of a productive working relationship between the two men, a relationship that several months later saw the Military Governor telling the General "No one will go further than I in vindication of your character." [8]

Slender, handsome, and optimistic, the 43 year-old Rosecrans, according to historian Allan Nevins, was "an excellent organizer and disciplinarian, and a tremendous worker." "He is sound to the bone on the great questions of the war and the way it should be conducted,"

Brigadier General James Garfield said of Rosecrans to Treasury Secretary Salmon Chase. [9]

Chase himself, who like Johnson, had grown wary of Buell's delays in Tennessee and urged Lincoln to put Rosecrans in Buell's place, told Rosecrans directly that he knew he was for "earnest, vigorous, decisive action," adding: "You now have a great—a glorious opportunity which other generals have foolishly thrown away." [10]

Rosecrans' determination to fight, so clearly seen in his retaking of Murfreesboro, allowed Johnson the freedom to absent himself from Tennessee for a period of three months beginning in late February in order to honor several speaking invitations he had received in the North, culminating in a triumphant return to Washington where he delivered a widely-covered pro-Union address in the House chamber, an event seeing Lincoln, members of the president's cabinet, and most of the major Senate and House leader in attendance.

Speaking initially on February 26 in Indianapolis before a massive crowd of more than 25,000 people on the grounds of the State House, Johnson developed the themes that he would expand upon for the next twelve weeks, one of the primary conceits of which was the basic inanity of the secession movement.

Reminding an entirely appreciative audience that lawmakers from the South held the balance of power in Washington at the time of Lincoln's inaugural, Johnson noted that the President most likely could not have secured confirmation of a single cabinet member without their consent. The members of the Southern caucus, Johnson declared, had it in their power to "make the whole cabinet."

"Where was the danger, then, from his administration?" Johnson asked, ridiculing the wholesale departure of Southern senators and representatives who exited Washington once their states seceded.

He then sought to turn on its head the long-standing Confederate claim that the war the South was waging was entirely defensive in nature.

"Who commenced this war, this damnable struggle to destroy the people's rights?" Johnson asked, before answering: "The South."

"Who struck the first blow, fired the first gun, shed the first blood?" Johnson continued.

Far from the South defending anything, countered Johnson, it was Lincoln who, once the Confederacy began hostilities, "called for men to defend the Constitution and the laws."

The war, Johnson continued, was entirely of the South's doing, a war that "set brother against brother, orphaned these children, widowed these wives, and filled the land with mourning."

"Lift up your hands," Johnson commanded of the Confederate sympathizers who most likely were not in attendance in Indianapolis, "and see if they are not crimsoned with the blood of the victims of the rebellion."

Johnson then introduced a topic that may have made his Northern listeners squirm: what to do about slavery?

"I have lived among negroes all my life and I am for the government under the Constitution as it is, if the Government can be saved," Johnson remarked. "I am for the government without negroes, and the Constitution as it is."

Although Lincoln had just weeks earlier given evidence of a profound evolution in his thinking in announcing a graduated policy of emancipation, Johnson wasn't there yet. But the thought of a United States without slavery was at the very least something he was now willing to contemplate. For the present, he argued, without a sense of irony, the larger "battle for human liberty" was of greater importance than the institution of slavery. [11]

Johnson spoke to another immense gathering in Cincinnati on February 27 and the Ohio Legislature on March 3, before arriving on Saturday,

March 7 in Washington and checking into the familiar surroundings of the St. Charles Hotel.

The following day he met with an entirely receptive Lincoln in the White House, bringing the President up to date on Tennessee matters. Not for the first time, Lincoln urged Johnson to schedule elections in the Volunteer State as soon as possible, with Johnson, also not for the first time, promising to do what he could at the next opportune moment.

Making the rounds in Washington, Johnson two days later received an urgent message from John Forney who told him it was imperative that he make an appearance the following evening for an event at Philadelphia's National Union Club. "For your own sake and for our country's sake, do accept the invitation of our hosts of loyal men." [12]

A native Pennsylvanian, Forney knew the political importance of his state, and as a Johnson supporter, wanted him to make contacts there that might prove useful should the Military Governor someday want to seek national office.

The thinking was always, and Johnson had heard it many times going back to his famous late 1860 anti-secession speech, that he would make for a formidable presidential candidate sometime in the distant future. Most often that distant future was mentioned as 1868, after Lincoln had served two successful terms. How seriously Johnson took such speculation was hard to say. An election more than five years in the future was a lifetime in the political world.

Still, Johnson was aware of his growing national fame, and had undoubtedly wondered just exactly what he would do once the war finally came to an end and his services as Military Governor were no longer needed. Plus, he had always believed in moving onward and upward in his career, and after his current position, where else was there to go except the White House?

Johnson agreed to speak before the Philadelphia gathering, and could not have been displeased to hear a military band in attendance play *Hail to the Chief* as he rose to speak.

What turned out to be a successful Philadelphia event meshed with other speaking engagements Johnson had committed himself to in the days ahead, including a speech on March 14 to the Loyal League at the Academy of Music in New York, an event that a correspondent for the *New York Herald* said was particularly notable for the "crushing and crowding and eager masses pressed forward to listen." [13]

One week later Johnson arrived in Baltimore for yet another Union-boosting rally, this one at the Hall of Maryland Institute where he spoke for the better part of two hours. Uncharacteristically, Johnson several times employed humor to make his points. Addressing himself to those criticizing Lincoln for his suspension of the writ of habeas corpus, Johnson told of a preacher whose axe had been stolen by someone in his congregation. Picking up a rock, the preacher said he was going to pitch it at the person who took the axe, only to all of a sudden see a "fellow dodge under the bench."

Similarly, Johnson told his audience, "whenever you want to find a traitor, just ask him about the suspension of habeas corpus." [14]

It was a clever remark, and one meant to cast ridicule particularly on the loud Northern Peace Democrat movement, a gathering of war dissidents including former president Franklin Pierce that often complained about Lincoln's selective suspension of habeas corpus in matters relating to criticism of his administration's war policies.

While Johnson's appearances in Philadelphia, New York, and Baltimore were entirely successful and well covered in the prominent newspapers of the East, none of them compared with the dramatic import of his participation in a pro-Union meeting held inside the U.S. Capitol's House chamber on the evening of March 31.

For the better part of a week leading up to the unusual gathering, the event was promoted in both the Washington and national press. But on the day of the gathering itself, Washington was hit with a violent rainstorm that pummeled the city throughout the afternoon and early evening hours.

The downpour, however, did little to stop visitors from flocking to the capitol, first arriving by the dozens, and then by the hundreds. The House chamber where Johnson would speak was soon "crowded to its utmost capacity, and the lobbies leading to the doors, both of the galleries and the floor, were thronged by those who could not obtain even standing room inside," noted one reporter. [15]

Just before the proceedings began, with a Marine band playing military tunes, Lincoln walked into the chamber accompanied by Secretary of State William Seward, Treasury Secretary Salmon Chase, Secretary of the Interior John Usher, and Postmaster General Montgomery Blair, all taking reserved seats to the direct front of the podium from where Johnson would speak.

Preceded by several speakers, including his old friend Horace Maynard, Johnson soon delivered one of the finest and most-tightly reasoned addresses of his career.

"Give it to them, Andy!" an audience member in the gallery yelled out to the amusement of the vast assemblage just before Johnson spoke. [16]

And give it to them he did.

As he began his address, Johnson quoted from Lincoln's 1861 inaugural address in which the President had defined the coming struggle as a "people's contest."

That struggle, Lincoln had said, would be waged against oppression by those whose leading object is to "elevate the condition of man, to lift artificial weights from all shoulders, to clear the path of laudable pursuits to all, and to afford all an unfettered start and a fair chance in the race of life."

Now, Johnson declared simply, "That single paragraph illustrates the contest in which the country is now engaged. It is a struggle for free government. It is a contest of the many on one hand and of the few on the other. Shift it and mystify it as we may, this is the plain naked issue, and the query is whether we will maintain and perpetuate a free government."

Johnson then derided the notion that the war was a "Republican war," before deliciously ridiculing Southern lawmakers who had left Washington during the early weeks of secession, one of his favorite topics of derision.

"What did you go for?" Johnson asked rhetorically. "While you were here the capital of the government was in your possession."

"You went South to join Jeff Davis—to do what?" Johnson asked. "To take Washington, the capital of the government? While you were here you had it, it was in your possession, it was under your control."

But, continued Johnson, hugely enjoying what he regarded as the absurdity of secessionist reasoning: "The Government was free and you had a Constitution. But you, for the purpose of getting your rights and carrying out Southern principles, gave up what you had, and went South for the purpose of fighting to get it back again."

Johnson then defended Lincoln's policy on habeas corpus, declaring that in a time of rebellion, it was "clear that it could be suspended," before saying that his only objection to Lincoln's policy was that "he has not arrested more of these traitors," a remark that must have amused the President.

Johnson finally eviscerated the notion that the federal government could at any time broker some sort of compromise with the Confederate government. "Compromise with whom?" Johnson thundered. "With our brethren of the South? Talk to me about my brother when he stands with his arms in his hand, with his bayonet against my bosom, and his sword point to my throat."

"Such a brother they ask us to compromise with," Johnson remarked acidly.

Better that a deity should compromise with the force of evil, thought Johnson. "Would you have him to have compromised with the devil instead of kicking him from heaven to the nether regions?" he asked.

This was not just rhetoric. In contemplating the decades of aristocratic rule in the South, in thinking of the barbarities committed by Confederate soldiers, especially against the residents of his beloved East Tennessee, and now even giving a second thought to the fundamental nature of slavery, Johnson had come to regard the Confederacy itself as the epitome of evil, a reference that Lincoln himself avoided.

Compromise now, he said, and "another compromise will be necessary and another compromise will follow; and we will go on until we are all compromised away."

It was noted by reporters that this last remark was greeted with both laughter and applause.

The response afforded Johnson the opportunity to conclude his address on a high note, roundly endorsing Lincoln's emancipation proclamation, not in the way that an abolitionist would have desired, but still as evidence of a change in his thinking.

"If slavery has to go as an incident to the preservation of the government, in the name of God, let it go." [17]

Johnson's speech sparked a standing ovation from a rapt audience. "There never was a meeting in Washington at all to be compared with this, in numbers, respectability, and enthusiasm," reported the *New*

York Times, before specifically describing Johnson's speech as a "burst of eloquence seldom equaled in the Representatives' Hall." [18]

It was, perhaps, his greatest moment in Washington.

Johnson's gradual appreciation of the racial component of the war would now even extended to a consideration of black men in the South serving as soldiers for the Union.

Few topics stirred as much controversy, with pro-Union Southerners worried that the sight of black men in uniforms bearing weapons would never be accepted by vast swaths of Southern white people. Union commanders, to a lesser degree, wondered about the impact black soldiers might have on their white counterparts: some white soldiers had even gone so far as to vow that they would never serve with blacks on an equal basis.

Whatever the objections, Lincoln had been pushing the idea on Johnson. "In my opinion the country now needs no specific thing so much as some man of your ability, and position, to go to this work," the President told Johnson while he was still in Washington.

"The colored population is the greatest *available,* and yet *unavailed* of, force for restoring the Union." [19]

As Johnson continued to make the rounds in Washington, a skirmish for control of the military was playing out in Tennessee with Rosecrans suddenly upset over the treatment of one William Truesdail, a 38 year-old businessman from New York who had secured a position as the head of a secret police force under the General's guidance.

Johnson soon picked up on rumors that Truesdail was engaging in abusive practices, harassing civilians, and even taking financial advantage of his position. It was probably this last charge that bothered the scrupulously honest Johnson more than anything else, eventually complaining that Truesdail was "deep in all kinds of plunder, and has kept the army inactive to enable his accomplices and himself to become rich by jobs and contracts." [20]

Rosecrans, not necessarily with the same rancor that would have spirited Buell, only naturally began to wonder about the extent of Johnson's powers not just in trying to get rid of Truesdail, but in all matters military.

Oddly suggesting to Halleck that perhaps Johnson could better serve the cause in the field, Rosecrans was quickly slapped down when Halleck, in response, sternly reminded him that Johnson's sole purpose in Tennessee was to "organize and administer the civil government of that State until a constitutional government could be organized." [21]

Upbraided, a repentant Rosecrans on April 4 attempted to reassure Halleck: "No one appreciates the sacrifice and the delicate and trying position of Governor Johnson more than I do." [22]

On the same day, Rosecrans wrote to Johnson to tell him that he remained entirely supportive of the Military Governor's efforts in Tennessee, remarking "You know how very well often I have assured you I would do all I could to build up and support civil authority and you in every way in my power." [23]

For his part, Johnson needed no such reassurances. Promising to meet with the General as soon as he returned to Tennessee, Johnson was affirming in a way he could never have been with Buell. "There has been nothing, there will be nothing desired by me but harmony and concert of action to put down this rebellion and restore to the people all their legal and constitutional rights." [24]

Impressed with Rosecrans' candor, Johnson would soon have an additional reason to appreciate the General's diplomatic nature. When Johnson's son Robert, serving as a colonel in the 1st Regiment Tennessee Volunteer Cavalry, appeared drunk on several occasions, Rosecrans took the 29 year-old aside and made him promise to mend his ways.

It was entirely possible that Robert had been drinking upon learning of the death of his 33 year-old brother Charles, who had fallen from his horse and died while serving as an assistant surgeon in the 10th Tennessee Infantry. It is not known when Andrew Johnson himself learned of his son's death, although Robert informed him on April 7 that Charles' body had been placed in a vault at the Mount Olivet Cemetery in Nashville.

"Please accept my thanks for the gentle admonition you gave my son," Johnson subsequently remarked to Rosecrans, "and the kind manner in which it was done." [25]

In his quest to define the full extent of his strictly military authority in Tennessee, especially in the wake of his disputes with Buell and Negley, Johnson won a major leadership victory on April 18 when War Secretary Stanton conferred upon him additional powers.

Stanton's directive, the securing of which was the reason why Johnson remained in Washington well into mid-April, officially gave Johnson the authority to seize property and take charge of "all abandoned slaves, or colored persons, who have been held in bondage, and whose masters have been, or are now engaged in rebellion," while also enrolling able-bodied men of both races in the state for military infrastructure projects. [26]

Roughly two weeks later Johnson left Washington, stopping in Louisville where Eliza Johnson had previously relocated. He was worried about his 52 year-old wife's unimproved consumptive state, and along with other members of the Johnson clan, made plans for a return trip to Nashville with her.

Meanwhile, having heard from General Ambrose Burnside, commander of the Department of the Ohio, that plans were moving along for re-taking East Tennessee, Johnson implored Lincoln to add the Third Division of the Ninth Army Corps to Burnside's force, better enabling the General to "prosecute with success the expedition into East Tennessee."

"This part of the State must be entered," Johnson once again declared, as he had been declaring for nearly two years now. "The oppressions and inhumanity inflicted are indescribable, and must be redressed." [27]

Lincoln replied immediately. He wanted the attack to begin against East Tennessee now more than anyone in the country, with the obvious exception of Johnson himself. But the Ninth Army Corps could not, for now, be spared.

"I am sorry to have to tell you this," a rueful Lincoln replied, "but it is true, and cannot be helped." [28]

At last, on May 30, Johnson, with Eliza and several other family members, was back in Nashville.

He spent the early summer weeks trying to drum up support for a volunteer force in Tennessee, working on prisoner exchange matters with Rosecrans, ordering the hiring of black laborers, and initiating a policy allowing for citizens primarily in the countryside who had lately been subject to robberies to bear arms.

Hiring ex-slaves to work was one thing. Actually coming out in favor of the end of slavery was something else. On August 29, Johnson, speaking to an outdoor rally of Unionists in Nashville, crossed that bridge, declaring slavery a "cancer on our society." Stretching the metaphor, he thought the "scalpel of the statesman should be devised for its total eradication from Tennessee."

Illustrative of his life-long concern for the condition of the South's white working class, Johnson additionally predicted that the outright end of slavery would be good for his own kind, inflicting a mortal wound on a slave aristocracy that has long "held its foot upon their necks." [29]

One week later, in a casual conversation with Charles Dana, assistant secretary of war and former influential editor of the *New York Tribune*, Johnson revealed a new determination: slavery must for once and all be completely destroyed.

"He is thoroughly in favor of immediate emancipation, both as a matter of moral right and as the indispensable condition of that large immigration of industrious freemen which is necessary to re-people and regenerate the State," an impressed Dana subsequently reported to Stanton. [30]

The following day came the great news from General Burnside. The soldiers of the XXIII Corps, on the road for more than two weeks and adroitly bypassing Confederate forces in the Cumberland Gap, had taken Knoxville with no resistance.

"We have been elegantly received by the whole of East Tenn.," an exultant Burnside wired Johnson on September 9, adding that "the whole people" of the region wanted to see Johnson return to his native land in this Union moment of triumph. [31]

Johnson was ecstatic, as was Lincoln, who quickly wired the Military Governor, advising him to "get every man you can, black and white, under arms at the very earliest moment, to guard roads, bridges, and trains, allowing all the better trained soldiers to go forward to Rosecrans."

Perhaps remembering Buell's resentments regarding anything Johnson tried to do in a military manner, Lincoln was quick to add: "Of course I mean for you to act in co-operation with, and not independently of, the military authorities." [32]

During these weeks of extraordinary activity, seeing more than 120,000 soldiers for both the Union and Confederate armies facing each other in the crucial Battle of Chickamauga, Johnson remained a Rosecrans enthusiast. But the General himself knew that his days were numbered after the Confederates emerged victorious at Chickamauga, resulting in the death of nearly 16,200 Union soldiers.

Ulysses S. Grant, just days earlier put in command of the Military Division of the Mississippi, a position giving the general, as his long-time aide John Rawlins put it, the "most important command in the

United States," swiftly replaced Rosecrans with the stout, 47-year old George Thomas. [33]

On his way to Chattanooga, Grant on October 20 passed through Nashville where he was greeted with cheers from Union soldiers and local officials. Checking into the St. Cloud Hotel, Grant was soon also hailed by Johnson in a public ceremony in front of that hotel, comparing his military record with that of "Napoleon or of Caesar himself." [34]

As Grant listened, he later ironically reflected, it became clear to him that Johnson's address "was by no means his maiden effort."

The speech, typical of nearly every Johnson presentation, remembered Grant years later, was long, "and I was in torture while he was delivering it, fearing that something would be expected from me in response."

Sardonically, Grant added that he was relieved once Johnson had concluded his remarks to note that the people assembled had "apparently heard enough." [35]

Although Johnson had indicated that he was willing to share the stage with Grant, the General modestly declined, remarking that he had "never made a speech in his life and was too old to learn now." [36]

How these two men upon their first meeting sized each other up is impossible to know. Johnson could not have been unaware of the 41 year-old Grant's rising star, his name daily mentioned in the national press, his face appearing on the cover of such popular and widely-read publications as *Harper's Weekly*.

But the adoration that the unassuming Grant attracted would have meant less to Johnson, at least then, than the fact that the General was always moving forward, soon to reorganize soldiers at Chattanooga and opening a vital supply line for them, before crucially beating back the Confederates around that city.

Grant's initial impression of Johnson seems to have been less favorable. Never enamored of politicians or long-winded speeches, Grant probably viewed Johnson as just one more of the bombastic class, although he was quietly impressed with the Military Governor's lone and brave Union stand during his 19-month administration.

Grant left the next morning by train for lower Tennessee, while Johnson returned to his duties in the statehouse, neither man realizing how much their lives would intersect in just a short few years, battling at the highest stations of national power in a manner that would prove less than inspiring for both.

Making a quick trip to Louisville where he discussed the completion of his long-desired Northwestern Railroad with Stanton, Johnson was back in Nashville by late October, penning a quick note to General Thomas.

"Permit me to congratulate you upon your new position," Johnson remarked. Then in a comment that would have probably surprised Rosecrans, Johnson said of Thomas' new station: "It is the one, as you know, that I have long desired you should occupy." [37]

Johnson may have felt a kinship with Thomas because, like Johnson, he had opted in favor of the Union despite the fact that, as a native born Virginian, he was clearly a Southerner. But Johnson also liked the General for the modern manner in which he organized his troops, putting in place an efficient communication system allowing him to know at any point where his forces were, and utilizing the latest maps to get an almost scientific feel for battlefield terrain.

Johnson let Thomas know that while work on the Nashville & Northwestern railroad was "progressing very well," it would help to have more men to pitch in on the project. Thomas was prompt, as Johnson no doubt anticipated he would be, replying that companies of the Michigan Engineers would be available for the project, and reassuring Johnson that he deemed the completion of the railroad "of vital importance." [38]

The railroad project, which would at last be completed in May 1864, additionally gave Johnson a first-hand view, as nothing before had, of the promise of black labor. In subsequent testimony before a federal commission set up to study the status of the new freedmen, Johnson said it was good to see black men getting paid for their labors. It gave them, he added, "an idea of contracts, and when the rebellion is over, they will be in a better condition than if they were put into camps."

While not in any way embracing black people as fully equal to whites, Johnson had begun to experience a sort of paternalistic regard for a race he hoped would meet with success once the war was over. This was particularly true with his views of black people engaging in agricultural pursuits. Hired at fair wages, he said, black farmers "would make more cotton" than they ever could have as slaves, while also growing wheat and raising cattle.

Johnson additionally lauded the service of black soldiers, noting that they were easier to discipline than whites, and had, overall, "performed better than I had anticipated." [39]

Out of nowhere, Lincoln in early December sent Johnson a brief message: "I still desire very much to see you. Can you not come?" [40]

Johnson left Nashville almost immediately, arriving in Washington at the same time that a nascent campaign to nominate him for the vice-presidency in 1864 was first beginning to make itself known.

Several smaller Republican-leaning newspapers in the Midwest and California had already endorsed Johnson for the second spot, an idea that would soon win the backing of the Union League of Nashville. The *Evansville Daily Journal*, reflecting Johnson's growing popularity in the Midwest, also went on record supporting the idea, while the influential *Chicago Tribune*, in a page one story, reported that party leaders "with striking unanimity" were behind Johnson for the number two position. [41]

In a letter from Nathaniel Taylor, who had unsuccessfully run against Johnson for Congress in 1849, Johnson was described not only as the "next vice-president of the United States," but the man whom voters would surely select to succeed Lincoln as president in 1868. [42]

Unlike Johnson's spring visit to the nation's capital, his stay in Washington this time was brief and nearly entirely unnoticed by the press. He was in the city only a few days, meeting with the President at least once. What the two men talked about is unknown, although certainly Lincoln's desire to see local elections held in Tennessee sometime in the coming months must have been discussed.

Undoubtedly aware of the talk to put Johnson on the 1864 ticket as a gesture of Union solidarity, Lincoln probably did not talk to the Military Governor directly about the idea, but used the visit, as he had so many times before in the past, to appraise Johnson on an up-close basis, seeing before him an inordinately serious and even grim presence who was nevertheless extraordinarily capable and unwavering in his devotion to the Union.

He could always talk frankly with Johnson, and Johnson always respectfully listened to his views, following Lincoln's directives with something close to alacrity. If only all of his generals had proved as responsive, Lincoln must have reflected, the cause of the Union army would probably be in a much better condition as 1863 came to a close. Ironically, perhaps the only other man currently fighting for the Union and possessing the same spirit of determination was the commander both men admired: Ulysses S. Grant.

Back in Nashville for the holidays, Johnson soon delivered before the city's Union League his most extensive remarks to date on slavery and its imminent end.

In an address that would have been entirely unthinkable for any major public official in either Tennessee or the larger South just a few months earlier, Johnson declared that slavery's end was now imminent, and warned those who still owned slaves to first turn them loose and then hire them as paid laborers. "By this means, you will do your part in this great transition to teach them self-reliance," Johnson declared. [43]

On January 26, Johnson at last issued a proclamation calling for county elections, but in doing so required would-be candidates to sign a loyalty oath before launching their campaigns. The move sparked resentment among Tennessee Unionists who, while understanding why candidates who were formerly Confederates should sign such a document, didn't see why it should apply to them, too.

Turnout on March 5 proved both underwhelming, with Unionist candidates for a variety of local offices generally winning in an election that appeared to be largely boycotted, or in some places ignored altogether. At best, 50,000 voters participated, a decided drop from the 146,000 voting in the 1860 presidential election. "The whole affair," Clifton Hall would later declare, "brought no credit to its instigators and placed the government in a weak and equivocal position before the people." [44]

Johnson encountered a second disappointment in early April when delegates to a state convention in Knoxville designed to ratify emancipation vigorously resisted the idea instead. "Things do not look as I would like to find them," Johnson admitted to Lincoln as he headed to the meeting where he would strenuously argue in favor of an emancipation endorsement. [45]

"Men sneer at the doctrine of emancipation," the Military Governor angrily told the angry delegates. "Let them sneer—but this I tell you, mark me, it is the *white* we propose to emancipate, and may heaven hasten the work of emancipation and carry it on until we all are free." [46]

But the simple fact was that many Tennesseans, perhaps even a majority, were not ready to embrace slavery's end with quite the same enthusiasm Johnson was bringing to the task. The meeting eventually adjourned with no decision made on the question at all.

Despite these setbacks, Johnson's name was continually floated throughout the late spring weeks as a vice-presidential nominee. The Republicans, meeting in early June under the banner of the newly-designated National Union Party, made quick work of matters. After swiftly nominating Lincoln for a second term, Johnson scored a surprising victory on the second ballot for the vice-presidential slot.

The whole thing happened with an efficient rapidity that must have startled Johnson himself.

"A better or a stronger ticket could not have been nominated," the *Cleveland Daily Leader* exclaimed the following day, echoing the now general Northern view of Johnson as a man who clung to the Union banner with a "fervent and devoted love through storm and danger, enduring much, suffering much." [47]

A massive crowd gathered outside Nashville's flag-bedecked St. Cloud Hotel on the night of June 9, with a band of musicians from the 18th Michigan Volunteer Infantry playing patriotic tunes.

Appearing before an estimated 2,000 cheering people, Johnson was buoyant, declaring: "Come weal or woe, success of defeat, sink or swim, survive or perish, I accept the nomination on principle, be the consequences what they may." [48]

Banners and posters bearing the names and faces of Lincoln and Johnson were soon distributed by the hundreds of thousands throughout the North boosting the new National Union ticket. One in particular, emphasizing the national theme of the campaign, proclaimed: "The Union forever. Hurrah, boys Hurrah! Down with the Traitors; Up with the Stars." [49]

CHAPTER SIX

THE PLEBEIAN

H is political hopes unfulfilled at both the 1856 and 1860 Democratic conventions, Johnson had been wary when it came to what might happen with the National Union Party convention in June.

Although the movement in his direction continued to pick up steam in the spring of 1864, with one Illinois newspaper, the *War Democrat,* going so far as to suggest that Johnson should actually be the party's presidential nominee, doing away with Lincoln altogether, Johnson remained silent on his prospects. [1]

When delegates from 25 states met in Baltimore's Front Street Theater on June 7 and 8, the vote for Lincoln was pre-ordained. In a sweeping first ballot victory, the President won the backing of every state delegation except Missouri, which cast 22 votes for Ulysses S. Grant.

In a swift subsequent tally after the first ballot was completed, John Hume, chairman of the Missouri delegation, rose to announce a recanvassing of his delegation, making the president's renomination unanimous.

The only real drama of the convention came on its second day as delegates settled down to the work of deciding who would run with Lincoln. For months, the early betting had been on current vice president Hannibal Hamlin of Maine, who had offended hardly anyone during his term in office.

For his part, Lincoln remained curiously silent on the matter, at one point even intimating that as the delegates obviously would have little choice in naming him to a second term, they should be given as much latitude as possible in deciding on his running mate.

Still, Lincoln's silence was interpreted by some as a swipe at Hamlin. Alexander McClure, a party leader and member of the Pennsylvania delegation, later thought Lincoln's failure to drum up support for Hamlin "may have reflected his awareness that Hamlin was very radical on questions relating to slavery and the South." [2]

Besides, the question must have more than once occurred to Lincoln: what exactly did Hamlin bring to the ticket? In 1860 he helped carry New England for Lincoln. In 1864, Lincoln could take for granted that he was going to sweep New England, with or without Hamlin.

Johnson, on the other hand, offered the possibility of not only carrying Tennessee in November, but also Missouri and Kentucky, pivotal states that Lincoln had lost four years before.

Johnson was also favored by the fact that he was still a registered Democrat and obviously ardently committed to the military defeat of the Confederacy. As a correspondent for the *Pittsburgh Gazette* put it: "There is strong pressure on all hands for a War Democrat as a candidate for vice-president." [3]

As the vice-presidential nominating speeches were delivered, it was quickly clear from the sounds of the cheers on the convention floor that only three candidates had significant support: Hamlin, former New York Democrat Senator Daniel Dickinson, and Johnson.

But long-time Johnson friend and associate Horace Maynard may have emotionally tipped the scales in the Tennessean's direction in an address outlining Johnson's record as the military governor of the Volunteer State, emotionally lauding his "position of determined and undying hostility to this rebellion." [4]

"It was that speech by Maynard that defeated Hamlin," Burton Cook, chairman of the Illinois delegation, later claimed. [5]

The first ballot showed the lay of the land: Hamlin scored 150 votes, with Dickinson coming in at 105. Johnson, however, led the way at exactly 200 votes, showing surprising support in the New York, Ohio, and Indiana delegations.

The strength of Johnson's vote prompted the Kentucky delegation, at the beginning of the second ballot, to switch its 21 votes from General Lovell Rousseau to Johnson, sparking an avalanche. In just a few more minutes, the big Pennsylvania delegation yanked its 52 votes out of the Hamlin column and gave them all to Johnson.

By the end of the second ballot the vote for Johnson at 494 swamped Dickinson at 17 and Hamlin at 9.

While Hamlin claimed to not be bothered by his rejection, a book published 35 years later by his grandson, Charles Eugene Hamlin, bitterly scored Johnson's vice-presidential win as a farce, claiming that an astonished Lincoln never thought that the National Union delegates would actually select Johnson. "He knew the real man, and his distrust and dislike of him were founded on a knowledge of his character and record," the younger Hamlin said of Lincoln's supposed actual attitude toward Johnson.

Additionally claiming that Lincoln thought Johnson had a drinking problem, the President, in this account, even hoped to boot Johnson from his post as military governor, but could not do so "without raising trouble in Tennessee." [6]

The younger Hamlin's account of the thinking that went into the vice-presidential selection was based, to some degree, on interviews he conducted three decades after the fact with delegates who had attended the National Union convention.

But the account could have also been influenced by Hannibal Hamlin himself, who died in 1891, giving evidence in his later years of being embittered by his loss to Johnson, and perhaps expressing that resentment to a loyal grandson.

A more immediate telling of the events of early June was presented by Ohio Republican Solomon Newton Pettis, who met with Lincoln on the morning of the first day of the convention and bluntly asked who he really wanted as his running mate. In what Pettis subsequently described as a "low, but distinct voice," Lincoln, leaning forward, responded: "Governor Johnson of Tennessee."

Pettis later told Johnson that he was once again with Lincoln on the afternoon of June 8 when it was learned that Johnson had won the vice-presidential nomination. "I need not tell you of the satisfaction felt and expressed by him at the result," Pettis said of the President's reaction. [7]

Johnson, who had known Hamlin personally from his years when they both served in the Senate, most likely never gave a thought to Hamlin's ignominious rejection at the hands of the delegates. Hamlin's defeat and Johnson's victory were politics, and the men of that world, as appreciated by Johnson, accepted the wins and losses as an inevitable part of the business.

Besides, Johnson must have, in the wake of the convention, had his head turned by the praise of the national press, with various portions of that press liking the Johnson nomination for different reasons.

The *Baltimore American* fondly remembered Johnson's anti-secession stand, proclaiming that his nomination was a "just tribute to a patriot who stood firm in the defense of right when all around him were faithless in their trust." *Harper's Weekly* said the nomination "reflects directly, in his wonderful career, the genius of our institutions, under which the humblest citizen may attain the highest honors of the republic." [8]

But the *New York Times* probably came closest to appreciating the nomination the way Johnson did, judging that he has a "far stronger hold upon the great popular heart of the North than he could have had had he been born in the North." [9]

While Johnson's nomination should have been celebrated throughout Tennessee, reaffirming the state's pivotal role in presidential politics reminiscent of the victories of Andrew Jackson in 1828 and 1832, and James K. Polk in 1844, many Tennesseans were put off by the choice. Some had become opposed to Johnson in general, regarding his military governorship as nothing more than an expression of his authoritarian impulses. Others thought that by joining a ticket fashioned by Republicans, no matter the new and temporary name of the party, Johnson was betraying the Democratic party that had always given him sustenance.

But perhaps the biggest gripe against Johnson's nomination came from Union-loving Tennessee conservatives who, studying the National Union Party's pro-abolition platform, were convinced that Johnson was now little better than a Radical Republican.

Curiously, many of these same detractors ignored Johnson's very clear exertions in favor of fully returning Tennessee to the Union, and instead complained that he hadn't done enough in this direction. "They charged that Johnson sought to delay Tennessee's restoration to the Union in order to give him time to consolidate his power in the state and to punish his political enemies," writes historian William Harris. [10]

Johnson was admittedly worried that in the November election Tennessee might actually reject the National Union ticket. After all, in six of the last seven presidential elections dating to 1836, Tennesseans had rejected the candidate Johnson backed, while Johnson himself in his two gubernatorial elections in 1853 and 1855 had won with less than 51 percent of the vote.

While Johnson had little respect for George McClellan either as a general or politician, he worried about the Democratic presidential nominee's level of support. On July 17, Benjamin Truman reported to Johnson of soldiers in the field who were likely to back McClellan over Lincoln, while also offering the curious observation that some of the officers he had recently interviewed "will vote the Union ticket on account of your name being upon it, although they say they do not fully endorse Lincoln—they argue that he doesn't deal with traitors as traitors deserve." [11]

In fact, Johnson himself was sometimes found wanting in this same regard, exhibiting a surprising degree of mercy, particularly when it came to the sins of the youngest Confederates. On August 17 he asked Lincoln to suspend the execution by hanging of one John Young, a Rebel soldier convicted by a military committee of the murder of a Union soldier.

Word had come to Johnson that Young was not directly involved in the murder, although he may have been a part of the gang that was. The circumstances bothered Johnson enough to urge upon Lincoln a sentence of life at hard labor, rather than an execution, noting that Young was a "very young man and was influenced to enter the Rebel Army by others contrary to his will." [12]

Lincoln, usually needing little prodding in such matters, responded just hours later that Young's death sentence would indeed be suspended "until further orders from me." [13]

Young was eventually released in a prisoner exchange deal one month before the end of the war.

Johnson also, a week before the scheduled execution of 30 year-old Confederate soldier Thomas Bridge, put on paper his desire that the man's life be spared due to the discovery of new evidence "which will go a great way in mitigation of the offense, if not to entirely exonerate him." [14]

Lincoln already knew the details of Bridge's case, suspecting that he might not be guilty of stabbing a man in the midst of a riot, as he was accused, and telling his secretary John Nicolay that if Johnson officially asked for a suspension of Bridges' sentence, he would grant it. Johnson did as requested, with the eventual result of Bridge being paroled in March of 1865.

In these matters, as in so many issues of military administration, Johnson and Lincoln revealed themselves as two men almost always working in concert and both more than willing to make a tough decision and be done with it.

Johnson by the fall of 1864 had every reason to believe that he enjoyed Lincoln's complete confidence, while the President had long since decided that Johnson, despite sporadic unconfirmed reports that he occasionally enjoyed a glass of the most expensive whiskey, was entirely reliable.

Even so, Johnson knew he needed to advance the process of finally officially establishing a civil government in the state, a process that Lincoln consistently advocated as a piece of a larger restoration policy he envisioned eventually applying to the entire South.

To that end, in September, Johnson helped spearhead a convention composed of delegates from around the state and tasked with laying out a roadmap for establishing a civil government. The meeting, which conservative Unionists subsequently boycotted, established the parameters for Tennessee's participation in the November presidential election, and once again, as with the disappointing county balloting earlier in the year, required that voters must swear an oath of loyalty before participating in the election.

Johnson was inspired enough by the results of the convention to issue several proclamations, one asserting the right of Tennesseans to vote in the November contest, while another proclaiming that ex-slaves should be treated as equal citizens in state court proceedings.

Confident that because Tennessee was moving in the right direction, he could focus his attentions elsewhere, Johnson in October honored several invitations to speak beyond the state's borders on behalf of the National Union Party.

That he was by now regarded as a potent political commodity was seen in a letter from Republican House Speaker Schuyler Colfax, who asked Johnson to come up to Indiana for a speech-making tour. "No one man living could do us more good in this State than you," Colfax implored. [15]

Henry Raymond, editor of the *New York Times* and chairman of the National Union Party Executive Committee, wanted Johnson to appear in Ohio, Pennsylvania, and New York, noting "your presence, reputation, and ability combines to give great weight & influence to your words." [16]

From Massachusetts, Senator Charles Sumner entreated Johnson to speak in New England, declaring, "You would cheer & strengthen us. Perhaps you would be cheered & strengthened also by the patriotic fervor which I am sure your visit would inspire." [17]

Johnson saved these letters, treasuring the admiration of men who, within the span of the next two years, would be singularly dedicated to his destruction.

In early October, as part of a ten-day tour of Indiana, a relaxed and confident Johnson appeared before a massive outpouring in Logansport. He had had fun with the notion that he was, as it had recently been said, a "boorish tailor." The description came from the *New York World* only hours after Johnson had received the vice-presidential nomination. In fact, the pro-Democrat *World* had attacked the Lincoln-Johnson ticket as one made up of a "rail splitting buffoon," and a "boorish tailor," and even went on to describe them as "from the backwoods, both grown up in uncouth ignorance." [18]

Johnson's delight upon reading the *World*'s attack, which was shortly reprinted in newspapers across the country, can only be imagined. He knew that there were millions of Americans raised in similar backwoods conditions, and rather enjoyed the notion that Lincoln's early years axing railroad ties and his own years as a tailor should be so lumped together as somehow being socially embarrassing.

Now, in Logansport, Johnson remarked: "Yes, I am a tailor, but I learned long since that if a man does not disgrace his profession, it never disgraces him." Johnson added, to laughs, "And I may be permitted to say that when I was a tailor, I made some pretty close fits." [19]

These were the comments of a man at peace with himself. Johnson always put great stock in how things felt, an instinctive response to external events allowing him to know when an election or a business deal was about to succeed or go belly up.

Now, in the sunny Midwestern fall of 1864, speaking before entirely admiring Indiana Republican farmers, Johnson could see victory in his future, not just in his first national political campaign, but also the more important military victory of the Union army over a continually shrinking Confederate army in all parts of the South.

This was indeed a great time to be alive, and Johnson relished the applause and cheers of the Northerners who had come to idolize him.

But sometimes, in an increasingly buoyant mood, Johnson's rhetoric would lead him into uncharted territory.

Such was the case on the evening of October 24 when Johnson appeared before a crowd of several hundred ex-slaves who arrived at the steps of the state capitol in Nashville to cheer him. The entire event, viewed from any historical perspective, was unreal. Just the idea of a large number of black men and women freely congregating in a major Southern city was hard enough to believe. But that these same people, coming to voice their support of Johnson, were expressing a political point of view, transformed the evening into what must have seemed to everyone a dream-like experience.

Johnson greeted his visitors by referencing Lincoln's Emancipation Proclamation and then declaring "Consequently I, too, have a proclamation to make, and standing here upon the steps of the Capitol, with the past history of the State to witness, the present condition to guide, and the future to encourage me, I, Andrew Johnson, do hereby proclaim freedom, full, broad, and unconditional, to every man in Tennessee."

He next suggested that blacks should be able to use weapons "if traitors and ruffians" attacked them, allowing them to "defend themselves as all men have a right to do."

As the only "traitors and ruffians" who could possibly have any interest in attacking an ex-slave would almost certainly be a white man, this meant that Johnson was giving his sanction to a black man shooting a white man, if it came to that.

But stranger things were to come. He talked of breaking up several large white plantations into smaller farms that could be worked by ex-slaves and then, astonishingly, reviled what was left of Nashville's Confederate aristocracy, noting that anyone happening by its mansions would see "as many mulatto as negro children, the former bearing an unmistakable resemblance to their aristocratic owners."

The fact that white plantation owners had for decades engaged in sexual acts with their black women slaves had always been whispered in both black and white circles. But publicly, for the most part, it remained the great unmentionable; except during this entirely exceptionable evening.

When Johnson then exclaimed that he hoped for the ex-slaves the presence of a Moses to lead them through the "storm of persecution and obloquy they are compelled to pass," several voices yelled out that Johnson was their Moses.

This was the sort or exclamation, an emotional outpouring of the most momentary kind, that Lincoln would have resisted, making the point that the ex-slaves would most likely provide their own protection and guidance as they went along.

Johnson, however, liked the idea, shortly responding: "Well, then, humble and unworthy as I am, if no other better shall be found, I will indeed be your Moses, and lead you through the Red Sea of war and bondage to a fairer future of liberty and peace." [20]

Listening to Johnson's address, William Furay, a young correspondent for the *Cincinnati Gazette* and long-time hater of slavery, wasn't sure he heard what he heard. The speech, Furay wrote, was "one of the most remarkable to which it was ever my fortune to listen. The time, the place, the circumstances, the audience, the man, all combined to make a powerful impression upon a spectator's mind." [21]

The speech received widespread coverage in both the national and international press, with Harriet Beecher Stowe later characterizing it's presentation as one "unequaled in moral grandeur." Reading a local account of it in Massachusetts, poet and abolitionist Lydia Maria Child, who had only weeks earlier confessed to Sumner her fears that Lincoln "with his slow mind and legal conscience," might be defeated in November, now said of Johnson: "He has completely taken me captive by his speech in Nashville." [22]

Child shortly dubbed Johnson "The Moses of the Colored People." [23]

Published accounts of Johnson's address found their way across the Atlantic, with Francis William Newman, the famed English classical scholar and abolitionist, declaring "Andrew Johnson's speech filled me with delight." [24]

Wanting the address to receiver a wider circulation, Newman promptly sent a copy of it to the London-based socialist newspaper, the *Morning Star.*

That the speech and entirely implausible event benefitted Johnson among Northern voters was without doubt. How it played in Tennessee was open to question. "All that night his name was mingled with curses and execration of the traitor and oppressor," Furay noted of the immediate white Nashville response to Johnson's remarks, "and with the blessings of the oppressed and poor." [25]

Despite these excited encomiums, Johnson admitted he was worried about the coming election. Of the four major candidates (the National Union presidential and vice-presidential nominees, and their Democrat counterparts), Johnson was the only one who actively campaigned, and was also the only one who, because he remained a registered Democrat, was working against the interests of his own party.

He viewed the possible election of McClellan and his running mate George Pendleton, an Ohio Congressman and Peace Democrat, with a sense of dread, recognizing that neither man would pursue the Union's war aims as laid out by Lincoln, and that both men would be entirely comfortable living with an unreconstructed South.

On the Sunday before the election, Johnson spoke before a flag-raising ceremony in downtown Nashville and took the occasion to ask of McClellan: "What has he ever done?"

Johnson then unfairly accused McClellan of being a traitor. McClellan was, in fact, an entirely loyal American, but, as a General, was one whose command hesitations continually limited the potential of the Army of the Potomac. The notion, made by many Radical Republicans, that McClellan was somehow actually working in concert with the Confederates was wide of the mark, and beneath Johnson for even suggesting as much.

Even so, Johnson said it was noted that McClellan was a gentleman. Johnson then reminded his audience that McClellan had also once described Jefferson Davis as a gentleman. Thus, said Johnson in an entirely odd leap of logic, "McClellan and Jeff Davis are on the same platform."

He then told his listeners that "there were but two parties in the country— traitors and patriots." Traitors, with "Jeff Davis at their head and McClellan for their candidate," seeking to "destroy the Government."

The "patriots party," it went without saying, was led by Lincoln and Johnson. [26]

It was an ignoble ending to Johnson's campaign effort, and one not likely to inspire Tennessee Democrats to abandon their standard bearer for the Lincoln-Johnson ticket.

Not until the Wednesday after the election did wire reports reaching Nashville indicate the success of the National Union party. By early Thursday it was clear that Lincoln had been re-elected and Johnson was soon to be the nation's new vice-president.

The Lincoln-Johnson victory was solid, with the ticket winning 55 percent of the popular vote and 212 electoral votes, to the 45 percent of the popular vote won by the McClellan-Pendleton ticket and its 21 electoral votes.

Turnout was exceedingly low in Tennessee, where Lincoln and Johnson also prevailed (although the state's electoral votes would not be counted as Tennessee was still not officially back in the Union).

What final impact Johnson may have had on the fortunes of the National Union party is difficult to say. In only two states did Lincoln's plurality over his 1860 vote improve. As both of those states, Maryland and Missouri, were border states, it's possible that Johnson's presence on the ticket accounted for something.

But more than likely, in explaining the reasons for Lincoln's re-election, the spectacular Union victories in both Atlanta and Mobile in September made all the difference.

Four nights after the election a large group of black residents estimated at more than four thousand called upon Johnson at his Cedar Street residence. As candidly as he had raised the issue of white plantation owners sexually forcing themselves on black slaves in his "Moses of the Colored People" speech, Johnson now bluntly told his visitors that it was incumbent upon them to energetically embrace the opportunities he was certain awaited them in a free labor economy.

He added: "And I warn you, my colored friends, to avoid the folly of which some black men and women, and I am sorry to add, some white ones, too, are guilty: of working six days industriously and then spending all your wages in a drunken revel." [27]

The advice was clearly paternalistic and, no doubt to some, obnoxious in its presumptions. But it vividly spoke to a central theme in Johnson's life. He had always been more than willing, even when he first arrived in Greeneville with just the shirt on his back, to work hard and save at least a portion of his income for reasons of security and future investments.

That he felt a desire to share this advice with a group of people who knew little, at this point, about economies and the vicissitudes of the labor market, showed, if anything, that Johnson had hopes for their eventual self-sufficiency and economic success.

As Johnson made the final preparations for a return to civil government in Tennessee, he was distracted by a last-ditch effort on the part of Confederate General John Bell Hood to retake Nashville in mid-December.

Hoping to attract the attention of William Tecumseh Sherman, just then in the throes of his historic March to the Sea, Hood made it to the southern outskirts of Nashville on December 2, only after seeing the Confederate Army of Tennessee lose nearly 7,000 of its 28,000 soldiers in a battle with General John Schofield's Union forces at Franklin, Tennessee.

Weakened, Hood nevertheless led his men to the southern hills just outside Nashville. Union General George Thomas, with more than 50,000 soldiers, at first hesitated, but finally moved on Hood, decimating the Confederates in a two-day battle ending on December 16.

By December 30, Thomas could happily report to Johnson that the Confederate Army had been "entirely driven out of Tennessee," adding that "all should now feel that the establishment of Rebel authority in the state of Tennessee is hopeless." [28]

Responding, Johnson told Thomas that a convention would be held in nine days tasked with establishing a civil government in the state, before adding: "It is not necessary for me to say that you have a nation's gratitude for what you have done in preserving the Government of the United States." [29]

That January 9 convention would prove the apex of Johnson's rule in Tennessee with more than five hundred delegates from across the state gathering for what was essentially a constitutional assembly, abolishing slavery, voiding secession, and officially disavowing the Confederacy.

Intricately involved in the workings of the convention, Johnson cajoled, pled, and argued with individual delegates, doing what he could to move the cumbersome proceedings along. When the delegates decided in favor of an abolition amendment that, like all of the amendments coming out of the gathering, would go before the people of Tennessee, Johnson immediately wired Lincoln, prematurely exclaiming "Thank God the tyrant's rod has been broken." [30]

Lincoln, in response, was entirely pleased, but asked: "When do you expect to be here?" [31]

Johnson replied that he wanted to stay in Tennessee at least until April when the "state will be organized & resume all functions of a state in the Union." [32]

Other vice-presidents, including most recently the ill William King, who was elected with Franklin Pierce and took the oath of office in Cuba in 1853, had been sworn in away from Washington, and now Johnson wondered if he could do the same.

On January 24, Lincoln, after discussing the matter with members of his cabinet, told Johnson that it is "unsafe for you not to be here on the 4th of March. Be sure to reach here by then." [33]

Why Lincoln felt so intent on the matter is not clear. Secretary of the Navy Gideon Welles thought that Lincoln believed the absence of his vice-president might be misinterpreted in Europe, an explanation that suggests an attention to international nuance that Lincoln had not always shown before. Perhaps it was just as likely that Lincoln simply believed, although he continued to deny it publicly, that his life in wartime Washington was always in danger, making the presence of his vice-president crucial.

John Forney, too, strongly urged Johnson to get to the nation's capital soon. "I think all of our friends will be greatly disappointed if you are not in Washington at a very early date. Not alone your own interests, but the interests of the country demand your presence."

Showing that he was nothing if not a consummate political animal, Forney, who had once been a Democrat but joined the Republicans in the late 1850s after a falling out with President Buchanan, reminded Johnson that he was in fact the "representative of the Democratic element without which neither Abraham Lincoln nor yourself could have been chosen." [34]

Johnson's presence in Washington, thought Forney, would mitigate against an entirely Republican national government, while inspiring Democrats to embrace a modern national philosophy.

In February, Johnson fell ill, run down by the stress of trying to do what he could to convince his fellow Tennesseans to approve the proposed amendments to the state's constitution, an effort that proved successful during the third week of the month. A wire service report out of Nashville noted: "Governor Andrew Johnson, who was confined to his room with a severe cold for the past two weeks, is improving, but he is still unable to attend to the duties of his office." [35]

Nevertheless preparing to leave Nashville, Johnson sent notice to War Secretary Edwin Stanton announcing his official resignation as both military governor of Tennessee and brigadier general of the U.S. Volunteers. In so doing, Johnson attached a cover letter expressing what he said was his "high regard" for Stanton, thanking him for "the uniform kindness which you have been pleased to extend to me personally and officially during my service as an officer under the War Department." [36]

The usually haughty and difficult Stanton responded within hours, hailing Johnson for his "patriotic and able services during the eventful period through which you have exercised the high trusts committed to your charge."

The War Secretary didn't stop there, declaring that Johnson's service as military governor and brigadier general had placed him in a "position of personal toil and danger, perhaps more hazardous than was encountered by any other citizen or military officer of the United States." [37]

This was a bit much. While undoubtedly Johnson's wartime service endlessly put him in the path of danger, revealing him as an extraordinarily courageous person, the idea that his life was more threatened than that of any other military officer was overstated.

Stanton's praise has to be seen for what it probably really was: a man who had an uncanny knack for toadying up to those in positions of power, the Secretary's stated admiration for Johnson was more than likely a preemptive move to win the allegiance of the new vice-president as part of a larger ongoing struggle to maintain his powerbase in the federal government.

Stanton was in every way one of the most treacherous and mendacious persons to have ever served in a presidential cabinet. He was unprincipled and dangerous and someone Johnson would have been well advised to steer clear of once he arrived in Washington. Johnson didn't play politics at that level, and, undoubtedly in the winter of 1865, could not have possibly imagined the degree to which Stanton would eventually betray him.

With a party made up of his private secretary, William Browning, brigadier general Alvan Gillem, and General Lovell Rousseau, among others, Johnson at last left Nashville on February 25. The party made it to Cincinnati by February 27, where, after checking into the Burnett

House, Johnson was called upon to speak to an outdoor gathering of supporters. He was still unwell, noted a reporter for the *Cincinnati Enquirer,* who thought Johnson "appeared to be suffering from severe physical weakness and could not remain long exposed to the keen night air." [38]

Finally, on the evening of March 1, the Johnson party detrained in Washington, registering at the Kirkwood House on the northeast corner of Pennsylvania Avenue and 12th Street.

Everything was moving fast. Perhaps too fast. Johnson was days away from becoming the nation's 16th vice-president, a post that had been held by such luminaries as John Adams, Aaron Burr, and John Calhoun, let alone John Tyler and Millard Fillmore, both of whom became president upon the deaths of the chief executives they had served.

He was also just days removed from his exhausting service as military governor, a job that had challenged all of his faculties, transforming him, in the process, into one of the most prominent regional and national figures of his day.

There were still loose ends to tie up in Tennessee, Johnson knew, as he nearly collapsed at the Kirkwood, simultaneously contemplating his new role in the national government. What would be expected of him? How close to the vital seat of power would he really be? How much of a helpmate could he possibly be for Lincoln, a self-sufficient chief executive who had shown that while he was always open to advice, never really needed it.

The end of the war was weeks away. The kind of a country, the kind of a South, that would emerge from the ashes of that conflict was almost impossible to envision. What role would Johnson, who perhaps better than anyone in Washington, knew the vicissitudes of Southern pride, hatreds, and dreams, be expected to play in bringing the region back into the Union? Indeed, what role *could* he play?

The questions and possibilities must have tired Johnson every bit as much as his recent illness.

But a yearned-for rest at the Kirkwood was not to be had. Members of Congress and administration officials stopped by to greet him at the very time that John Forney was pushing Johnson to make the social rounds.

On the Friday evening of March 3, the night before the inauguration, Johnson finally attended a party given by Forney at his New Jersey Avenue residence. Unlike Johnson, Forney was an inveterate drinker, holding his liquor better on some occasions than others. He had been seen nearly entirely inebriated during the ceremonies culminating in Lincoln's Gettysburg Address. But on other occasions, at parties where the drinks flowed freely, Forney conducted himself well enough, always showing up on time for his Senate secretary duties the next day.

How much Johnson and Forney drank on the night of March 3 is not known. What is known is that the following morning, Johnson, sporting a new black frock coat, black pants, and black ribbed silk vest recently ordered and purchased from a Washington tailor, arrived at the capitol feeling worse for the wear.

Talking with outgoing vice-president Hamlin in his office, Johnson downed several shots of whiskey in quick succession, perhaps following the popular 19th century "hair of the dog" practice dictating that the best way to get rid of a hangover was to drink more alcohol, and fast.

Hamlin later said seeing Johnson drink so quickly made him feel "a little apprehensive," but claiming that he knew Johnson was a "hard drinker," he "supposed that he could stand the liquor he had taken." [39]

As the time neared for his swearing in, Johnson, noted a reporter for the *New York Herald*, "walked unsteadily, probably from excitement," into the Senate chamber. [40]

What happened next would change perceptions of Johnson forever among both friends and foes. After being sworn in by Hamlin, with Forney standing nearby, Johnson turned to a chamber populated with the President and First Lady, members of the Supreme Court and diplomatic corps, and Senate and House leaders, and launched into a nearly 20-minute harangue emphasizing his pride in becoming the nation's new vice-president and his roots as a commoner.

He had always liked the word "plebeian," and now repeated it throughout a speech that seemed to have no beginning or end: "Plebeian as I may be," "I, a plebeian," "I, though a plebeian boy," he yelled out several times.

He lauded the Constitution, the Government, the people, and reminded everyone that "a person could not exist here 48 hours if he were as far removed from the people as the autocrat of Russia is separated from his subjects," a remark that most likely didn't thrill Eduard de Stoeckl, the Russian minister, sitting in the audience. Johnson referred to the cabinet secretaries, but forgot the name of Gideon Welles, and, leaning in Forney's direction, audibly asked "Who is the Secretary of the Navy?" [41]

He then turned to Attorney General James Speed and bluntly declared that, despite opinions to the contrary, Tennessee was and always had been in the Union. "She is now as loyal, Mr. Attorney General, as is the state from which you come."

Loudly, Johnson added: "Thank God, Tennessee has never been out of the Union!" and that he was "here today, as her representative." [42]

His face flush, his movements unsteady, Johnson gave every appearance of being thoroughly and entirely drunk.

"Such a speech!" remarked the *New York Herald* reporter, who provided one of the first full accounts of the address. "It might have been appropriate at some hustings in Tennessee, but it certainly was far from being appropriate on this occasion."

The reporter, knowing that readers were aware that Johnson had just recently traveled to Washington from Tennessee, added sardonically: "He evidently did not skip Bourbon County, Kentucky on his way here." [43]

Lincoln closed his eyes, undoubtedly wondering how much longer Johnson was going to speak.

"His manner was that of a stump orator, and his language such as would be unworthy of even an ordinary ward politician," thought the *New York Tribune,* noting that "at one moment his voice would swell until it could be distinctly heard in the lobby and on the stairs leading to the gallery, not in the sonorous tones of an orator, but in a wild, backwoods shout, and suddenly drop so low as to be inaudible in the reporters' gallery immediately above where he stood." [44]

Johnson embarrassed himself further when he failed to properly swear in eleven new members of the Senate, holding out a Bible for them to repeat their oaths, only to wave the men away before they voiced those oaths, prompting Forney to properly perform the ceremony instead.

As the ceremonies moved to the outside of the capitol for the President's swearing-in and inaugural address, Lincoln quickly instructed Missouri Senator John Brooks: "Do not let Johnson speak outside." [45]

Once outside, Lincoln at some point in the proceedings saw Frederick Douglass and briefly talked with him. At that very moment, Johnson noticed both men briefly staring at him. What Douglass saw in return startled him: "The first expression which came to his face, and which I think was a true index of his heart," Douglass noted as Johnson glanced at him, "was one of bitter contempt and aversion."

Johnson may have in more sober moments regarded himself as the "Moses of the Colored People," but clearly when drunk was entirely disgusted with the idea that a black man should be treated as an equal during a presidential inauguration.

Johnson quickly "tried to assume a more friendly appearance," Douglass later recalled, who nevertheless remained convinced that Johnson's initial response revealed the essential man, while his second response was nothing more than the "bland and sickly smile of the demagogue." [46]

Johnson's Senate chamber speech seemed even more maudlin when compared with Lincoln's inaugural address, an address that historian Doris Kearns Goodwin has said "fused spiritual faith with politics." [47]

Reaching a highpoint with a classic peroration, Lincoln declared "With malice toward none, with charity for all," as he urged a binding of the nation's wounds by finally ending the war, caring for the widows and children of soldiers who had died on the fields, and doing everything possible to "achieve and cherish a just and a lasting peace, among ourselves, and with all nations." [48]

Johnson was seen at a White House inaugural reception later that afternoon, but shortly afterwards moved out to the quiet two-story brick mansion of Francis and Elizabeth Blair in Silver Spring, Maryland, some 6 miles to the northeast of Washington, arriving there as "the most mortified sick *hurt* man I ever saw," Elizabeth would later note. [49]

In the days to come nearly everyone offered a take on Johnson's inaugural performance. The poet John Greenleaf Whittier kindly thought Johnson's "lapse of the 4th ult. was exceptional, as I cannot learn that he has ever before been charged with excess." [50]

The *Daily Evening News* of Falls River, Massachusetts, declared: "It would be unfair to make one error outweigh all the able, unselfish, and loyal labors he has performed, and the sufferings he has endured for the sake of the country." [51]

But this was decidedly the minority view.

Johnson was for the most part roundly cut up in the papers across the country for what had happened. The *Brooklyn Daily Eagle* remarked that "Johnson drunk is but Johnson sober with the mask off; at heart a boastful, low-bred, time-serving braggart." The *Chicago Tribune,* influential in Republican circles, announced: "We are of the opinion that Vice-President Johnson should resign his office and allow the Senate to elect a sober presiding officer." [52]

The Washington correspondent for the *London Times* quoted a Democrat senator worried that if Lincoln died and Johnson replaced him, the country would sink to a depth not seen "since the Roman Emperor made his horse a consul." [53]

Agreed the *Nottinghamshire Guardian*: "His behavior was that of an illiterate, vulgar, and drunken rowdy, and could it have been displayed before any other legislative assembly in the world, would have led to his arrest by the sergeant-at-arms." [54]

Pennsylvania Representative Thaddeus Stevens, unenthused about Johnson's presence on the National Union ticket in the first place, now suggested a Congressional inquiry looking into the vice-president's impeachment. After all, said Stevens, "he has already suffered the high penalty of public disgrace and permanent loss of character and influence." [55]

Charles Sumner was ready to act. The same man who just six months earlier had invited Johnson to speak in New England, now confided to abolitionist Wendell Phillips his desire to see Johnson impeached and removed from office "in order to redeem the national name & republican institutions & to save the country." [56]

Sumner and Stevens' efforts were frustrated by the fact that the House was only in session until March 11, with members declining to take the matter up. Sumner and fellow Massachusetts Republican Henry Wilson, however, did succeed in quickly pushing through a resolution in the Senate aimed to remind the world of Johnson's speech, banning all intoxicating liquors "in every form from the Senate portion of the Capitol." [57]

Trying to regain his strength at the Blair estate, Johnson at some point contacted Richard Sutton, chief reporter of the Senate, asking to see the printed version of his March 4 speech as it would appear in the *Congressional Globe*. Sutton complied, allowing Johnson to considerably clean up his remarks for the record. Dutifully, Forney then ran a copy of the revised speech for the readers of his *Daily Morning Chronicle*. [58]

Johnson remained at the Blair estate well into late March, with Elizabeth eventually reporting that he "now enjoys his food hugely—his breakfast particularly—and now that there are but few of us at the table talks well & a great deal & is getting happier in his feelings." [59]

As early as March 8 Johnson had, by note, informed Lincoln that the "prostration of my health" made it impossible for him to visit with the President. The two would, in fact, not meet for another four weeks. But Lincoln had early on come to Johnson's defense, telling Treasury Secretary Hugh McCulloch that the Vice-President was in no way an alcoholic, although he acknowledged that Johnson's March 4 behavior was in every way a "bad slip." [60]

But the *New York Herald* reporter's comments that Johnson, on his way to Washington, "didn't skip Bourbon County, Kentucky," greatly amused Lincoln, who subsequently cautioned General Joseph Hooker, about to leave Washington to return to his command of the Northern Department in Cincinnati, to be cautious about one particular county in the Bluegrass State. When Hooker asked the President what he meant, Lincoln, with a smile, replied "I mean Bourbon County. You must avoid it." [61]

By the end of the month Johnson was itching to get back into the action in Washington, while at the same time making plans to return to Tennessee for the inauguration of the new governor, William Brownlow. But he put off his plans, moving out of the Blair mansion and back into the Kirkwood House, where he rented a two-room suite on the first floor. With time on his hands, its not hard to imagine that Johnson renewed the habit of his senatorial years, walking over to the Library of Congress to satiate his voracious reading habits and checking out books that he could enjoy in the privacy of his Kirkwood suite.

In early April came word of Jefferson Davis' abdication of Richmond and the fall of the Confederate capitol. Johnson was ecstatic, wiring Brownlow on April 3: "The rebel Army routed and in full retreat—the enthusiasm here is perfectly wild."

Johnson, for no particular reason, made a point of adding: "The *Colored* troops first entered Richmond." [62]

Johnson walked two blocks to the front of the Willard Hotel on that same afternoon to listen to speeches celebrating the end of the war, before being asked to give one himself.

Lincoln would soon deliver an impromptu address noting that the "surrender of the principal insurgent army give hope of a righteous and speedy peace whose joyous expression cannot be restrained."

His remarks were entirely reverent and aspirational, and served as a reminder of the post-war struggles ahead: "We must simply begin with, and mold from, disorganized and discordant elements. Nor is it a small additional embarrassment that we, the loyal people, differ among ourselves as to the mode, manner, and means of reconstruction." [63]

Johnson's remarks in front of the Willard were entirely different in tone. Recalling his service in the U.S. Senate during the winter of 1860-61 when the country was coming apart, Johnson said he had then labeled secessionists as traitors and was happy to now do so again.

He had been asked back then "what I could do with such traitors, and I want to repeat my reply here. I said, if we had an Andrew Jackson, he would hang them as high as Haman."

"Humble as I am," Johnson now continued, "when you ask me what I would do [with the Confederate leadership], my reply is that I would arrest them; I would try them; I would convict them; and I would hang them."

His remarks were both unforgiving and class conscious. "I hold, too, that wealthy traitors should be made to re-numerate those men who have suffered as a consequence of their crime." [64]

Johnson in the weeks since his March 4 speech had renewed a friendship with former New York Senator Preston King, whom he may have encountered while recuperating at the Blair estate. A leader in the founding of the Republican Party in New York and strong anti-slavery advocate during his one term in the Senate, which ended in 1862, the 58 year-old King was frequently commented upon because of his size. Only 5 feet, 6 inches tall, he weighed at least 250 pounds, if not more, and was sometimes known for falling asleep at Washington parties after a big meal.

Rigidly honest, King was also a bachelor and a lonely man. Johnson genuinely liked King, recalling the times that the New Yorker had engaged Jefferson Davis in angry debates on the Senate floor. Johnson was also not unmindful of the fact that King, during the 1864 Baltimore convention, had beseeched his fellow New York delegates to vote for Johnson as Lincoln's running mate.

Now, in the aftermath of the Confederate retreat from Richmond, Johnson and King, along with several other men, traveled to the former Confederate capital, touring a city that had been ransacked by residents fleeing before the Yankees moved in. With broken windows, smoldering fires, and trash lining the streets, Richmond was a forlorn, decimated place now primarily populated with ex-slaves who had wildly cheered Lincoln when he had visited the city only two days before.

It was later asserted that during their trip to Richmond, Johnson and King also attempted to meet with Lincoln, who was staying at the massive Union encampment at City Point, some 22 miles to the southeast, and that upon learning this, the President supposedly exclaimed: "Don't let those men come into my presence. I won't see either of them; send them away." [65]

But the person who claimed to have heard these comments was Admiral David Dixon Porter, who in relating these remarks in his memoirs published two decades later had long since become a Johnson foe. Besides, Lincoln rarely spoke in such a didactic manner. Much more probable is the recollection of Colonel William Cook, who served as a bodyguard to both Lincoln and later Johnson. Crook said that when Lincoln heard Johnson might on his way to City Point, he remarked "Well, I guess he can get along without me." [66]

Crook later mused: "I do not know whether this meant that the President did not like Mr. Johnson or not. It may have been merely that he felt he was at City Point for a certain purpose and had no time for other things." [67]

Johnson made no public comment during his brief visit to Richmond, returning to the Kirkwood where in the days to come he sporadically entertained guests and received mail, primarily from friends in Tennessee updating him on the transition to a civil government there.

One correspondent, Catherine Melville, a former Tennessee school teacher who had moved to Washington during the war, working as a clerk in the quartermaster general's office, stopped by to visit, later asking the Vice-President if he could find employment for her companion, Eliza Jane Gay, whom she described as "always & ever a Loyal woman." [68]

Melville, 55 years old, and Gay, 30 years old, were lesbians who shared housing in the 400 block of 13th Street NW. Whether Johnson knew of their sexual orientation or even cared, it was clear that he admired both women for their work as educators.

He wrote a note to himself: "A letter must be written for Miss Gay." Shortly afterwards, Gay was hired as a clerk in the federal post office department. [69]

Not until the afternoon of April 14 did Johnson meet with Lincoln. It was two days after the formal signing of documents making official the

Confederate surrender of General Robert E. Lee to Ulysses S. Grant that had taken place on April 9.

The President was in an understandably joyous mood, presiding over a late morning cabinet meeting attended by Grant, who was upset that he did not yet have word of the surrender of Confederate General Joseph Johnston to Union General William Tecumseh Sherman in North Carolina, putting an end to the last significant rebel action.

What Johnson and Lincoln talked about during their mid-afternoon meeting is unknown, although a sense of celebration must have filled the air, along with a brief discussion on the need for an efficient restoration of the Southern states, a subject near to the hearts of both men.

Johnson was back at the Kirkwood by early evening, while Lincoln and the First Lady, along with their guests, socialite Clara Harris and her fiancé Major Henry Rathbone, headed in a carriage to Ford's Theater on 10th Street NW to watch a performance of the comedy *Our American Cousin* starring Laura Keene.

Lincoln had earlier invited Grant and his wife Julia to attend the show. In fact, a small notice in the morning's *Washington Evening Star* announced: "Lieut. General Grant, President Lincoln and Mrs. Lincoln have secured the State Box at Ford's Theater tonight to witness Miss Laura Keene's 'American Cousin.'" [70]

But Grant begged off after Julia sent him a note asking that he instead go with her to their residence in Burlington, New Jersey.

Grant, weary of the pressing public attention he had been subject to for the last 24 hours after arriving in Washington from Virginia, was only too happy to have an excuse not to go to the theater.

The Lincolns could have at this point invited Johnson instead, but it is not known if the President, who had spent hours with him during any number of meetings in the last four years, actually regarded the business-like Johnson as an enjoyable companion for a night on the town.

Besides, Mrs. Lincoln, who disliked many of Lincoln's associates with a sometimes unreasoning passion, seemed to have developed a particular contempt for Johnson, partly spirited by his behavior at the March 4 inaugural, which she regarded as deeply embarrassing to the President.

Earlier this same afternoon the actor John Wilkes Booth had entered the Kirkwood and asked the registration clerk for a blank calling card. Booth then wrote a message for Johnson that was really meant to confuse anyone on his trail: "Don't wish to disturb you. Are you at home." He signed the card, "J. Wilkes Booth." [71]

For months Booth, a passionate supporter of the Confederacy and slavery advocate outraged over the possibility that Lincoln's Emancipation Proclamation might lead to the social and legal equality of the races, had been stalking the President, hoping, at the very least, to kidnap him.

Once so captured, Lincoln would be used as the supreme bargaining chip in a move to force the federal government to release captured Confederate soldiers.

With a mesmerizing presence, the 26 year-old Booth, regarded by reviewers as one of the country's most gifted Shakespeareans, talked a small group of malcontents into first seizing Lincoln and then, finally, as the plot evolved, assassinating him.

One of the group under Booth's spell was 30 year-old carriage repairman George Atzerodt. Later described by the *Washington Evening Star*: "Short, thick-set, round-shouldered, light-colored mustache [and] unpleasant green eyes," Atzerodt soon found himself in the middle of a plot to not just hold Lincoln hostage, but to take down the entire federal government. [72]

Lincoln would be assassinated, and so would Secretary of State William Seward, as well as General Grant, and...Andrew Johnson.

Atzerodt later claimed that once he realized Booth's murderous intentions, he wanted no part of the scheme. But Booth, in response, laughed, pointing out that whatever happened, it was certain to be "the death of everyman that backed out." [73]

Left with the job of killing Johnson, Atzerodt checked into the Kirkwood and was assigned a room on the second floor, above Johnson, who was residing in Room 68. Once in his quarters, Atzerodt stuffed a loaded pistol under one of the bed's pillows, and bowie knife under the bedsheets. He hung on a hook his black coat which contained in one of its pockets a bank book belonging to Booth.

By early evening, a clearly addled Atzerodt, after drinking at the nearby Union Hotel, returned to the Kirkwood and drank some more at the bar there, asking odd questions regarding Johnson's whereabouts and whether the Vice-President carried a gun.

At around the same time, Lewis Thornton Powell, another of Booth's minions, knocked at the three-story Lafayette Square residence of Seward. Powell announced to a servant that he was there to deliver medicine to the Secretary, who, recovering from a brutal fall he had taken during a carriage ride nine days earlier, was wearing a heavy metal brace around his upper neck and mouth.

When the servant hesitated, Powell brushed past him and ran up the staircase to the second floor where he first shot at Seward's son Frederick, and, upon missing, violently smashed the gun on the younger Seward's head, rendering him unconscious. Powell then knocked down a military aide before running into the Secretary's bedroom and stabbing at Seward's face with a large knife.

Powell was soon enough pulled back by the military aide and another Seward son, Augustus, before breaking free of both men, running downstairs and out the front door yelling "I'm mad! I'm mad!" as he disappeared into the darkness. [74]

At Ford's Theater, meanwhile, all was pandemonium as Booth, well-known to the staff of the theater, gained admittance to the balcony containing the presidential party and overlooking the stage, shot Lincoln in the back of his head.

In a blur of events that soon almost every American would remember by heart from the first time they read of it, Booth pulled out a knife and stabbed in the chest Major Rathbone, who had tried to seize him, before jumping from the balcony to the stage some 15 feet below, the spurs on his boots catching in the folds of one of the American flags decorating the balcony, causing him to land, very briefly, on his hands and knees.

Athletic, Booth quickly jumped up and yelled to a confused and soon to be hysterical audience "Sic semper tyrannis," the Latin phrase meaning "thus always to tyrants," as he exited off stage to an outside passageway and waiting horse. [75]

In the midst of a scene of frenzied chaos, audience members, having heard Mary Lincoln scream that the President had been shot, rushed into the aisles and out onto the lobby, with others, unthinking, clogging the stairwell and trying for no particular reason to reach the President. One of those audience members, meanwhile, suddenly thought of Andrew Johnson.

Leonard Farwell, the former governor of Wisconsin, had the presence of mind to wonder about the Vice-President's well-being. He had casually spoken with Johnson several times at the Kirkwood in the previous weeks and had earlier in the evening invited him to the *American Cousin* performance. But Johnson had declined, saying he preferred to spend the evening reading.

Now Farwell ran from the theater to the hotel where he told the desk clerk to secure guards for the front of the hotel, lobby, and outside of Johnson's room, before loudly knocking on the Vice-President's door.

By this time, Atzerodt had entirely lost his nerve, drunkenly leaving the Kirkwood and riding a mare through the streets of Washington before, after midnight, checking into the Pennsylvania Hotel on C Street where he spent what was left of the evening.

"Governor Johnson, if you are in the room, I must see you," Farwell announced just before Johnson tentatively opened the door and heard for the first time the news of Lincoln's shooting. Farwell later said that both he and Johnson were overcome at that moment thinking of what had just happened. Farwell then decided to go back to the theater in the hope of learning more about Lincoln's condition. [76]

Once near the theater, Farwell was confronted by a mass of confusion as hundreds of people crowded to the front of the Peterson House, across the street from the theater, where an unconscious Lincoln had been carried. Farwell encountered 25 year-old James O'Beirne, the city's provost marshal, and told him that Johnson was in need of protection. O'Beirne, a former captain in the 37th New York "Irish Rifles" Infantry, immediately appreciated the danger Johnson might be in, soon joining up with John Lee, a member of the military police force, who, upon arriving at the Kirkwood, searched Atzerodt's room for clues.

Johnson could only sit still for so long. He wanted to go the Peterson House, having no idea what he would see. A concerned O'Beirne suggested the protection of several troops, but Johnson preferred to go virtually unprotected, wearing a heavy coat and hat somewhat pulled over his face, as he walked the two and a half blocks to the Peterson House with O'Beirne and Farwell.

The three men sliced through the crowd at the house where Johnson saw the dying Lincoln stretched diagonally across a small bed. The room was thick with doctors, aides of the President, and politicians. Earlier, Secretary of War Stanton had entered, saw Lincoln's condition, and quickly commandeered a back parlor where he began to send out a series of orders virtually locking down Washington in an attempt to capture Booth and his fellow conspirators.

Johnson stayed at the Peterson House less than half an hour, briefly talking with Stanton before he left. Various reports indicate that Johnson also looked in on Mrs. Lincoln, grieving in a separate room of the residence. The First Lady had spent most of her time at the Peterson with

Charles Sumner, with whom she had always felt comfortable. Sumner knew that Mrs. Lincoln roundly disliked Johnson and perhaps may have signaled to Johnson that it was not at all a good idea to say anything to the First Lady.

Quietly, Johnson left the Peterson, walking back on what were now rainy streets to his hotel.

At three in the morning, Stanton sent out a wire: "The President still breathes, but is quite insensible, as he has been ever since he was shot." Stanton continued to issue directives and bulletins until sunrise when he wrote: "Abraham Lincoln died this morning at 22 minutes after 7 o'clock." [77]

Back at the Kirkwood, there was no doubt in Johnson's mind that Confederates, whether he meant amateur devotees or high-level officials, were behind Lincoln's murder and the assault on Seward. "They shall suffer for this," Johnson exclaimed to no one in particular. "They shall suffer for this." [78]

The rain continued. At 9 a.m., Chief Justice Salmon Chase arrived at the hotel, somberly shaking hands with Johnson, and later describing him as "full of sorrow & anxiety." [79]

Attorney General James Speed and Treasury Secretary Hugh McCulloch also entered Johnson's suite to observe the formal swearing in of Johnson as president. The men were shortly joined by Senators Solomon Foot of Vermont, Alexander Ramsey of Minnesota, and John Hale of New Hampshire, along with old friends Francis Blair and his son Montgomery.

The blinds to the windows of the suite remained drawn as the men found their places around Johnson, who, in a low voice, repeated the words as recited by Chase. Upon the conclusion of the oath, the Chief Justice remarked: "You are President; may God support, guide & bless you in your arduous duties." [80]

McCulloch thought Johnson appeared "oppressed by the suddenness of the call upon him to become President." McCulloch added that what he called the "unfavorable impression" Johnson had made upon many of the same men in the room as a result of his March 4 spectacle, "had undergone a considerable change." [81]

Johnson then delivered brief and general remarks, and in the context of those remarks said something that could be interpreted differently by different people. "As to any indication of any policy which may be pursued by me in the administration of the government, I have to say that that must be left for development as the administration progresses," he quietly commented. [82]

Nearly forty years after running away as a tailor's apprentice, a poor boy without a friend; four years after bravely standing up to the entire South as it seceded from the country; and just six weeks after his humiliating vice-presidential inaugural speech, Andrew Johnson, 56 years old, was now the President of the United States.

CHAPTER SEVEN

THE VANQUISHERS AND THE VANQUISHED

E ven as Johnson was being sworn in, Edwin Stanton was laying the groundwork for the new President's first cabinet meeting.

Where exactly the meeting would be held was of no small consideration. The White House, with a grieving Mary Lincoln, was obviously out. Navy Secretary Gideon Welles suggested instead the use of the office of Treasury Secretary Hugh McCulloch, an idea that made sense to all concerned.

At noon a somber Johnson entered that office, which would soon be draped with the flag that had decorated the front of Lincoln's box at Ford's Theater, exchanged brief greetings with the cabinet members, and said only that his intention was to keep Lincoln's team intact. "He desired the members of the cabinet to go forward with their duties without any interruption," Welles recorded in his diary. [1]

Stanton's biographer, William Marvel, would later assert that the War Secretary took charge of the meeting, attempting in the process to fill in for a recovering Seward. For his part, Johnson said he would appoint William Hunter, long-time State Department functionary, as acting Secretary of State, while also asking all of the Cabinet members to coordinate their efforts organizing the massive funeral ceremonies for Lincoln. [2]

The details of the funeral would provide Stanton with a new opportunity to command. Already having ordered that Lincoln's body be taken to the White House, Stanton soon even oversaw the late President's embalming. When a local undertaker suggested removing a bruise on Lincoln's face that had probably been caused when he fell after being shot, Stanton declared "No, this is part of the history of the event." [3]

Stanton, who on this very day was also coordinating the search for John Wilkes Booth, also ordered that Lincoln's funeral service should be held in the East Room. The following morning, at a subsequent cabinet meeting, once again in the Treasury Department, Stanton handed out a detailed plan for the reconstruction of the South, a plan putting an emphasis on establishing military rule in every state except Virginia, which already had a Unionist governor in place.

How Johnson felt about Stanton's activities at this point is difficult to discern. He was undoubtedly distracted by a hundred different concerns, including, for the moment, setting up his own administrative staff, and trying to get a feel for what had become, under Lincoln, a massive federal bureaucracy.

More than likely Johnson was probably relieved that Stanton was willing to take on so much work. But, accustomed to calling his own shots, Johnson may have also been put off by Stanton's blustery manner and his seeming belief that he was always the smartest man in any room.

Days later a friend of Orville Browning predicted that Johnson and Stanton "would not agree and that the Cabinet will be reorganized within thirty days." [4]

Johnson, meanwhile, sought to allay fears regarding his own reconstruction policies, agreeing to meet on Sunday, April 16 with members of the Committee on the Conduct of the War, the same committee he had briefly served on in the early winter of 1862.

Michigan Senate Zachariah Chandler, Indiana Congressman George Julian, and committee chairman Benjamin Wade had long since given up on Lincoln. The men, determined to protect ex-slaves, had decided that the best way to achieve this end would be to promulgate a harsh and unflagging control of the entirety of the south. That control would see the punishment, by death if need be, of former Confederate leaders, and a general seizure of their property, to be divided and distributed to the slaves who had for decades been forced to work those lands.

Johnson met with the men in his Treasury Office and said all the right things. He promised a vigorous prosecution of the fading Confederate leadership, prompting an excited Wade to declare "By Gods, there will be no trouble now in running the government." [5]

Charles Sumner, too, was uncharacteristically happy. The same Massachusetts Senator who had half a year earlier invited Johnson to campaign in New England, and then called for his impeachment after Johnson's drunken vice-presidential speech in March, could now not say enough for him, telling a correspondent that Johnson had "glided quietly into his duties, with a simplicity & modesty which are admirable." [6]

Johnson had told Sumner, as he had remarked many times before, that those committing treason "shall be punished." The voraciousness of Johnson's stand now prompted Sumner to wonder: "How many must be executed in each state?" [7]

On the afternoon of the day Lincoln died, Johnson's 36 year-old daughter Martha Patterson wrote her father a heart-felt letter expressing her sorrow over the assassination and telling the new President: "How I long to be with you this sad day, that we might weep together at a *nation's calamity,* and be ever mindful of *Him,* who watches over and preserves us from all harm." [8]

Johnson wanted his daughter, undeniably the only Washington-savvy member of his family besides himself, to get to the nation's capital as soon as possible. He also understandably wanted the rest of his family with him, although he couldn't provide more permanent quarters until he was finally able to move into the White House, an event that would not happen until early June after Mary Lincoln, with the help of her son Robert, had at last moved out.

With almost every newspaper in the country disclosing Johnson's residence as the Kirkwood House, Johnson shortly moved, with Preston King, into the relatively more private residence of Massachusetts Congressman Samuel Hooper at the intersection of 15th and H streets.

On April 17 Johnson and King visited a White House draped in black, where Lincoln's casket rested upon an ornate catafalque in the East Room. Two days later, also with King, but this time nicely joined by former vice-president Hannibal Hamlin, Johnson entered the East Room at precisely noon for Lincoln's initial funeral service.

It had been an odd day, slightly gray with a hint of rain in the air. Johnson rode by carriage to the White House on streets packed with tens of thousands of mourners, all orderly, all quiet. The blinds to the East Room were closed, with only a hint of light streaking through the windows.

Johnson looked around and saw doors, chandeliers and mirrors covered in black muslin. The ever-silent Ulysses S. Grant stood silently next to Lincoln's catafalque, some noticing tears in the General's eyes.

Saying nothing, Johnson approached the catafalque and for several moments just stared at the face of the deceased president, his movements closely observed by White House aides, members of Congress, visiting state delegations, and reporters.

Johnson's thoughts contemplating the corpse of a man he had known for nearly two decades, a transformational and historic figure who had dramatically changed Johnson's life forever, were unknown. He never told anyone what was on his mind just then, nor did he talk very much in the many years to come about his relationship with Lincoln, his thoughts, his memories, and Lincoln's profound legacy.

Johnson was not an unemotional man. His close relationship with his family and never-ending concern for their welfare, was proof enough of that. The many impoverished and harassed Tennesseans he endeavored to protect militarily during the war, let alone the occasional young captured Confederate soldiers he sympathetically tried to understand and excuse, was evidence of a man whose heart was very much in functioning order.

But Johnson could also, at times, be coldly functional. As such, his feelings in the days and hours after Lincoln's death were all entirely unemotional. Lincoln had been president. But now he was dead. Johnson was the new president, and had a lot of work to do.

Two days after the White House funeral ceremony, Johnson was handed a document by Stanton and Grant detailing a surrender agreement worked out between Union General William Tecumseh Sherman and Confederate General Joseph Johnston. In his zeal to bring this final conflict in the Carolinas to an end, Sherman had offered exceedingly liberal terms, providing a general amnesty to all ex-Rebels, the restoration of property, and, most alarmingly, imminent federal approval of all existing state governments in the South.

Scanning the document, Johnson was concerned. But Stanton was apoplectic, angrily holding forth in a subsequent cabinet meeting, wildly accusing Sherman of disloyalty and strongly urging that Grant be assigned to go immediately to the South to straighten matters out.

It was true that the surrender terms were unrealistically generous, as well as political dynamite: "Almost unanimous against the Sherman armistice," John Forney wired Johnson once the document was reported in the press, "Feeling tremendous." [9]

Rhode Island Governor William Sprague told Johnson: "Loyal men deplore and are outraged by Sherman's arrangement with Johnston. He should be promptly removed." [10]

But what Stanton did next gave Johnson his first real view of how the War Secretary operated. Instead of being satisfied with Grant quietly trying to work with Sherman to come up with a more realistic agreement, Stanton released to the press the entirety of the Sherman-Johnston document, along with a biased account of the matter, stopping just short of calling Sherman, one of the greatest Union commanders in the war, a traitor.

Making the point that Sherman had no authority to enter into any agreement with anyone, Stanton, also in his press release, made sure to note that the "action of General Sherman was disapproved by the President, by the Secretary of War, by General Grant, and every member of the Cabinet." [11]

Reading the newspaper accounts, Gideon Wells reflected that he was not sorry to see the details of the Sherman-Johnston agreement disclosed, although the "manner and some of Stanton's matter was not particularly commendable or judicious." [12]

To say the least. Sherman, upon reading of Stanton's move to defame him, was rightly outraged. His mood only darkened when he learned of an additional letter that Stanton had sent to Grant proclaiming that the agreement had been met with "universal disapprobation. No one of any class or any shade of opinion approves it. I have not known as much surprise and discontent at anything that has happened during the war." [13]

Sherman now felt compelled to write Stanton, acknowledging that his agreement with Johnston had been an error, but adding: "I had flattered myself that by four years' patient, unremitting, and successful labor, I deserved no remainder such as is contained in the last paragraph of your letter to General Grant." [14]

Grant did his best to calm Sherman down, standing respectfully in the background after the Union General and Johnston cobbled together a more appropriate agreement along the lines of the one Grant had earlier made with Robert E. Lee.

If Sherman was angry over Stanton's treatment of him, Grant was outraged. "It is infamous! Infamous!" he declared privately to aide Adam Badeau, "after four year of such service as Sherman has done, that he should be used like this." [15]

Johnson had remained curiously passive throughout the entire affair. He had initially agreed with Stanton that the original Sherman/Johnston agreement was inappropriate, although whether he also agreed with the War Secretary that Sherman was an actual traitor seems unlikely. Johnson had been unimpressed with Sherman's service at the beginning of the war when he failed to launch an assault on East Tennessee. But as the war continued, particularly with Sherman's heroic March to the Sea, Johnson's respect for the General's bravery and acumen increased accordingly.

The two men, in fact, in the months to come, would become friends, although never sharing the kind of emotional bond that Sherman enjoyed with Grant.

Ultimately, the contretemps over the Sherman/Johnston agreement told Johnson very little about Sherman himself, other than his being at times both impetuous and generous of spirit. The contretemps told Johnson much about Stanton, who was jealous of Sherman's popularity and his potential future as a presidential candidate.

Johnson was given another opportunity to see how Stanton worked when presented with a document requiring his signature and declaring that Jefferson Davis and several other Confederate leaders, still on the run after the fall of the Confederate government, were wanted for arrest as conspirators in the assassination of Lincoln.

The matter had been discussed by the full cabinet, with a reward of $100,000 offered for Davis' capture.

Whether Johnson ever actually believed that Davis was involved in Lincoln's murder is unknown. All that really mattered was that Stanton did. While John Wilkes Booth had been shot and killed by Union soldiers on April 26, the net had been cast for Booth's conspirators, with Stanton in a public statement declaring that "all good citizens are exhorted to aid public justice on this occasion. Everyman should consider his own conscience charged with this solemn duty, and rest neither night nor day until it will be accomplished." [16]

Once those conspirators were rounded up, Stanton successfully urged Johnson to call for a military trial that would be conducted behind closed doors. To this end, Stanton was instrumental in making certain that the prosecution would be headed up by Judge Advocate Joseph Holt, a man, if possible, even more determined to see the accused conspirators quickly disposed of.

Although political leaders and newspapers across the country urged a civil trial, a military trial began on May 9 and ended on June 29, with three men sentenced to death, "the proceedings findings and sentences" sent to Johnson for his approval. [17]

The military commission additionally sentenced 32 year-old Mary Surratt, mother of John Surratt, one of the conspirators still at large, to death. There was a very real doubt regarding Mrs. Surratt's guilt. While it seemed clear that she knew most of the conspirators, her involvement in any plot was unproven, creating enough doubt in the minds of several of the commission members to suggest she should instead be given a sentence of life in prison.

Holt visited Johnson in the White House on July 5, handing him the findings of the commission. In reviewing the papers, Johnson most likely did not see an attached recommendation for Mrs. Surratt's alternate sentencing, or so he would one day assert. She was hung two days later with the other male conspirators, an ending that entirely satisfied both Stanton and Holt.

But the matter would become a public controversy months later when Johnson said he had recently gone through the commission documents and only then discovered the clemency plea for Mary Surratt. Holt would angrily deny that he had done anything in any way to conceal the information. But given that Holt, like Stanton, was entirely fired with seeing to the swift execution of the conspirators, and also, like Stanton, had a history of vindictiveness, it seems safe to assume that Johnson never saw the document in question.

Stanton's eagerness to prosecute the Booth conspirators, knowing from the start that there was no chance any of them would be found not guilty, may have appeared unseemly. But he and the new president were also at this time giving every appearance of being in agreement on the need to try and execute the captured leaders of the Confederacy, redeeming Johnson's bellicose pledge to "hang them as high as Haman." [18]

But when Johnson included General Robert E. Lee in the select number of Confederate leaders he most wanted to see arrested, tried, and executed, he found himself confronted with the stalwart opposition of Grant.

Grant, years later, said he frankly told Johnson that "so long as Lee was observing his parole, I would never consent to his arrest." Grant added that had Johnson ordered him to arrest Lee or "any of his commanders who obeyed the law," he would have resigned from the Army. [19]

This was exceedingly blunt language coming from the seemingly quiescent Grant, and was perhaps the first planted seed in what would someday prove to be Johnson's almost obsessive resentment of the General.

In the end, Lee was never arrested, with Johnson, grudgingly, eventually dropping charges against him and nearly forty other Confederate leaders.

On the morning of May 23, Johnson seated himself on a reviewing stand to witness the extraordinary spectacle of nearly 200,000 soldiers over the course of the next two days parading down Pennsylvania Avenue. The soldiers were primarily of the Army of the Potomac and the Army of the Tennessee, and comprised a cavalcade nearly 20 miles long.

The event had been anticipated for days, inspiring an air of joyous celebration throughout the city as tens of thousands of Washington residents and visitors from other places filled both sides of the avenue, waving flags, and cheering the end of a war that had at times seemed on the verge of destroying the country, but in the end made it more unified and stronger than ever.

In some ways, the review, with Johnson sitting next to Grant and a host of cabinet members, was a shining moment of American exceptionalism, a recognition on the part of everyone involved, including an untold number of awestruck school children watching from the sidewalks, that America clearly was the greatest country on earth.

"Though the city is so crammed, it is yet gay and jovial with the good feeling that prevails," a reporter for the *New York Times* wrote, capturing the sheer merriment of the event. [20]

Just days before leading his men into Washington, General Sherman had sent Johnson a quick message informing him that "if there by any matter on which you desire to see me personally, I will hasten to see you." [21]

Johnson did, indeed, subsequently meet with Sherman, a meeting in which Sherman later said the President had proven himself "extremely cordial." [22]

His good feelings towards Johnson notwithstanding, Sherman made a point, as he joined the dignitaries on the reviewing stand, of saluting the President and Grant and shaking their hands. But when an expectant Stanton, amazingly, also sought to shake Sherman's hand, Sherman glared at the portly War Secretary and turned away, leaving Stanton, as his biographer William Marvel put it, to "grasp the air" in front of him. [23]

Upon hearing that some of Sherman's officers, drinking later that night at the Willard Hotel, had loudly maligned Stanton, Grant gently suggested that Sherman should for the immediate future keep his men confined to camp in order to "preserve quiet and decorum."

Sherman, in response, promised to do a better job of controlling his soldiers, but still angry over Stanton's libel, pointedly noted: "I could not maintain my authority over troops if I tamely submitted to personal insult." [24]

Forever disenchanted with Stanton, Sherman nevertheless admitted to Grant that he had come to highly admire Johnson. "The President only has to tell me what he wants done and I will do it," Sherman declared. [25]

Parade-watchers and reporters taking in the review all agreed that Johnson appeared in exemplary form, repeatedly saluting the various units as they marched by, nodding to some, and taking his hat off to others.

The poet Walt Whitman, who had revered Lincoln and spent untold hours caring for wounded soldiers in several local Army hospitals, was profoundly impressed seeing Johnson in the reviewing stand, deciding that it was "wonderful that just the plain middling-sized ordinary man, dressed in black, without the least badge or ornamentation, should be master of all these myriad of soldiers." [26]

Increasingly, leaders of this or that party faction now looked to Johnson as the determined and calm leader who could somehow seamlessly usher in a massive political, societal, and economic reconversion to a peacetime nation.

Perhaps foremost among those expressing the most enthusiasm for Johnson's course so far were the Radical Republicans, certain that the new President fully embraced their idea of a subservient South for the time being, which could mean months or years, governed from Washington via a massive federal troop and bureaucratic presence.

Sumner was hopeful, telling Columbia University professor Francis Lieber that Johnson was entirely committed to the idea that "colored persons are to have the right of suffrage; that no state can be precipitated into the Union; that the rebel states must go through a term of probation."

"I had looked for a bitter contest on this question," continued Sumner, "but with the President on our side, it will be carried by simple *avoir du pois* [by its own weight]." [27]

The good feelings were substantially shattered just four days after the conclusion of the Grand Review when Johnson issued two historic proclamations. One provided a general amnesty to nearly all ex-Confederates, with the exception of those who held a high rank in either the Confederate military or government or owned more than $20,000 in property.

The second appointed a provisional governor of North Carolina, the beginning of a process that Johnson pointedly described as a "restoration," eventually returning the Southern states to their familiar relationship as independent satellites of the federal government. [28]

On the question of giving black people the right to vote, Johnson was silent, having decided that because voting issues were handled at the state level, he had no real authority to act.

Sumner was astonished by Johnson's announcement, but uncharacteristically urged calm, telling Chief Justice Salmon Chase: "Thus far there is a disposition to treat him tenderly & to avoid a break, but some of my correspondents anticipate a break." At the same time, he frankly told Gideon Welles, "I tremble to think how much of agitation, trouble & strife the country must pass through in order to recover from the move which has now been made." [29]

One of Sumner's correspondents was Thaddeus Stevens, leader of the Radical Republicans in the House, who quickly convinced himself that it had been Johnson's intention all along to return the South to its pre-war condition, and damn the blacks.

Earlier, Stevens had tried to gently remind the President that all reconstruction issues were a "question for the Legislative power exclusively." [30]

Now Stevens plaintively asked Sumner: "Is it possible to devise any plan to arrest the government in its ruinous career?" before telling Johnson, "Among all the leading Union men of the North with whom I had intercourse, I do not find one who approves of your policy." [31]

Not until June 9, meanwhile, was Johnson finally able to move into the White House, roughly two weeks after a distraught Mary Lincoln had left and White House staffers readied the executive mansion for the new President. With Johnson came his extended family, who joined him at different points over the course of the next several weeks. First Lady Eliza Johnson, due to her ongoing consumptive state, declined to involve herself in very many ceremonial functions, leaving those tasks largely to Martha Patterson, Johnson's 37 year-old daughter and most probably his favorite child; and 32 year-old Mary Stover, whose husband Daniel had died the year before in the war.

Both women gradually gained favor among the White House staff and federal officials for their unassuming and modest ways. "I like them both very much," remarked Benjamin Brown French, the federal commissioner of public buildings. "Mrs. Patterson is one of the very nicest and most amiable ladies I have met with for a long, long time. It will be a pleasure to attend to her, I know." [32]

French soon found himself equally impressed with the President, who sought to impose an exacting system organizing all documents and correspondence coming into the White House, expecting at the same time for his staff to work every bit as hard as he did.

Johnson not only courteously took the trouble to assure French, despite rumors to the contrary, that his job was secure, he also casually talked with the surprised commissioner about general events, sitting with him on a bench under a tree on the White House grounds, and talking "on the condition of the country and what ought to be done, for at least an hour." [33]

Others were impressed with Johnson's extraordinary honesty. He had always been for frugality in government, and even more, wanted every penny spent to be accounted for. It was perhaps for this combination of reasons that money, the mother's milk of American politics, had no role in the way Johnson conducted affairs. "Offices were not merchandise," Treasury Secretary McCulloch later noted of Johnson's approach to patronage. "The President never permitted himself to be under personal obligations to anyone." [34]

On the contrary, anyone suggesting that a financial contribution might be Johnson's for the asking should he appoint a favored person to a government post would realize that the suggestion had royally failed when the President swiftly showed his visitor to the door.

William Crook, who had served Lincoln as a body guard, was not initially sure that he liked the new President. Crook had heard rumors that Johnson was perhaps an alcoholic and given to moments of irrational anger or exuberance.

How could this man, Crook wondered, conceivably replace Lincoln?

But as the days turned to weeks in the summer and fall of 1865, Crook found himself admiring Johnson's no-nonsense work ethic, seeing him spending hours at his desk just trying to stay on top of his job.

"I grew to follow his directions with alacrity and to welcome his rare and laconic remarks," Crook later recalled, adding that "all of the employees began to feel his influence. He was a man who, through association, swayed insensibly the men who were with him." [35]

Eventually, Johnson and Crook would ride out together to the tree-lined Glenwood Cemetery on the outskirts of the city where Johnson enjoyed the peaceful surroundings, walking between the graves and now and then stopping to read a headstone or two.

One day Johnson laughed after looking at the inscriptions of two headstones. One was the stone of a buried woman proclaiming: "Sacred to the memory of my wife—by her disconsolate husband." The next marker read of the death of the man's second wife, only two years later.

"It didn't take that fellow long to get over his first affliction, did it?" Johnson, with a morbid delight, asked. [36]

On top of the question of what to do about ex-Confederate leaders, at the very top, was the problem of Jefferson Davis. Captured by Union soldiers in early May, Davis and several other high-ranking Confederate leaders, including former Alabama Senator Clement Clay, were transported by steamer to Fort Monroe, the forbidding fortification built during the War of 1812 that was now serving as a Union prison.

Davis, noted a report immediately filed by Assistant Secretary of War Charles Dana, "bore himself with a haughty attitude. His face was somewhat flushed, but his features were composed and his step firm." [37]

For a while Davis was immobilized with iron clamps fastened about his ankles, as officials in Washington endlessly debated what should be done with the first and only president of the Confederacy.

Johnson had despised Davis for more years than he could probably remember. He despised him for his aristocratic pretentions, his annoying and probably uncontrollable tendency to look down on the kind of poor Southern white stock from which Johnson rose, and his outrageous decision to join what Johnson had always regarded as a treasonous movement against the U.S. by agreeing to lead the Confederacy.

Now this man who annoyed Johnson as few other men had before, was a pathetic, yet still stubbornly proud inmate whose fate was in the hands of the federal government, and in particular, Andrew Johnson.

Johnson had long talked of Davis and other Confederate leaders being hung for their deeds, and undoubtedly the fact that Johnson could now entirely determine Davis' fate had to have at the very least satisfied Johnson at some level.

But much of Johnson's rhetoric regarding the execution of Davis was just that: rhetoric. He had never actually imagined that the time would come when he could push for a trial of Davis that might led to his death sentence. Johnson was in every way a tough, unremitting, and many times merciless foe. But he wasn't bloodthirsty. He no more intended to be responsible for playing a part in Davis' execution than Davis would have had their fortunes been somehow reversed.

On the contrary, Johnson soon began to realize what a problem an imprisoned Davis was for his new administration. The President was talking about the importance of bringing the South back into the Union, with the concurrent hope that Southerners might eventually embrace the idea of now being Americans and not Confederates.

But this hoped-for attitudinal change could hardly be helped if the federal government should end up executing Davis. Making the matter more cloudy was the question of where Davis would be tried. Obviously Virginia was the most likely place. But because the federal military was still in control of the Commonwealth, a new problem cropped up when Chief Justice Chase, traveling the federal circuit, announced that he would not preside over any such proceedings until Johnson declared that the "judicial is not subordinate to the military." [38]

While Johnson declined to make any such determination, it seems clear that the visits and entreaties of Varina Davis, the 39 year old refined and attractive wife of Davis, played some role in his thinking on the matter. Varina had written to Johnson as early as August 30 and may have sent him a quick note several weeks before asking that she be allowed to visit her husband. "Before you refuse me, pray remember how long I have been separated from him and how much I have suffered," she said to Johnson. [39]

Varina Davis's approach to Johnson, as well as a handful of other federal officials, was eloquent of the woman herself. Always she was respectful and reasonable. If she felt any anger regarding the depleted fortunes of Davis and his ironic fate at the hands of Johnson, she never recorded them. Simply trying to get on with life, Varina Davis did not regard herself as an aggrieved party, nor was she incapable of accepting the South's defeat at the hands of the North.

Much more difficult was the likes of Virginia Clay, the wife of Clement Clay, who later frankly admitted her outrage having to request anything from Johnson, a man she clearly regarded as her social inferior. "I had no reason to respect the Tennessean before me," she later recalled of one meeting with the President. "That he should have my husband's life in his power was a monstrous wrong."

Mrs. Clay added: "I would not have knelt before him to save a previous life." [40]

Even so, Mrs. Clay proved exceedingly solicitous of the President, asking, like Varina Davis, to be allowed to visit her husband at Fort Monroe and adding that should Johnson grant that permission, or even more, order her husband's actual release, "I will fly to you with words & tears of grateful thanks for your justice, magnanimity & clemency." [41]

That was probably more than even Johnson, who clearly enjoyed the praises of women, especially those of the blue blood predilections, could stand.

Mrs. Clay was given permission by the end of the year to visit her husband at Fort Monroe. In April of the following year, Johnson ordered that Clement Clay be freed, while still trying to make a decision in the much more symbolically important matter of Jefferson Davis.

While contemplating the travails of the Confederate leadership, Johnson was also increasingly hearing stories of grinding Southern poverty, and what some said was the continued oppression of white Southerners at the hands of the victorious Union soldiers tasked with maintaining order. All too typical was a letter from a man named William Moore, residing in Vicksburg, Mississippi, who complained that even Southern whites who had long since declared their fealty to the Union were being harassed, their land confiscated. "Without property or other means, persons who have always been Union men, are left to wander about the streets like paupers and vagabonds," reported Moore. [42]

A correspondent from Alabama, Anna Powell, told Johnson that "the Negroes are threatening us with midnight assassination and massacre," while another letter writer, also from Alabama, didn't regard the ex-slaves as a threat, but thought it likely that the white people of the South would eventually be forced to "take care of the many thousands of them." [43]

Johnson soon wondered why it was that the Radical Republicans, as concerned as they were for Southern blacks, never seemed to have much to say about the depleted fortunes of Southern whites, even those who had never been a part of the old aristocracy, or had been compelled to join the Confederate Army.

The lectures from the likes of Stevens, long one of the largest landowners in southern Pennsylvania; Zachariah Chandler, who had become enormously wealthy as an investor in Michigan; and Sumner, exceedingly comfortable due to an inheritance; also felt more and more to Johnson like the patronizing airs of the Confederate aristocrats, men who disdained their social inferiors, and regarded the impoverished whites of the South with a barely disguised contempt.

On the evening of December 2, Sumner paid a call on Johnson at the White House, and in the course of what must have been a heated discussion for both men, told the President that black people in the South were "frequently insulted by the rebels."

Johnson challenged the Massachusetts Senator, asking if people were ever assaulted or murdered in his state. When Sumner acknowledged as much, Johnson pounced: "Would you consent that Massachusetts should be excluded from the Union on this account?" [44]

Sumner said no, but was astonished by the exchange, and even more stunned that Johnson could employ such an argument, which appeared to make light of the increasing reports of white-on-black violence in the South.

"Much of what he said was painful, from it's ignorance & perversity," Sumner told Francis Lieber the following day, failing entirely to consider Johnson's point. [45]

In the midst of his many other concerns, Johnson had also been listening for word of what had happened to his friend Preston King. Recognizing King's unimpeachable integrity, Johnson had several months earlier appointed him as the new Collector of the Port of New York, a position reeking of patronage. In mid-November, Johnson learned that King was dead, leaping from a ferryboat in the New York Harbor. Exactly why King had committed suicide was not known. He left no note behind. But it was thought that the bad system of payoffs that had for so long been a part of the collectorship simply overwhelmed a good man.

Johnson sent his first formal Message to Congress on December 4, a document whose written elegance was partially attributable to the input of historian George Bancroft. Given the President's decided view that only Southerners should be in control of the South's destiny, encouraging the establishment of state conventions designed to create governments reaffirming their devotion to the Union and ratifying the 13th Amendment abolishing slavery, it should have come as a surprise to no one that Johnson would emphasize what he called "the greatness of the States," balancing themselves off against the "encroachments of the Federal Government."

He argued against the establishment of federal military governments in the South, a particular Radical Republican priority, contending that ultimately they would divide the people into the "vanquishers and the vanquished," creating "hatred, rather than restored affection."

"The willful use of such powers, if continued through a period of years, would have endangered the purity of the general administration and the liberties of the States which remained loyal," Johnson asserted. [46]

This was entirely a constitutional argument, framed in a calm manner that placed Johnson in the ranks of Andrew Jackson, James K. Polk, Franklin Pierce, and other pre-Lincoln presidents. The government could solve problems, Johnson suggested, but woe to a people who habitually looked at it to solve *all* of their problems. Washington, by the very fact that it had an army and massive treasury, would always only naturally be more powerful than any single state. But it was the collective power of the states together that gave Washington its real might.

From his earliest untutored readings of the Constitution, Johnson got this. An ascending line could be drawn throughout the entirety of his career, from his earliest days as a state official to his service in Congress through to his tenure as military governor of Tennessee, showing a consistent embrace of the states and federal government as partners in perpetuity.

Where Johnson failed, and failed spectacularly, was in his inability as presented in his Message to Congress, and subsequent public statements, to embrace the move to legally permit ex-slaves to vote.

Until the freedmen could participate in the franchise, they would never be full citizens, denied a basic and fundamental right enjoyed by whites, and thus forever floating in a kind of constitutional limbo.

Johnson, again, turned to his understanding of the Constitution. "It is one of the greatest acts on record to have brought four millions of people into freedom," he said, celebrating the end of slavery in America. [47]

But he could not simply grant these same people the right to vote, Johnson claimed, because there was no provision for such action in the Constitution.

Besides, noted Johnson in an obvious reference to white opposition to black voting rights in states well beyond the South, "a concession of the elective franchise to the freedmen, by act of the President of the United States" would equally apply to the North. [48]

This was a sore point to many Radical Republicans who knew that white Northerners were as hostile to black voting rights as were white Southerners: a glaring hypocrisy Johnson was only too happy to exploit.

Even so, Johnson's stand puts him forever in history as a president hostile to the best interests of African-Americans. Sandwiched between the racially enlightened administrations of Abraham Lincoln and Ulysses S. Grant, Johnson would historically appear a sad and mean-spirited interlude between the presidencies of two men who listened to their better angels.

The Radical Republicans did not comprise a strict majority in either house of Congress as 1866 dawned. But they were united in purpose and with the help of moderate Democrats and Republicans were confident that they could effectuate reconstruction policies beyond anything Johnson most likely envisioned. "We are really stronger radically in both branches & that makes a strong temptation," House Speaker Schuyler Colfax, an enthusiastic Radical Republican, confided to a friend in the early days of the new year. [49]

That temptation would soon be seen in a decision by House leaders to deny sitting any member elected from an ex-Confederate state, a group that included Johnson's long-time friend, Tennessee Congressman Horace Maynard, who had remained a loyal Unionist throughout the war.

This clearly hostile action was joined by a House vote to set up what came to be known as the Joint Committee on Reconstruction, a signal to the President that the radicals had every intention of formulating reconstruction policies, putting Johnson in the position of being a mere observer.

Within days, Congress passed legislation extending the life of the Freedman's Bureau, the agency set up to help ex-slaves transition into freedom through financial support and educational programs, while once again pushing for black voting rights.

Both Sumner and Stevens were now openly criticizing Johnson, criticism that was joined by such activists as the famed abolitionist Wendell Phillips, precipitately launching a national grass roots campaign urging Congress to begin impeachment proceedings against a president who had only been in office nine months.

It was generally assumed that once Congress reauthorized the Freedman's Bureau, Johnson would most likely sign on. The legislation's sponsor, Illinois Senator Lyman Trumbull, had spoken several times with the President, convinced that while he wasn't happy with the whole thing, he would more than likely support it. And what was there to oppose? Trumbull later noted of the ex-slaves: "They have become free without any of this world's goods, not owning even the hats upon their heads or coats upon their backs, without supplies of any kind, not knowing often where to obtain their next meal and to save them from starvation." [50]

Johnson knew the Freedman's Bureau was hugely important to the Radical Republicans. Lincoln had supported it, so did Grant. The Northern press couldn't say enough about it. But after consulting with several members of his cabinet, Johnson, in a lengthy veto message, said he saw no reason to keep the bureau going, even arguing that the enabling legislation contained "provisions which in my opinion are not warranted by the Constitution and are not well suited to accomplish the end in view." [51]

While Johnson received some small amount of praise for his veto, the overwhelming response was negative. Sumner and Stevens were in high dungeon. Wendell Phillips, who seemed to have a particular talent for getting under Johnson's skin, proclaimed that the veto was proof that the Confederates had actually won the war.

Three days after his message, Johnson, in an angry frame of mind, played host to a large outdoor gathering of more than 1,000 people celebrating George Washington's birthday. The event had worried Hugh McCulloch, Secretary of the Treasury, who liked Johnson, but noticed that on some occasions he had a tendency to talk too long and too emotionally about his policies.

Knowing that Johnson was in a peevish mood, McCulloch warned him against saying anything very sensational at the Washington celebration. "Don't be troubled, Mr. Secretary," Johnson replied. "I have not thought of making a speech and I shain't make one." [52]

But in fact, Johnson did just that. After politely thanking the celebrants, he launched into a lengthy address defending his policies, noting that he had fought traitors in the South during the war, and now as he sized up those "at the other end of the line," regarded himself as back at the battlefield again.

When someone in the crowd asked him to name three people "at the other end," Johnson blurted out: "Thaddeus Stevens of Pennsylvania is one; I say Mr. Sumner of the Senate is another, and Wendell Phillips is another."

"I know it may be said 'You are the President and you must not talk about these things,'" Johnson continued. "But my fellow citizens, I intend to talk the truth and when principle is involved, when the existence of my country is in peril, I hold it to be my duty to speak what I think and what I feel, as I have always done on former occasions."

Johnson then presented his view of himself as a man misunderstood and victimized, a hubristic self-portrayal that had now and then emerged in his public addresses back in Tennessee, but never in such a prominent national forum: "I stand for my country. I stand for the Constitution. There I have always placed myself from my advent in public life. They may traduce me, they may slander, they may vituperate me, but let me say to you all this has no influence upon me. Let me say further, that I do not intend to be overawed by real or pretended friends, nor do I mean to be bullied by my enemies." [53]

What essentially turned into a nearly hour-long harangue prompted condemnation across the country. "The manner of the President was, to say the least, most undignified," charged the *Chicago Tribune*, "and the speech contained the bitterest personal abuse. Many are attempting to excuse it, but it was cool and deliberate from beginning to end." [54]

"A more shameful and humiliating spectacle could scarcely be presented," said the *Louisville Daily Courier*, charging that Johnson was attacking leaders of a party who had put him in the White House in the first place. [55]

"Instead of calling names and indulging in personalities, he would have done well to have imitated the patience with which Abraham Lincoln bore the bitterer gibes, far ruder attacks, from the same men," thought the *New York Evening Post*. [56]

Four weeks later, Johnson further widened the breach between himself and the radicals with his veto of a new civil rights bill, complaining in a long message that provisions of the legislation created "for the security of the colored race, safeguards which go infinitely beyond any that the general government has ever provided for the white race." [57]

Johnson continued to hammer on the theme that if the South could be just left alone, it could work out its own problems. Although various correspondents sent him reports throughout the spring warning of racial unrest in his native region, he either refused to believe those reports or simply ignored them.

During the first week of May it became suddenly more difficult to feign ignorance. A confrontation between recently discharged members of the Third Regiment of the U.S. Colored Authority and the local police in Memphis sent shock waves across the country when it quickly escalated into massive violence resulting in the deaths of nearly fifty African-Americans and the burning of property.

Less than two months later nearly three dozen black citizens were killed during a rampage in downtown New Orleans after white policemen and firemen attacked a large group of African Americans and some white Radical Republicans who had gathered to formulate a new state constitution that would, among other things, permit black voting.

"To see the Negroes mutilated and literally beaten to death as they sought to escape was one of the most horrid pictures it has ever been our ill-fortune to witness," said the *New York Times*. In a subsequent report sent to Grant, General Philip Sheridan, who arrived in New Orleans after the riot was over, but conducted interviews trying to piece together what had happened, said the police action was done in a "manner so unnecessary and atrocious as to say it was murder." Sheridan subsequently called the riot "an absolute massacre by the police," adding that it was "perpetrated without the shadow of necessity." [58]

All the while, Johnson was under assault in Congress. On June 20, the Joint Committee on Reconstruction officially declared that it was the province of the legislative branch, not the executive, to handle all reconstruction matters. Two days later Johnson announced his opposition to submitting the equal protection 14th Amendment to the states, an opinion that Congress entirely ignored as the amendment advanced without his support. On July 15, he vetoed a new version of the Freedman's Bureau bill, only to see Congress override that veto the next day.

By early August, battered but not defeated, Johnson decided to fight back, promoting the launching of a third party to support his administration, and making preparations for what would prove the most disastrous personal tour by a president in American history.

CHAPTER EIGHT

Traduced, Slandered, and Maligned

O n the afternoon of August 13, the dashing 25 year-old General George Armstrong Custer stopped by the White House to pay his respects to Johnson, following up on a plea he had made several days earlier to be sent into the field again.

"I respectfully ask to be assigned to a regiment of white troops," Custer had written, "as I have never served with any other." [1]

Named brigadier general of volunteers in June of 1863, making him the youngest general in the Union Army, Custer soon won the devotion of his men for the gallant manner in which he rode into battle, riding ahead of them with his gold shoulder-length hair waving in the wind, wildly brandishing a shiny saber.

The traveling press, taking note of Custer's flair for the dramatic as well as his accomplishments as a commander, soon gave him the kind of coverage that would transform the young warrior into a national hero, appearing on the cover of the popular illustrated *Harper's Weekly* and the front page of the *New York Times*.

After the war, Custer served in Texas, later testifying to a general distrust of the ex-Confederates he daily encountered in the Lone Star state. The young General thought that while the former rebels appeared to have accepted their defeated status, "They acknowledge that it is from a desire to obtain the benefits of the government, rather than to give the government any support." [2]

But, like Johnson, Custer was opposed to the Radical Republican notion of an ongoing federal military presence in the South, remarking "For the government to exact full penalties simply because it is constitutionally authorized to do so, would, in my opinion, be unnecessary, impolitic, inhuman, and wholly at variance with the principles of a free, civilized, and Christian nation." [3]

The national public interest in Custer made him an enticing political property. Radical Republican Senator Zachariah Chandler several times encouraged him to run for office in his native state of Michigan, having no idea that Custer was a Democrat and Johnson supporter.

Chandler's enthusiasm for Custer did not prevent him from several times trying to seduce the General's attractive 24-year old wife Libbie. After one such encounter, Libbie characterized the 42 year-old Chandler as an "old goosey idiot," adding in a letter to her parents, "now [that] his wife is away he is drunk *all* the time. And O, so silly." [4]

Michigan Democrats, too, were hoping Custer would run under their banner for Congress, an idea that Custer was considering, discussing it's merits with the astute Libbie.

On August 4, delegates in Monroe County, Michigan named Custer as head of a new veterans group called the Soldiers and Sailors Union. The group called for an end to all federal involvement in the South, demanding in the process that the region be returned its full representational rights in Congress.

After his talk with Johnson, Custer sent to the President a letter with a small news clip attached at the bottom quoting him as saying: "Andrew Johnson is my commander-in-chief and he speaks for me." [5]

Five days later Custer called to order an informal preliminary gathering of the Soldiers and Sailors Union in Washington. Meeting in a parlor of the Willard Hotel, the purpose of the conclave, as made clear by Custer, was to plot strategy for a planned September convention of the group while also debating the merits of inviting Southern soldiers to attend.

Although no final decision was made, it was clear that Custer, along with attending generals Lovell Rousseau and James Steedman, wanted to do something to get in front of the reconciliation movement, and by so doing, telegraph their support of the President.

Two days later Custer, in case anyone still had doubts, issued a statement pointing out that the country was in the midst of an historic transformation and that in that process he entirely backed administration efforts to bring the South fully back into the Union, calling Johnson "the highest authority that we recognize on earth." [6]

This was one of the most blatantly political statements ever made by Custer and he admitted as much, acknowledging a discomfort for "departing from what I have ever considered a judicious custom" of not being involved in politics as a military man. But the issues, he maintained, were too important not to become involved. Johnson's policies were the best and quickest way to return a South with no slaves to the Union, ushering in an era of peace. "As for myself," Custer proclaimed, "I have had enough of civil war." [7]

If he had not been before, Johnson was now clearly impressed with Custer. On August 24, Custer sent a short letter to Libbie to tell her the big news: he would be back in Michigan the following day in order to prepare for another trip in "two or three days to accompany the President to Chicago." [8]

The jaunt to Chicago was, it soon became clear, much more than that. For more than two months Johnson had been playing with the idea of taking a trip to the largest city in the Midwest to lay the cornerstone to a monument to Stephen Douglas, the late Democrat senator from Illinois and staunch Unionist. In subsequent weeks, as Johnson began to also view the excursion as a good opportunity to go before the public and explain his policies, the parameters of the journey became increasingly larger with supporters inviting him to appear in New York, Cleveland, Indianapolis, and St. Louis, among other cities.

And the number of passengers grew, too, particularly after Johnson told Secretary of State William Seward and Navy Secretary Gideon Welles that "we should have plenty of company." [9]

Included on the guest list was Admiral David Farragut and his attractive wife Virginia, at 43 years of age, some two decades younger than her adoring husband; generals John Rawlins, George Stoneman, and James Steedman; Postmaster General Alexander Randall; and both Seward and Welles.

Edwin Stanton, who throughout late 1865 and most of 1866 was increasingly at odds with the President, charting, behind Johnson's back, his own course with the Radical Republicans, begged off, saying that his wife was too sick for him to leave her side. Cynically, Welles recorded in his diary: "I think Mrs. S may be some but not seriously indisposed, but at no time have I entertained a thought that Mr. S himself would be with us." [10]

Delighted by the invitation, but not certain what was expected of him, Matias Romero, the 29 year-old Mexican minister to the U.S., agreed to be a part of the excursion. A skilled diplomat with an uncanny knack for making friends, Romero had connections throughout the White House and with the Radical Republicans. But perhaps his most important association came in the person of Ulysses S. Grant, who regarded the Mexican as a young man of principle correctly worried about France's increased involvement in Mexico through the imposed regime of the Archduke Maximilian.

Also along for the ride: reporters from at least three dozen newspaper and wire services, including Johnson's old friend Benjamin Truman, writing for the *New York Times,* Sylvanus Cadwallader with the *New York Herald,* and Lawrence Gobright with the Associated Press.

While this was all nice, Johnson would not be satisfied until securing Grant's pledge to be a part of what would soon be popularly known as the "swing around the circle," an allusion to Johnson's many campaign forays back in Tennessee when he traveled the circle of a given legislative or congressional circuit giving speeches. The only difference this time, from Johnson's perspective, was that the circle had been considerably expanded, with parameters running from Washington to New York, New York to Chicago, Chicago to St. Louis, and St. Louis back to Washington, altogether a more than 2,700-mile mile excursion.

On August 19, the President received a group of delegates returning from a pro-Johnson National Union Party conclave that had just wrapped up its business in Philadelphia. The convention was framed to provide Johnson with a third way: keeping intact, at least in name, the party that had nominated the Lincoln-Johnson ticket in 1864. The effort was also designed to bring together moderate Republicans unenthused with the radical wing of their party, and moderate Democrats in the North who had proven to be generally supportive of the President.

For two days, beginning on August 14, the National Union Party enthusiasts, with an energized Custer in attendance, hammered out a platform declaring their support for a South without slavery; a withdrawal of remaining Union soldiers in the South; and enhanced federal aid for Union veterans and their families.

The emotional highpoint of the gathering was undoubtedly it's opening moments when delegates from Massachusetts and South Carolina walked arm in arm into the Philadelphia conclave, accompanied first by the musical strains of "Yankee Doodle Dandy" and finally "Dixie."

Every plank in the party's platform, Wisconsin Senator James Doolittle wired to Johnson, had been adopted "amid the greatest enthusiasm without a dissenting voice from the North or South, East or West. Thanks were returned to Almighty God for the good order & fraternal feeling which prevailed & at one p.m. the convention adjourned with nine cheers for the President." [11]

Now a group of National Union Party committeemen crowded into the East Room of the White House to officially present to Johnson the convention's resolutions. Johnson had ever so casually invited Grant to attend the ceremony. Walking into the room and greeted by a loud round of cheers, Grant, finding no place to sit, shook Johnson's hand and for the duration of the ceremony stood next to him, which was exactly where Johnson wanted him to be.

Everything Grant did at the ceremony, which additionally included being positioned by Johnson at the door to shake hands with each departing delegate, seemed to indicate "I am with you, I endorse your proceedings," wrote Truman in an article that appeared on the front page of the *New York Times* the following morning. [12]

After the happy delegates left the White House, Johnson took Grant aside and specifically asked him to be a part of the caravan to Chicago. Grant was non-committal, subsequently discussing with his staff what he should do. Grant aide Colonel Horace Porter observed that Grant thought Johnson's request was most likely "merely an invitation," which he could decline "as politely as possible."

But something about the way that Johnson, who undoubtedly knew what he was doing, worded the request made it seem, in the end, as though it was "in the form of an order," finally giving Grant no choice but to comply. [13]

Less than two weeks later, on an overcast morning, Grant arrived in front of the White House to join a large and boisterous group of people excitedly climbing into a series of carriages destined for the downtown Baltimore & Ohio depot. Everyone seemed in a good mood, in particular Johnson, who greeted his fellow travelers warmly. Only Grant was subdued.

The excursionists got off to a good start, arriving in Baltimore several hours later where a crowd estimated by reporter Cadwallader at "probably not less than 100,000 people" greeted the president, not just from the street, but also from the roofs of old row houses. A reporter for the *Baltimore Sun,* catching sight of a field of waving handkerchiefs, could not help but also observe the "lively interest taken by the gentler sex" in seeing Johnson in person. Leaving the train at the Camden Station and briefly traveling in a series of carriages to the President Street Station, the party was nearly overwhelmed by admirers massing around the vehicles. [14]

Awed by what they had just witnessed, Johnson and his companions climbed into their newly transported cars taking them up through Delaware, and a brief pleasant stop in Wilmington, where again another crowd of mostly working people gathered to cheer the visitors.

By late afternoon Johnson and his companions were in Philadelphia. Mayor Morton McMichael, a strong Radical Republican, found it more convenient to be out of town just then on business. Members of the city council, meanwhile, publicly declared their refusal to meet with the President.

But the lack of an official welcome may have been more than compensated for by the appearance of Colonel James Page, former collector of the Port of Philadelphia, who hailed Johnson for "binging us together as one people," adding that he had inspired "any and every sacrifice for the common good and national welfare." [15]

The party was booked into the downtown Continental Hotel for the night. Hours later, Johnson found it impossible to not address a large crowd that had gathered outside, demanding that he speak to them. For the most part he was pacific, only once launching a political volley when he seemed to refer to the Philadelphia Union League, which had also made a point of snubbing him, declaring: "Let each man belong to the great national league and let the Constitution of the United States be the constitution of his league." [16]

His speech hit all the right notes with his audience. He made his points and only benignly criticized his opponents, but by declining to name any one foe in particular, he managed to preserve his presidential allure.

Later that night, Truman, in a dispatch to the *New York Times,* reported that "thousands of Philadelphia's hard-fisted sons" had turned out to greet Johnson. Surely, they returned to their homes with a better opinion of him, thought Truman, than "that through which they have been lately entertaining through the medium of the Radical press." [17]

All in all, it had been a splendid first day on the road.

As the Johnson party settled in for a night's rest at the Continental, New York officials were putting the final touches on what one reporter thought was destined to be the "grandest affair of the kind ever witnessed in this country." [18]

A large wooden platform in front of the famous Delmonico's restaurant on Fifth Avenue had been erected, upon which the presidential party would review an extensive welcoming parade, while Major General Charles Sanford of New York's First Guard division had sent out meticulous orders instructing a cavalry brigade to "receive the President at Battery Place and escort him up Broadway and Park Row to City Hall." [19]

As the presidential party sped across New Jersey, a reporter for the *New York World* thought the excursionists were in a happy mood, even when it came to the tiring task of greeting crowds. "General Grant and Admiral Farragut kept up a continued bantering of each other, the General insisting upon putting the Admiral forward and the Admiral protesting that the General was shirking the responsibility."

Grant, delightedly, finally suggested that Farragut should simply be "lashed to the roof of the car" so that admirers could get a better view of him. [20]

At the Jersey City depot, packed with more than 30,000 people, the party was escorted to the steamboat *Colden* by various city and Tammany Hall officials as it set off across the Hudson River. It was a spectacular scene: "Ferry boats, yachts, pilot-boats, the little steam-craft that play up and down our waters, in fact everything that could command a piece of bunting, displayed it in honor of the patriot President," observed the *New York World*. [21]

Reaching the other side, the party was greeted by Mayor John "Toots" Hoffman and escorted to a line of open carriages taking them down Broadway. Altogether, more than 200,000 New Yorkers watched and cheered the caravan as it made its dense way to City Hall, where Johnson was briefly introduced to every conceivable Tammany Hall official, remarking of the reception "I am free to say this occasion overwhelms me and language is inadequate to give utterance to my feelings." [22]

On to Delmonico's: sitting in the reviewing stands, Johnson, Grant, Farragut, Seward, Welles and the other members of the party smiled and waved as more than 9,000 troops marched by. Taking in the reception, Welles turned to the President and asked what he thought. Never diverting his gaze from the procession, Johnson replied "It is wonderful." [23]

Some three hours later, the party entered the grand hall of Delmonico's, illuminated with calcium lights, the tables decorated with lavish bouquets and candles. More than 250 prominent New Yorkers had showed up for the feeding, including financier Cornelius Vanderbilt, Republican party boss Thurlow Weed, and *New York Tribune* publisher Horace Greeley (once a Johnson supporter, but now increasingly wary).

Taking it all in, Matias Romero could hardly believe his fortune. "I was invited and assigned a seat of honor," he later wrote. But when subsequently asked to speak, he caught sight of Seward, who wasn't crazy about the Mexican ambassador saying anything at all. The Secretary, increasingly concerned that Romero and Grant were conniving to send U.S. troops to Mexico, while he thought matters with Maximilian could be settled through diplomacy, privately just wanted Romero to disappear. "I attempted to say nothing that could have displeased him," Romero later said of his perfunctory remarks. [24]

Finally, two hours into the dinner, Hoffman introduced Johnson, who soon launched into one of the better speeches of his presidency, vigorously defending his restoration program. Speaking for nearly an hour, Johnson began by acknowledging Grant and Farragut. "Here is the Army," he said, pointing to Grant on his right. "And here is the Navy," pointing to Farragut on his left. Johnson's purpose was more than just trying to remind everyone that two of the nation's greatest heroes were with him. Johnson also sought to illustrate a larger point: that every part of the federal government had been united during the Civil War.

Now such unanimity was elusive, Johnson remarked, noting that the Radical Republicans had denied seats to legislators from the South and wondering if their actions were designed to precipitate a new civil war: "Are we again prepared to see these fair fields of ours, this land that gave a brother birth, again drenched in a brother's blood?'

"The country, gentlemen, is in your hands," Johnson soon concluded. "I stand here tonight not in the first sense in the character of the Chief Magistrate, but as a citizen, defending the restoration of the Union and the perpetuation of the Constitution of my country." [25]

Had Johnson concluded his journey here, he could have returned to the White House in triumph. Hundreds of thousands of admirers had cheered him up the East coast, local politicians (with the exception of committed Radical Republicans) hailed him, and the newspaper coverage had been overwhelmingly positive.

But in heading west the next day, the journey would prove all downhill in a way that neither Johnson, his admirers, or even his foes could have imagined.

Now joined by George and Libbie Custer, the party made a stop in Schenectady, where a platform attached to the back of the presidential train collapsed just as the dignitaries stepped onto it, causing no serious injuries even as Johnson, Grant, Seward, and Farragut tumbled onto each other. Arriving at the Seward family mansion in Auburn later that day, the party was royally entertained at an outdoor banquet, before returning to carriages that would take them back to the train.

A young boy rushing to the carriage carrying Grant, slipped and fell underneath. One of his legs was crushed and later had to be amputated. A startled Grant subsequently paid a call on the boy, whose name was Willie Richardson, promising to stay in touch by letter.

It had only been three days, admittedly three full exhausting, hot, and overwhelming days, since the party had left Washington, but already the excursionists were weary. Grant, in a quick note to Mrs. Grant, admitted: "I am getting very tired of this expedition and of hearing political speeches." Romero privately talked of what he called the "torment" of the journey, noting that "almost all of the people who came with the President are indisposed, since, besides excitement we have necessarily had a great irregularity in the meals." [26]

Welles, also bedraggled, would soon wonder if Johnson might eventually just collapse from the strain: "For it seemed as though no one possessed the physical power to go through such extraordinary labor day after day," the Navy Secretary pondered. [27]

Before the presidential party crossed the New York border, it stopped in the town of Westfield. Local residents arrived at the train station there on horseback and in wagons to see the President. Oddly, Johnson delivered part of his remarks in the third person: "Andrew Johnson, your fellow citizen, never deceived the people. They are the ones in whom he ever trusted." When a heckler tried to interrupt, Johnson yelled "Keep quiet 'till I have concluded. Just such fellows as you have kicked up all the rows of the last five years." [28]

There would be more of this to come.

Still in southwestern New York, the train was visited by a reception committee from Cleveland which came onboard carrying large quantities of drink and food. Grant, out of his mind with boredom, went for the liquor. A man who got drunk easily when he drank, and for that reason generally avoided all alcohol, he was soon so drunk as to be "compelled to lie down on a pile of empty sacks and rubbish" in one of the baggage cars of the train, reporter Cadwallader later recalled, noting that long-time staffer General John Rawlins kept a watchful eye on Grant, protecting him from observation "as far as possible." [29]

By the time the train reached Ohio, both Grant and Rawlins boarded a steamer for Detroit where he sobered up in a downtown hotel. Mentioning nothing at all about drinking, Grant wrote a quick note to Julia merely saying that the overnight stop in Detroit "has given me a fine chance to rest." [30]

The other members of the presidential party, meanwhile, arrived in Cleveland by mid-evening. Checking into the Kennard House, they enjoyed an elegant dinner in a dining hall decorated with gas-lit chandeliers and a long table bearing bowls of peaches and goblets of wine.

A band was playing patriotic and military tunes outside the hotel where a large group of people had gathered. Once dinner was consumed, Johnson appeared on the hotel's balcony delivering what he intended as merely perfunctory remarks. But then an odd exchange took place: when Johnson made a reference to Lincoln, calling him "a distinguished citizen, now no more," the remark prompted someone in the crowd to yell out "Unfortunate." Johnson quickly shot back: "Yes, unfortunate. The ways of providence are mysterious and incomprehensible, controlling all those who exclaim 'unfortunate.'" [31]

This started an avalanche. As Johnson tried to continue, William Hudson, a reporter for the *Cleveland Leader*, noted he was "interrupted by cheers, by hisses and by cries." [32]

Angered, Johnson challenged his audience to name one act he had ever done "in violation of the Constitution," at which point several people yelled out "New Orleans."

This was no random chant. Radical Republicans had for weeks been talking about the recent riots in the Crescent City, blaming Johnson for having coddled what they regarded as vicious, violent Southern racists. As more and more people picked up the "New Orleans" chant, Johnson began to yell back, but was shortly stunned by a new refrain from the crowd: "Hang Jeff Davis."

Were these the words of a simple desire, or an effort to ridicule Johnson, who, in fact, had said the same thing many times before? "Hang Jeff Davis! Hang Jeff Davis!" he responded, almost in disbelieve, before making an unbelievable comment of his own. "Why don't *you* hang him?"

Exasperated, Johnson soon also strangely suggested: "Why don't you hang Thad Stevens and Wendell Phillips?"

The back and forth now descended into a discordant mixture of sounds, with reporters having a difficult time catching who said what. Vainly trying to regain the upper hand, Johnson was left in the humiliating position of responding to every taunt, every goad, even telling one of his detractors: "If you ever shoot a man you will do it in the dark and pull the trigger when no one else is by to see." [33]

Angry that he was unable to win control of what soon appeared to be a mob, Johnson turned back into the hotel, where an equally surprised James Doolittle bluntly told the President that such an exchange could only damage the dignity of his office. "I don't care about my dignity," Johnson almost spitted in a voice loud enough to be heard by several reporters. [34]

Gideon Welles and William Crook were among the onlookers who thought that Johnson had made a mistake arguing with the crowd. The nation's press soon enough agreed, with newspapers from the *Cleveland Leader* to the *New York Times* condemning Johnson. The *New York Herald*, which had consistently supported the President, soon observed: "It is mortifying to see a man occupying the lofty position of President of the United States descend from that position and join issue with those who are dragging their garments in the muddy gutters of political vituperation." [35]

The next morning an air of resignation hung over the excursion. "The entire party appeared weary and unrefreshed by their brief repose," observed reporter Cadwallader. [36]

The excursionists made their way to Monroe, Michigan, where hometown hero Custer was loudly cheered. On to Detroit, where Johnson once again, this time briefly, exchanged words with a detractor who said he wasn't worth the $25,000 a year he was getting as president. "Has it increased since I came into office?" Johnson somewhat pointlessly asked. [37]

Johnson knew he faced hostile territory as the party headed to Chicago. The *Chicago Republican* had advised local residents to avoid Johnson "as they would any other convicted criminal," although the paper never said exactly what Johnson had been convicted of. Illinois Governor Richard Oglesby flatly declined to be on hand to greet the President. The Chicago Common Council passed a resolution declaring their opposition to taking part in the proceedings. [38]

The party did not reach what would soon be popularly known as the Windy City until late in the evening, checking into the Sherman House. Cadwallader made a note of the travelers' departure from the hotel the next day around mid-morning, but also mentioned for his vast readership that he had overheard Grant remark "I am disgusted with this trip. I am disgusted at hearing a man make speeches on his way to his funeral." [39]

With Seward, Wells, Custer, and Farragut, the President was soon walking on the fresh grass of a clearing located off of E. 35th Street on the south side of the city, finally set to take part in the cornerstone unveiling ceremonies at the Douglas monument created by sculptor Leonard Wells Volk, the supposed purpose of the whole trip in the first place.

The ceremony was proper and quiet. Johnson lauded Douglas as a "man who died and toiled for the people and the union of the states." Oddly, Johnson suggested that if Douglas could suddenly "rise from his grave," he would undoubtedly proclaim "The constitution and the union—they must be preserved." [40]

The party returned to the Sherman House for the evening. Custer, perhaps sick of the very little of retail politics he had witnessed on the journey in the last few days, penned a letter that night to the *Detroit Free Press* disavowing any desire to run for Congress, before declaring that national "peace, harmony, and prosperity" could best be realized through the National Union Party. [41]

That same evening Romero plotted to absent himself from the duration of the journey, confiding to Sebastian Lerdo de Tejada, the Mexican minster of foreign relations, that when he first agreed to be a part of the trip, "One could not believe, with any foundation, that it would take the turn which the President has given it." [42]

He said he would tell Seward that he was feeling ill, giving him an excuse to head back to Washington the following day.

The Johnson party, without Romero, visited Lincoln's marble vault in Springfield the next day. The city's *Daily State Journal,* reporting on a decided lack of local enthusiasm for the presidential visit, remarked: "Were he the Andrew Johnson of 1864, he would have had a different welcome." [43]

The occasion was shrouded in memories of Lincoln, with all of the visitors taking off their hats as they quietly stood before the late president's tomb and signed the official visitor's book. By evening, the party rested at the St. Nicholas Hotel, another place shadowed with Lincoln's memory, where he had often met with political associates.

The following morning seemed bright with promise, an early fall Midwestern day, both sunny and cool. Arriving in St. Louis by late afternoon, after an inspiring escort of twelve steamers decorated with flags and banners took them across the Mississippi River, the party was startled to see a crowd of several thousand happily cheering their entry to the city. Riding in a series of carriages, Johnson and party passed beneath a massive arch on Chestnut Street decorated with large portraits of Johnson, Grant, and Farragut, and only one unfriendly banner from a storefront window reading "A. Johnson, the Apostate." [44]

Receiving guests that evening at the Southern Hotel, Johnson, surprisingly tentatively, decided to briefly greet from the building's balcony a crowd gathered outside, and got off on a good note. When he said he was "proud to meet so many of my fellow citizens," a man yelled out: "How about British subjects?" For once, the President responded with humor: "We will attend to John Bull after a while, as far as that is concerned."

The quick rejoinder prompted laughter. But no sooner did Johnson dispense with this interruption than another voice yelled out the refrain that had so unnerved the President in Cleveland: "New Orleans. New Orleans."

This time, Johnson insensitively responded: "The riot at New Orleans was substantially planned." By planned, of course, Johnson meant that the perpetrators were the Radical Republican activists and blacks of New Orleans, not the city's white and armed Democrats.

But no sooner did Johnson make this sensational charge than someone in the crowd called him a traitor. Johnson angrily answered back: "I have been traduced. I have been slandered. I have been maligned. I have been called Judas; Judas Iscariot and all that."

The crowd now maddeningly picked up the refrain: "Judas. Judas. Judas."

Johnson pushed on: "If I have played the Judas, who has been my Christ that I have played Judas with? Was it Thad Stevens? Was it Wendell Phillips? Was it Charles Sumner? Are these the men that set up and compare themselves with the Savior of men, and everybody that differs with them in opinion and tries to stay and arrest their diabolical and nefarious policy is to be denounced as Judas?"

When someone yelled out "Hang Jeff Davis," Johnson responded much as he had in Cleveland, to similar bad effect: "Why don't you hang Thad Stevens and Wendell Phillips? A traitor at one end of the line is as bad as a traitor at the other."

The idea that the President was suggesting that a Congressional leader and prominent citizen should be executed, only naturally excited the crowd. For Johnson, it just seemed a natural part of a rhetorical give and take. But his remarks, the more he was worked up, became increasingly personal and bitter: "When they talk about tyranny and despotism, where's one act of Andrew Johnson's that ever encroached upon the rights of a free man in this land? Because I had stood as a faithful sentinel upon the watch tower of freedom to sound the alarm, hence all of this traduction and detraction that has been heaped upon me." [45]

Johnson then rather abruptly wrapped up his remarks and went back inside the hotel. Reporters hurriedly transcribed their notes, realizing that the President had yet again provided them with a great story. An observation soon made by a correspondent for the *London Times*, that Johnson's St. Louis speech was "remarkable for its bitterness," seemed to encapsulate the feeling of reporters and columnists across the country now coming to the conclusion that Johnson had become his own worst enemy. [46]

Undeniably, Grant felt this way. The next morning during a heavy rainstorm, Grant wrote to Julia: "Tomorrow morning the party starts on its course East and will reach Washington on Saturday. I will be glad enough to get there. I have never been so tired of anything before as I have been with the political stump speeches of Mr. Johnson from Washington to this place. I look upon them as a national disgrace."

There could be no return for Grant now. He had tied to support the President and still generally agreed with the administration's reconciliation policies. But he detested demagoguery in all forms, and having heard too many excited and seemingly out-of-control speeches from Johnson, finally decided that the President was bad news.

Yet, Grant had to be careful, for a dozen different reasons. "Of course," he warned Julia, "you will not show this letter to anyone for as long as Mr. Johnson is President. I must respect him as such, and it is in the country's interest that I should also have his confidence." [47]

Leaving St. Louis early on September 10, the presidential party stopped in a series of small southern Illinois and Indiana towns before arriving early in the evening in Indianapolis. From the moment the excursionists left the depot in Indiana's capitol city, heading for the Bates House hotel, there was trouble: gangs of young men repeatedly tried to block the carriages carrying the presidential party. After city police officers pushed the boys away, the party arrived at the hotel and heard a brief speech from former Union General and wealthy Indiana farmer Solomon Meredith welcoming the party.

But when Johnson began to speak, his voice was immediately drowned out by a cascade of jeers. It had to be clear by now that his detractors, inspired by the reports of Johnson's increasingly intemperate and chaotic speeches in other places, were working in concert, engaged in a fun ritual of trying to enrage a President easily enraged.

From the crowd came the taunts: "We want nothing to do with traitors," yelled one person. "We don't want to hear from you, Johnson," exclaimed someone else. One reporter heard a man threaten to shoot Johnson if he continued to speak. [48]

For once, Johnson, who had gestured for silence, gave up, turning around and walking into the hotel. But his quick exit did nothing to placate those in the crowd looking for trouble. People holding up Johnson signs had them ripped from their hands. Others were attacked and beaten. From an upper window of the hotel, an outraged Custer saw a man on horseback he later identified as a city marshal giving some sort of signal to several other men, who then used clubs to beat peaceful Johnson supporters. One man loudly offered $1,000 to anyone who successfully assassinated the President.

Soon there were gunshots, with a member of the crowd dying after being shot in the mouth, and other bullets flying in the direction of the hotel. Grant, oblivious to the danger, walked out onto hotel's second floor balcony and yelled: "Gentlemen, I am ashamed of you. Go home and be ashamed of yourselves." Farragut, watching the melee, wondered "what manner of people" there were in Indianapolis. [49]

One bullet shattered a lantern hanging from Johnson's window, entering the President's room where it lodged in a wall. Grant quickly decided that the shot was not random, but a "deliberate attempt to assassinate Mr. Johnson." [50]

The next day, Cadwallader interviewed a man described as a "gentleman belonging to the Republican party," who confided to him that the violent disturbance had been substantially planned by local party leaders. A reporter for the *Indianapolis Herald* went even further, saying that members of the pro-Republican Grand Army of the Republic had planned to hold Grant, Seward, and Farragut hostage, while at the same time running Johnson out of the city. [51]

Several days later, that same paper published a long list of prominent local citizens, most of them Radical Republicans, who were said to have encouraged the rioters.

One thing was certain: in the aftermath of the Indianapolis riot, which clearly included an attempt on the President's life, there were no Congressional calls, unlike in the days after the New Orleans riot, to find out who had done what. Clearly, any riot where Johnson was the victim was not worthy of investigation.

The following day, the understandably rattled party headed south to Louisville, Kentucky, where it was warmly received. Enjoying a dinner hosted that evening in their honor by the city's Democrats onboard the steamer *Uncle Sam*, the party partook of a splendid all-night journey up the Ohio River.

In Newark, Ohio the next morning, a group of men began to call out for Grant just as Johnson began to speak. Custer thought it was just the latest attempt by the Radicals to rattle Johnson, and yelled out "You cannot insult the President through General Grant." In the town of Scio, Custer heard something he didn't like from someone in a crowd gathered to listen to Johnson. Jumping to the ground from the train, Custer confronted the heckler: "I was born two miles and a half from here, but I am ashamed of you." [52]

When the train stopped at the small village of Cadiz, Custer said of Johnson's ongoing detractors: "I have not seen a worst class of people." When someone yelled out, "Except the rebels," Custer retorted: "The rebels have repented." [53]

Listening to Custer, Johnson may have wondered if there was enough room on one train for two hot heads. When the young General began to berate another group of hecklers in Steubenville, Johnson quickly stopped him: "Let them alone. They know not what they do." [54]

Custer and Libbie got off the train in Steubenville, leaving behind the other, older members of the party who had enjoyed their youthful energy and spirit. The Soldiers and Sailors Union Convention was set to begin in four more days, with Custer expected to take a prominent part.

In Pittsburg that night, Seward declined to attend a banquet held in the presidential party's honor at the St. Charles Hotel. For the jovial, wine-drinking Secretary of State to miss such an event could only mean that he was seriously sick. A cholera pandemic, most likely originating in the Middle East, had slowly made its way to the U.S. by the summer of 1866, eventually killing tens of thousands of people over the course of the next five years.

The 65 year-old Seward appeared to have all the signs of infection, physicians determining that he should be taken by special car to Harrisburg where the presidential party would catch up with him.

The excursionists on September 14 stopped briefly in a series of villages in mostly southern Pennsylvania on the way to the mill town of Johnstown on the crest of the Appalachian Mountains. Several thousand people there had climbed onto a long wooden platform bridging a vacant canal some 20 feet below, waiting for the presidential party. Just moments into that visit, the platform gave way, causing well more than half of them to fall to the canal, with planks and boards from the platform landing on top of them.

"Men and women were seen with helpless children in their arms," reported Benjamin Truman, "their clothes and faces blackened by the coal dirt against which they had fallen." Johnson and Grant asked that the train be kept in place in order to transport the injured, but were told by the conductor that the route ahead had been cleared for them for only a scheduled period of time, making it necessary for the party to move on. [55]

As it was, at least six people died in the accident, while dozens suffered broken arms and legs. A local journalist confided in a letter to Johnson the next day that some of the President's detractors had condemned him for showing "anything but a humane feeling" for having left the scene of the disaster. [56]

In fact, Johnson had ordered one aide to stay behind and help with relief efforts, while writing out a check for $500 designed to assist "the most needy of the bereaved and wounded." [57]

The Johnstown disaster very obviously dampened the mood of the presidential party. There were four more stops to make in south central Pennsylvania that afternoon before the excursionists arrived in Harrisburg in early evening for what would prove a melancholy ending to a melancholy day.

There, Johnson received the alarming news: William Seward was dying. "Father was very cold and purple when we first saw him," wrote William Seward, Jr. to his wife Jenny after seeing the Secretary the following morning, "and could only make himself understood by signs." [58]

A somber Johnson, Grant, and Welles visited the greatly weakened Seward in his train car. Johnson could not help but be touched when the Secretary leaned forward and whispered to him: "My mind is clear and I wish to say at this time that your course is right." [59]

Preparing for the last leg to Washington, Johnson wired Stanton, informing him of Seward's condition. Stanton responded quickly, noting that "All necessary arrangements have been made at Mr. Seward's house for his comfort."

Referencing welcoming ceremonies being planned for the President's return, Stanton, with little evident enthusiasm, added: "The People here have made arrangements for your reception." [60]

What was left of the presidential party departed from Harrisburg early on the morning of Saturday, September 15, following in the path of a separate train transporting the ailing Seward.

Once finally back in Washington, Seward was lifted by stretcher to a carriage that returned him to his Lafayette Square home. The presidential party, meanwhile, was delayed in Baltimore due to the size of a welcoming crowd estimated at more than 100,000 people. Grant, long past the point of endurance, decided to take a separate train to Washington, with Cadwallader putting a good face on matters when he wrote that the General had left simply to "avoid being the recipient of the complimentary demonstrations which have greeted him all along the route." [61]

Due to the protracted Baltimore reception, the presidential party did not make it back to Washington until early evening. Riding in an open carriage, Johnson was cheered by thousands as the procession first put in a ceremonial stop at City Hall before being escorted to the grounds of the White House.

As a military band played, Johnson gingerly walked up the steps to the building's south portico, crowded with smiling staffers and supporters. Thanking those who had turned out to receive him, the President delivered brief remarks, perhaps shocking some when he declared: "All I can promise you for the future is that it will be a continuance of my conduct in the past." [62]

With that, he entered the White House, perhaps willfully ignorant of the serious damage the nearly three-week journey had done to his presidency.

CHAPTER NINE

THE GREATER BURDEN

U pon his return to Washington, Johnson tried to pick up where he left off, greeting visitors, meeting with Congressional delegations, and talking casually with reporters. "His manner was absolutely as when he first took upon himself the cares of the office," recalled William Crook, who was pleased to discover that Johnson also wanted to resume his afternoon carriage rides.

But Crook also noticed something different about the president, who was daily becoming more aware of how many people objected to his behavior during the "swing around the circle."

"Never after this, as far as I remember, was he betrayed by the warmth of feeling into an unwise public utterance." On the contrary, thought Crook, Johnson's "habit of bandying words with the mob was overcome." [1]

If there really was a change in Johnson's behavior, it was only because he knew that a much larger change had occurred regarding his reputation. In the national press, Johnson was now undergoing a transformation from a leader who had previously been seen as mysterious but strong, to a man who was nothing more than an intemperate and unreasoning demagogue.

The avalanche of criticism flowing into the White House in the days and weeks to come must have been sobering and depressing. These stump diatribes had always worked for Johnson in Tennessee. Why had they now failed so spectacularly when he tried the same methods on a national scale?

Observing Johnson's quickly-declining fortunes, Thaddeus Stevens was delighted, referencing to a group of supporters in late September what he called a "remarkable circus that traveled through the country," featuring the President and Seward as clowns.

"In order to attract attention they took with them a celebrated general and an eminent naval officer whom they chained to the rigging so that he could not escape," Stevens continued in an obvious reference to Grant and Farragut.

Hugely enjoying himself, Stevens noted that Johnson had frequently alluded to his past jobs as a tailor, local official, congressman, and senator, before adding: "He had been everything but a hangman, and now asked leave to hang Thad Stevens." [2]

More seriously, Stevens wondered if Johnson, who had several times during his journey suggested that the people should simply ignore Congress, was thinking of some sort of new legislative configuration. "The President contends that the body of men known as a Congress has no constitutional power," Stevens wrote in a public letter during the last week of September, suggesting that Johnson wanted to form his own Congress dominated by representatives from the South. Clearly, Stevens perceived that while Johnson was in political trouble, he was still nevertheless dangerous. [3]

Unlike Stevens, Charles Sumner saw nothing amusing in Johnson's behavior, calling him "perverse, distempered, ignorant, & thoroughly wrong." [4]

On October 2, Sumner did what he did best and gave a very long speech to a packed Boston Music Hall on Johnson's declining fortunes. Entitled "The One Man Power vs. The Congress," Sumner's address, as later distributed in pamphlet form, was fully footnoted with an abundance of references to constitutional laws, statutes, and previous acts of Congress.

The address was also personally bitter, with Sumner at one point suggesting that Johnson was suffering from a form of "Presidential madness" when he threatened the lives of his opponents and "stimulated a mob against them."

Sumner then called upon his audience to "arrest this madness."

"Your votes will be the first step," Sumner declared as he reached a rhetorical high point in remarks that would also be reprinted in newspapers nationally. "The President must be taught that usurpation and apostasy cannot prevail. He who promised to be the Moses and has become Pharaoh must be overthrown." [5]

The enmity of the likes of Stevens and Sumner, Johnson could handle. In a perverse way, he had stoked it, and seemed to even enjoy their hatred. But what happened next was beyond his understanding, with strange voices in even stranger venues, people he didn't know and had never met, eviscerating him in a way that no previous president had endured.

For a man desperate for the respect and admiration of those he habitually assumed were beyond his social circle, the weeks to come, in which Johnson was repeatedly held up to relentless and even vicious ridicule, were not only the most depressing in his presidency, but perhaps his entire life.

The descent was first seen in the nation's press with the *New York Times,* which had until now been neutral in its Johnson coverage, taking a decided critical tone. As early as September 7, the paper registered its disappointment, noting of Johnson's fights with hecklers: "The President of the United States cannot enter upon an exchange of epithets with the brawlers of a mob without seriously compromising his official character." In the weeks to come, the paper would no longer have much positive to say about Johnson at all, and would maintain a rather wary appraisal of Johnson for the rest of his days as president. [6]

Far more alarming was the loss of the more influential *New York Herald,* which had steadfastly advocated for Johnson since the first day of his presidency. In a confidential correspondence, William Phillips, chief editorial writer for the paper, told Johnson that the *Herald* had "commenced a new course, and one less cordial to your administration."

Always reflecting the opinions of its brilliant but mercurial owner, James Gordon Bennett, the paper now saw Johnson as a loser, with Phillips telling the President that Bennett "thinks your trip to Chicago was unfortunate, and has done you no good." [7]

The support of major newspapers was important not just because millions of people read those publications, but also because Washington lawmakers regarded them as weathervanes indicating a president's popularity. There was no official polling in 1866, but the rapid decline of Johnson's support among the most influential publications clearly indicated trouble.

Improbably, it was Johnson's decline within the literary community that was likely the most severe. In a time when regular working people read, analyzed, and treasured books, writers had an outsized influence on the thinking of the country and a soulful, transcendent relationship with followers that Johnson could never hope to duplicate.

The poet John Greenleaf Whittier, whose hugely successful narrative poem *Snow-Bound* had been published earlier in the year, had once liked Johnson, but now remarked: "What a ridiculous fiasco was the President's tour. If he left Washington the ninth part of a man, what a pitiful decimal fraction he brings back." [8]

Henry Wadsworth Longfellow pondered: "Mr. Johnson grows worse and worse, and if he is not checked by an overwhelming majority in the Fall elections, will perhaps try something in the old Cromwell style, and we shall have another Civil War." The President, thought Longfellow, "is capable of any iniquity." [9]

On September 14, Longfellow received a letter from an old friend, the essayist and poet James Russell Lowell, who cleverly exclaimed "What an anti-Johnson lecturer we have in Johnson! Sumner has been right about the *cuss* from the first." As Lowell sent his letter, an essay on Johnson he had written for the *North American Review* was being mailed to subscribers. A nearly 30-page exploration of the administration's policies over the course of the past year, Lowell's article was also a bitter and at times remarkably personal indictment of Johnson as a man.

Well known for his humor, Lowell was anything but funny now, revealing his own class pretentions when he predicted that Johnson would be remembered in history as the "first, and we trust the last of our chief magistrates who believed in the brutality of the people and gave to the White House the ill-savor of a corner-grocery."

Recalling that Johnson had repeatedly characterized himself as a tribune of the people, Lowell exploded: "*He* a tribune of the people! A lord of misrule, an abbot of unreason, much rather!"

On the contrary, Lowell argued, Johnson corrupted any principle he claimed to believe in. "Every word he uttered must have convinced many, even those unwilling to make the admission, that a doctrine could hardly be sound which had its origins and derives its power from a source so impure." [10]

A biting assault, Lowell's attack on Johnson was nothing compared to the two essays published by the critic Edwin Percy Whipple in the September and November issues of the *Atlantic Monthly*. Like Lowell, Whipple, usually known for his satirical talents, lost all comic perspective when it came to Johnson, describing him in the first essay as "insincere as well as stubborn, cunning as well as unreasonable, vain as well as ill tempered, greedy of popularity as well as arbitrary of disposition, veering in his mind as well as fixed in his will."

Whipple wondered about Johnson's stability, a topic Sumner had already introduced, suggesting that the President was "egotistical to the point of mental disease," and charging that his worldview was alarmingly distorted: "He sees hardly anything as it is, but almost everything as colored by his own dominant egotism." [11]

As harsh as these observations seemed, Whipple saved his most damning remarks for the November issue of the *Atlantic Monthly*, charging that the speeches Johnson made on his swing around the circle were a "volcanic outbreak of vulgarity, conceit, bombast, scurrility, ignorance, brutality, and balderdash."

"Never was a blustering demagogue led by a distempered sense of self-importance into a more fatal error," continued Whipple, adding that Johnson's behavior on the journey had left Americans "mortified and indignant," as they read of the President's "impolitic and ignominious abandonment of dignity and decency in his address to the people he attempted to alternatively bully and cajole." [12]

The humorist David Ross Locke soon joined the chorus of ridicule. The creator of the amusing character Petroleum Nasby, a bumbling Southern bigot and schemer, Locke penned a series of fictional letters narrating Nasby's participation in the presidential caravan. The letters soon revealed that the fictional Nasby cared little about Johnson's policies, but just wanted to be in the inner circle to hold on to his cherished postmaster job.

The jabs at Johnson were for the most part gentle, but still pointed. When Nasby expressed relief that no supporter of the President was killed during the disastrous Johnston, Pennsylvania platform accident, the train's conductor, referencing the dearth of actual Johnson supporters, is said to remark: "They'd have to import for that purpose." [13]

Locke's series soon appeared in the form of a book entitled *"Swingin Round the Cirkle,"* reflecting the spelling inadequacies of the ignorant Nasby, and containing a series of anti-Johnson cartoons, one of which showed him getting increasingly smaller in size as the caravan made its way across the country, while another portrayed a rush of admirers gathering around Grant as the train arrived in Cleveland, all ignoring a bewildered Johnson.

While newspaper readers were digesting the Locke/Nasby letters, the 25 year-old cartoonist Thomas Nast was putting his pen to a series of cartoons soon to appear in successive issues of *Harper's Weekly* that would represent the most detailed and brilliant visual assault on any president in history.

A gifted newspaper caricaturist during the Civil War, Nast saw his cartoon portraits of Grant, Farragut, and others going for about $1,000 each in a New York art gallery. He had recently even sold a drawing of Johnson for $5,000, an innocuous portrait comment on the President's veto of the Freedman's Bureau bill showing Johnson kicking another kind of bureau, in this case a chest of drawers, down the steps of the Capitol. As he does, a handful of black people were seen falling out of the drawers onto the ground. [14]

That cartoon, pointed but not harsh, represented Nash's thinking for most of 1865 and early 1866: sympathetic to the Radical Republican cause, the cartoonist was was disappointed with Johnson, although still hopeful. But the president's increasingly rancorous confrontations with Congress and the riots in Memphis and New Orleans soon changed the cartoonist's thinking.

On September 1, Nast's cartoon "Reconstruction and How it Works," appeared. The drawing was not a one-picture comic hit, but rather a series of images and script all revolving around a theme, in this case the many sordid things going on around the country that seemed to have some connection with Johnson. The core of the illustration was a depiction of black people being brutalized by whites, with Johnson variously appearing as smarmy but apparently undisturbed by the violence. [15]

On October 27 came Nast's triumph: "Andy's Trip," a visual indictment of Johnson's behavior during his swing around the circle, divided by two dozen panels, with Johnson at the center wearing a halo and smiling beneath the words, a takeoff from his New York speech, "Who has suffered more for you and for this Union than Andrew Johnson?" [16]

Nast's final anti-Johnson broadside appeared several days before the November election, entitled "King Andy," it suggested the lush surroundings of a monarch with Johnson reigning while an executioner raises his axe over the head of a manacled Stevens. In line behind Stevens, waiting their turn to die, are Sumner and Wendell Phillips, among others. [17]

Nast's biographer, Fiona Deans Halloran, would later note that *Harper's Weekly* editor William George Curtis had, like the cartoonist, grown increasingly disenchanted with Johnson, particularly after the trip to the Douglas monument. Curtis, in awe of Nast's talents, writes Halloran, "placed his faith in reasoned argument. Nast preferred the hammer-blow of satire." [18]

With a circulation surpassing the 250,000 mark, the impact of *Harper's Weekly,* and the decided damage Nast now inflicted upon Johnson, had probably less to do with the actual number of people who purchased the publication and much more with the many who passed the publication around to friends and family, studying Nast's images over and again, and undoubtedly enjoying the artist's literary allusions, very fine pen, and relentless portrayal of Johnson as a sort of evil simpleton.

Very soon, *Harper's* dared to even broach the subject of impeachment. While stopping short of recommending that Johnson be removed from office, the publication nevertheless determined that he was "entirely unfit by natural capacity and training for the office he holds." [19]

That the publication felt compelled to discuss impeachment was no accident. Almost as soon as Johnson's swing around the circle was over, came calls that Congress should consider the beginning of impeachment proceedings against the President. The *National Anti-Slavery Standard* announced simply: "If the present emergency does not demand a recurrence of this constitutional method of protection, it is impossible to conceive one which would." [20]

In late September, Republican Congressman George Boutwell of Massachusetts told the *Daily National Intelligencer* that "articles of impeachment will be offered and carried by the House at the next session." Boutwell's Republican colleague, Ohio's John Bingham, declared: "So help me God, I will neither give sleep to my eyes nor slumber to my eyelids until I have drawn bills of impeachment against Andrew Johnson." General Benjamin F. Butler, running for a congressional seat in Massachusetts, promised that his first order of business, if elected, would be to vote out articles of impeachment, maliciously asserting that in the event of a trial, Johnson could be even jailed by the Senate until the results were known. "The right and form are clear," declared Butler. "Let us have this thing be done with." [21]

The problem with these early Radical Republican initiatives were simple: for what was Johnson going to be impeached? The President's detractors pointed to his frequent use of the veto in attempts to frustrate Radical Republication legislation he regarded as excessive. Yet, this was an entirely constitutional tool available to any chief executive, with nine of the previous sixteen presidents using the veto power at least once, and Andrew Jackson showing the most presidential muscle with a record twelve regular and pocket vetoes.

The second gripe was that Johnson, as seen by his splenetic performance during the Douglas monument journey, was not "presidential." Yet, while in most instances, Johnson's comments clearly were incendiary and decidedly lacking in the statesmanship department, those comments in the final analysis were nothing more than expressions of his own opinions. All of which meant that even in the early going, impeachment proponents were playing a hand with two exceedingly weak cards.

Cooler heads within the Radical Republican caucus soon realized they would need more, much more, to mount a serious impeachment effort.

Their cause was in no small way helped by the results of the fall mid-term elections which saw the Republicans ending up with a massive numerical advantage in the House of 134 to 41; while holding the Senate 42 to 8.

As the Republican victories multiplied, Wendell Phillips was one among many Radical Republicans who believed that Johnson, through his intemperate rhetoric and unyielding policies, had become an unwitting ally for the opposition. "Let us pray to God," Phillips proclaimed to a New York audience, "that the President may continue to make mistakes." [22]

No sooner was the 2nd session of the 19th Congress gaveled to order on December 3 than the Radical Republican assault on Johnson began. Sumner immediately brought up a bill he knew Johnson opposed, granting voting rights to blacks in the District of Columbia. Stevens introduced a measure limiting Johnson's ability to remove public officials from office, while Ohio Senator Benjamin Wade thought it might be a good idea to constitutionally limit the presidency to one term.

On January 5, Ohio Representative John Ashley called for an impeachment inquiry, which he hoped to head up. Ashely was in reality impeachment obsessed and had been talking about removing Johnson from office for months. But his fellow Radical Republicans weren't sure Ashley was equal to the task ahead. "He could make nothing of it but a malicious and vindictive partisan crusade," judged one correspondent to the *New York Times*. [23]

What made talk about impeachment in the coming weeks less of an abstraction, despite the likes of Ashley, was the unprecedented and growing standoff between the President and Congress on a series of issues, beginning with Johnson's veto of the District of Columbia voting bill, which was swiftly overridden on January 8.

On March 2, Johnson more than happily vetoed the Tenure of Office Act, a constitutionally dubious piece of legislation prohibiting him from removing any civil officer, including members of his own cabinet, without the consent of the Senate. That same day, the veto was overridden. Practically in response, Johnson vetoed the first Reconstruction Bill, which divided the South into five military districts to be governed from Washington, only to see that veto also overridden.

Three weeks later, Johnson displayed his stubborn determination by vetoing a second Reconstruction Bill, which was also instantly overridden.

For Johnson supporters, the endless warfare was interpreted as a brave lone man standing up to the tyranny of a power-mad Congress. For his opponents, the continued confrontation was nothing more than a sign of Johnson's unfitness for office, with the press increasingly portraying him as a president incapable of compromise.

Johnson received minimally good reviews in late June, attending the dedication ceremonies of a Masonic temple in Boston. Throughout the trip, which included several stops along the East coast, Johnson displayed a new-found discipline, speaking mostly from prepared texts. "The people of New England," thought the anti-Johnson *Springfield Daily Republican* newspaper, found the President "cordial, affable, desirous of pleasing, easily pleased, patriotic and generous in his speeches." The *New York Herald* was equally approving, pointedly noting: "The country will agree with us that the contrast between the Chicago trip and this Boston trip is of good cheer. For all those savage diatribes, the bandying of unworthy epithets, those disgraceful scenes, which every memory will recall, we have only parties and welcomes." [24]

But whatever good feelings Johnson earned from the Boston trip disappeared six weeks later when he decided to do what many of his friends had been advising for more than two years in getting rid of the treacherous Stanton. "The cabinet is not and has never been a unit," Gideon Welles had frankly told Johnson on August 4. It was common knowledge now that the always-manipulative War Secretary was shamelessly consorting with Radical Republican leaders in a daily effort to undermine Johnson, while, out of an almost perverse desire, contradicting and arguing with Johnson over all matters of policy. Stanton's purpose had little to do with any kind of principle. He was a man, indeed, entirely devoid of principle. Instead he had decided to join the Johnson opposition simply because, addicted to power, he astutely realized that power was daily seeping away from Johnson, while the Radical Republicans were entirely ascendant. [25]

One day after Johnson's conversation with Welles, he decided to cut Stanton loose. "Public considerations of a high character constrain me to say that your resignation as Secretary of War will be accepted," Johnson informed Stanton by way of a hand-written latter. [26]

Even more, in the days ahead, Johnson removed General Philip Sheridan, long suspected of collusion with the Radical Republicans, from his New Orleans post, and also axed General Daniel Sickles, who had several times urged upon the President a more moderate course with Congress, for the same reason.

Sarcastically, Stanton had a ready response for Johnson, parroting the President's note of dismissal: "I have the honor to say that public considerations of a high character, which alone induced me to continue at the head of this Department, constrain me not to resign the office of Secretary of War before the next meeting of Congress." [27]

That next meeting of Congress, beginning on December 2, Stanton knew, would fully sustain him as any number of Radical Republican leaders loudly declared that Johnson, by trying to sack Stanton, was in violation of the Tenure of Office Act. But Johnson had been smarter than many of his opponents appreciated. Five days after Stanton refused to step down, Johnson ordered instead that he be suspended from office (an order Stanton also rejected out of hand), and appointed in his place an entirely uncomfortable Grant as "Secretary of War *ad interim*."

Grant had earlier warned Johnson that getting rid of Stanton, Sheridan and Sickles would be more than the "loyal people of this country (I mean those who supported the Government during the great rebellion) will quickly submit to." [28]

Johnson reacted angrily to Grant's suggestion, and dared even to deride the General's ability to discern anything that the loyal people of the country wanted.

One thing was certain: by this most recent action Johnson had effectively, if chaotically, put nearly everyone in a bind; the Radical Republicans, because Johnson was now following the Tenure of Office law by submitting the Stanton suspension to Congress; Stanton, who was uncertain where he stood; and Grant, maneuvered into a job he didn't want, and suddenly viewed suspiciously by many Radical Republicans (including Stanton) for taking it.

By the fall of 1867 the Radical Republicans realized that the movement for impeachment had been fully re-ignited. "I have never doubted that the President would be impeached," Sumner said in an interview on August 30 from Boston, adding "There is but one thing the country cannot stand, and that is misrule, which is precisely what we have now." House Speaker Schuyler Colfax revealed that he was counting the days until Johnson "would be brought before the Senate for impeachment." Meanwhile, the November issue of the *Atlantic Monthly* happily predicted: "The House of Representatives, which has the sole power of impeachment, will in all probability impeach the President. The Senate, which has the sole power to try impeachment, will in all probability find him guilty." [29]

One week into 1868, the Senate dramatically voted in a night-time executive session to reinstate Stanton. Johnson, in an interview with the *New York World,* one of the last major newspapers to still support him, said he was unmoved by the upper chamber's actions. Noting that the Senate had passed a resolution saying it did not concur in Stanton's suspension, Johnson remarked "But this does not reinstate Mr. Stanton according to the law." [30]

In fact, Johnson maintained that the Senate had actually played into his hands. By continuing to uphold a law that he believed unconstitutional, the upper chamber had paved the way for Johnson to challenge it in court. From Johnson's point of view, Stanton was still suspended and Grant was still his temporary replacement. But Grant, feeling the pressure from all sides, announced that it had never been his goal to replace Stanton. The General also said he was convinced that Johnson was bad mouthing him behind his back for not being a better ally in the struggle against Stanton and the Radical Republicans, adding that he didn't appreciate the "many and gross representations, affecting my personal honor," which he had read in the press and were said to have come from the White House. [31]

Soon came a series of increasingly vituperative letters between Johnson and Grant, with the President crafting long and hopelessly combative arguments allowing for no possibility of the battle ending any time soon. Grant, in return, gave as good as he got, barely concealing a steadily increasing contempt for Johnson.

Johnson now appeared to everyone who worked with him to despise Grant in the sort of all-consuming manner he had once reserved for Jefferson Davis. The parallels only went so far, however. Grant was not an aristocrat and never looked down his nose at Johnson or anyone else for that matter. But he had something that Johnson now entirely lacked: the affection not just of the masses, but of the rich and connected.

In December more than a thousand people had packed themselves into New York's Cooper Institute to officially launch the campaign to make Grant the next president on the Republican ticket. Among those present was not only a bevy of the city's political leadership, but also millionaire retailer Alexander Stewart; Moses Grinnell, successful shipper and merchant; William Dodge, lumber and railroad baron; William and John Jacob Astor, Jr., who maintained their family's extensive real estate holdings, and a sprinkling of Roosevelts. These men were among the most wealthy business leaders not just in New York, but the entire country.

It was a class devoted to the unassuming Grant, who had also been given a fully furnished house in Philadelphia by the well-heeled of that city, and another home in Galena, Illinois, where he and Julia had lived before the war.

No one, Johnson was quick to note, was giving him a house. And when loyal Democrats attempted in late January to stage a competing show of support for him at the same Cooper Institute, none of the city's upper crest could find their way to the hall. Meanwhile, the only political figure of note to say anything nice about Johnson at the spiritless rally was Wisconsin Senator James Doolittle, and he actually didn't appear but sent a letter of endorsement instead.

On February 21 Johnson at last outright dismissed Stanton, and giving up on Grant, appointed in the Secretary's place the less assertive 64 year-old General Lorenzo Thomas.

That was it for the Radical Republicans: instantly cries were heard in both chambers that Johnson had to go. "Correspondents flew from end to end of the Capitol as if shot out of guns," reported the *New York Times* as news of Stanton's firing reached Congress. [32]

No story seemed too far-fetched, including the very real one that Stanton refused to leave his office, barricading himself behind a locked door as he ordered the arrest of Thomas.

Much more sensational was the vote on February 24 impeaching the president. The words "high crimes and misdemeanors," describing the acts for which a president could be removed from office, were suddenly on the lips of every congressman, making their way into the print of the nation's newspapers.

Two weeks later, the Senate accepted eleven articles of impeachment. Ten of the eleven articles dealt with various aspects of Johnson's attempt to remove Stanton. Article X mostly centered on Johnson's speeches during the swing around the circle, final proof of how corrosive the trip had become for the president.

"Is telling the truth to the people in a public address a 'high misdemeanor'?" Johnson wondered several days later in an interview with Jerome Stillson of the *New York World*. [33]

The president, in looking over what was supposed to be a copy of his St. Louis speech attained by his defense team, noticed that portions of it had been removed, "perhaps by a pair of convenient scissors," raising the suspicion that the impeachment managers had framed their Article X arguments around only certain sections of certain speeches, never their entirety. [34]

Johnson's legal counsel was soon delighted by the existence of Article X, primarily because it created so many more questions for the managers than it solved: how could anyone actually prove that Johnson's words constituted a high crime or misdemeanor? In other words, could the President's accusers really divine the intent of Johnson's speeches and thereby remove him from office for the things he had said?

Although even some impeachment supporters questioned the wisdom of proceeding with Article X, Massachusetts Congressman Benjamin Butler, part of the prosecuting team, contended "We are too apt to overlook the danger that may come from words."

"But words may be and sometimes are things," Butler continued, "living, barring things that set a world on fire." [35]

Butler then attempted to recreate the sensations at Cleveland and St. Louis, claiming that Johnson had threatened to hang Stevens and Sumner, when in fact he had just suggested that his antagonists in the audience should do the honors. When the president causes the "cheek to burn with shame, exposing to the taunts and ridicule of every nation the good name and fame of the chosen institution of 30 millions of people, is it not the highest possible crime and misdemeanor in office?" demanded Butler. [36]

The impeachment managers brought forth as witnesses reporters who had listened to Johnson's speeches in Cleveland and St. Louis, a mistake that Johnson's defense team easily exploited when it was revealed that none of the reporters had heard the entirety of the President's remarks, thus leaving their testimony open to the charge of being incomplete. [37]

Although in the days to come the impeachment managers moved onto other examples of what they regarded as Johnson's unfitness for office, they couldn't seem to leave Article X alone, with Congressman Boutwell in mid-April single-mindedly focusing on what he imagined was the intent of the President's remarks, which he characterized as "calculated and designed to impair the just authority of Congress."

In the final analysis, Boutwell's argument, as he laid before the Senate each of the articles of impeachment, suggested less that Johnson had done any one particular thing wrong and more that he was just a very bad human being. "He has injured every person with whom he has had confidential relations," Boutwell said, "and many have escaped ruin only by withdrawing from his society altogether." [38]

When the senators, in mid-May, at last rose to declare how they would vote, it was not entirely certain that Johnson would escape conviction on every article. But the managers' continuing focus on Article X foolishly allowed pro-Johnson members of the Senate to make a much larger constitutional argument. "It cannot be reasonably expected that the president should be removed for exercising a privilege enjoyed by every American citizen: the first amendment to the Constitution declares that Congress shall pass no law abridging the freedom of speech or of the press," said Maryland's George Vickers. [39]

It was the observations of Justin Morrill, a slender Maine Republican known for his integrity, however, that were perhaps the most cogent. Never a fan of Johnson, Morrill pointed out that his speeches were in the end only evidence of a "bad taste and violent temper, such as are not infrequently exhibited in political discussions and sometimes, it is to be regretted, have appeared as foul blots in legislative discussions."

Johnson's speeches, thought Morrill, were to be deplored for the "stigma and scandal thereby brought upon the nation." But, in the end, they were simply expressions of opinion, nothing more.

Reaching his conclusion, Morrill both cynically and astutely remarked: "To President Johnson, it will be a cruel and unavoidable punishment, unparalleled in our history, that such speeches are to be perpetuated as a prominent feature of his future presidential fame."

"I do not desire," Morrill added, with no small amount of irony, "to place any greater burden on his back." [40]

When members walked into the Senate chamber on May 16, Johnson's fate remained unknown. There had been hundreds of pro and anti-impeachment rallies that had taken place across the country in recent days, with nearly all of the nation's major newspapers filling up columns of space either promoting Johnson's removal or acquittal.

White-gloved policemen stood guard in the packed corridors and stairways outside the chamber, while dozens of well-dressed women filed into the gallery, waving fans in the heated atmosphere, determined to bear witness to the historic moment. The nation, and indeed, the world waited upon a verdict.

Within minutes came the shocking news: the catch-all Article XI was defeated by a one-vote margin. Reporters ran from the gallery to wire the results to their home papers, all of which declared that the historic, unprecedented effort to remove a President of the United States from office had failed.

True, the effort had met defeat by the thinnest of margins, with 35 Republicans and no Democrats voting to convict Johnson on Article XI, one less than the required 36. But Congressional observers immediately recognized that the result would be the same for any new votes on the other articles of impeachment, which turned out to be the case.

Johnson, ordering whiskey from the White House cellar for his lawyers and friends, celebrated his acquittal. Those who had stood with him to the end suggested that this acquittal was a one-of-a-kind triumph, secured against the most improbable odds.

But for the President, it was only a precursor to imagined glories to come. In less than two months, the Democrat National Convention would be meeting in New York, and Johnson had every intention of ending up as the party's presidential nominee.

CHAPTER TEN

THE MOST MAGNIFICENT
PERSONAL TRIUMPH

U lysses S. Grant was nominated by a united Republican convention
meeting in Chicago less than a week after Johnson was acquitted
in the Senate. The Chicago conclave was heavy on a love of the General,
with speakers repeatedly lauding Grant's Civil War leadership and
potential as a man who would bring the country together after the
clamorous reign of Andrew Johnson.

Formally accepting the nomination several days later, the usually
circumspect Grant, who rarely spoke more than a few words in his
public addresses, was characteristically brief, promising to maintain the
laws and promote economy in government, before simply remarking in
words that would animate the Republicans' fall campaign: "Let us have
peace." [1]

It was all enough to make Johnson sick. If he hadn't been sure of
wanting to be the 1868 Democratic presidential nominee before Grant's
coronation, he was entirely certain of it afterwards.

To this end, Johnson was entirely prepared to launch a personal
assault against Grant. In fact, in early April, he had given readers of
the *Cincinnati Commercial* a taste of what might be coming when he
told reporter Joseph McCullagh that Grant had been drunk during the
ill-starred swing around the circle. "He went to Detroit, but it wasn't

because he was disgusted with my politics at all. In fact, he wasn't in a condition to know much about politics just then," Johnson asserted.

Given Johnson's inebriated 1865 inaugural performance, the subject of drinking seemed a volatile one for the President. But it was one more sign of his uncontrolled loathing for Grant that, by inference, he additionally decided to summon up memories of the 1865 event, telling McCullagh: "It's very strange that some men will be abused like the devil for drinking a glass of whiskey and water, while others in equally important stations may almost roll in the gutters, and not a word is said about it." [2]

There was, of course, little evidence that Johnson had enjoyed only a single "glass of whiskey and water," in the hours leading up to his disastrous inaugural address, nor could anyone remember Grant "almost" rolling in the gutters, whatever that meant.

But the remarks underlined Johnson's increasing contempt for the General, a contempt only nourished by the fact that Grant had never held an elective station, unlike Johnson who had run for and won offices at every level of government. How could, Johnson wondered, this political nonentity be viewed as a favorite to become the next president?

While history records Grant as one of the most popular presidents ever, and Johnson as one of the most discarded, none of this was overwhelmingly apparent in the early summer of 1868. On the contrary, certain that the Radical Republicans had moved out too far ahead of the public, and that Grant was now seen in some quarters as not their leader, but rather their captive, Johnson soon became convinced that he could soundly finish off Grant in the general election.

As the subsequent election returns would prove, while Grant was clearly an emotional favorite with millions of Americans, his embrace of a party that, at least since the assassination of Lincoln, seemed obsessed with reordering society in a way that had never been spelled out in the Constitution, left many voters uneasy, thus explaining why Grant would ultimately win only 52% of the vote.

The most immediate challenge for Johnson was securing a two-thirds vote of the Democrat delegates meeting in New York between July 1 and 9.

"Why shouldn't they take me up?" Johnson wondered of those delegates, telling a group of New Yorkers who visited him in the White House that the idea that he belonged to no party because he had run as Lincoln's ticket mate in 1864, was off the mark. Such assertions, Johnson claimed, missed his more important service to the country. "Caesar had a party, and Pompey and Crassus each had a party, but the commonwealth had none." [3]

But those who doubted Johnson's party bona fides had a point, at least in so far as his reluctance went during the last three years to provide federal jobs for favored Democrats.

What should have been a positive reason to support Johnson, that he was refreshingly resistant to the pressures of patronage, was early on seen as a negative by Democrats who overstated the complaint that the very least thing Jonson could have done was hand out a few postmasterships.

"I believe you will receive the nomination at New York," a Tennessee enthusiast wrote to Johnson in mid-June, adding that once so anointed, "there will be an enthusiasm in your favor, which will spread like wildfire over the land." [4]

"You deserve the nomination from the Democrats for the gallant stand you have made for the Constitution," enthused Lillian Foster, a New York author and political activist who confided to Johnson her belief that his record as president would be "warmly endorsed" at the convention, while nevertheless still doubting that he would emerge as the actual nominee. [5]

An initial challenge confronting Johnson was whether he should actually declare his candidacy for the nomination. Tradition held against it. As with the curious practice of 19th century presidential candidates not actually running for the office they sought, so, too, history proscribed a virtually non-existent role for a president hoping to be re-nominated. Lincoln said nothing about his desire for an additional four years in office as the National Union Party met in the summer of 1864, nor did Franklin Pierce when the Democrats met in 1856. But both men dearly wanted a second term, Lincoln winning the prize due to a convention smoothly run by his operatives, Pierce falling short after delegates decided that his support of the Kansas-Nebraska Act would be too great a burden for them to bear in the fall elections.

Johnson wasn't initially sure how to proceed, with his operatives meeting in New York candidly telling him the odds didn't look good. Even so, Johnson finally decided to break with tradition, coyly admitting that should there be a popular clamor for his nomination, "I shall cordially acquiesce." [6]

This was probably as close as any incumbent president at the time could come to admitting that he wanted another term. But Johnson added fuel to what he hoped would be a fire for his effort on July 4 by issuing a general amnesty for all Confederates not currently under indictment in the federal courts. This was a popular move among Democrats in general, but particularly with the Southern Democrats attending the New York meeting. The President's proclamation, thought the *New York Times,* was clearly "an overture to the convention." [7]

In the opening hours of the convention delegates approved a resolution lauding Johnson for "resisting the aggressions of Congress upon the Constitutional rights of the States and of the people." Reading wire service accounts of the proceedings, Johnson was additionally pleased to learn that there were cheers from the floor when old friend and former Tennessee Congressman Thomas Nelson put his name in nomination, declaring that even though the President had been "persecuted by the Radical party," he had nevertheless "stood up nobly for the principles of the Constitution." [8]

But such tributes were about as good as things would get for Johnson at the convention. He showed well during the first balloting, placing a strong second at 65 votes to Ohio Congressman and 1864 vice presidential nominee George Pendleton at 105 and General Winfield Hancock with 33. But in subsequent balloting, Johnson's vote continually declined, with neither Pendleton nor Hancock showing much traction.

Finally, in one of those inexplicable moments that animated so many conventions of the day, members of the Ohio delegation bolted for former New York Governor Horatio Seymour, starting an avalanche. On the 22nd ballot, Seymour won the nomination overwhelmingly.

Sometimes derided as the "Great Decliner" for the number of times he turned down offers to run for this or that office, the 58 year-old Seymour gave no evidence of being an enthusiastic candidate, preferring in the weeks ahead to avoid the kind of in-person campaigning that Johnson relished.

While the Democrats in the days after the convention united with varying degrees of enthusiasm behind the New Yorker, Johnson fell into a gloomy silence. The loss of the nomination meant the imminent loss of the White House. But even more for this still active and vital 59 year-old, it meant the imminent lack of a public station, a dreadful prospect for a man who had constantly held office, always in the middle of action and endless controversies for the last three decades.

The silence in the White House troubled Democratic officials who soon launched a concerted effort to rally the President to the party's cause. But it wouldn't be easy going. Convinced that Seymour had never really supported his administration, Johnson privately grumbled that he had no intention whatsoever of helping the Democratic nominee. The President, reported New Yorker John Van Buren, was "not only cross, but implacable." [9]

He was equally put out by suggestions that he could help Seymour by asking for the resignations from his cabinet of Secretary of State William Seward and Navy Secretary Gideon Welles, on the theory that neither man was a Democrat. Amazed, Johnson said getting rid of his two loyal and able department heads would amount to an "acknowledgment of weakness and an abandonment of our cause which would inspire the adversary with hope and confidence." [10]

Loyal, Johnson would not have dismissed Seward or Welles even if he had somehow won the Democratic presidential nomination. That he should now do it for another candidate, seemed absurd.

Johnson's indifference to Seymour eventually weakened when other New Yorkers, including most prominently the enigmatic Samuel Tilden, chairman of the state Democrat party, assured him that Seymour had always been one of his most steadfast admirers.

More important, by late October, Johnson realized the obvious: there was only one person standing in the way of Ulysses S. Grant moving into the White House, and his name was Horatio Seymour.

On October 22, in a public letter, Johnson told Seymour that he was encouraged to learn that the New Yorker was planning to actively campaign in the final days of the election. "The mass of the people should be aroused and warned against the encroachments of despotic power now ready to enter the very gate of the citadel," Johnson told Seymour, as he not for the first time also revealed his low opinion of Grant. [11]

Johnson's public correspondence with Seymour prompted his friends to contemplate what might have been. "Every day's experience leads me to a more & more confident belief that we should have been more likely to success if you had been our candidate for the Presidency," Connecticut Senator James Dixon told Johnson on October 29. [12]

Undoubtedly Johnson agreed, although he sensibly steered clear of a bizarre and utterly impractical suggestion made by the *New York World* in the waning days of the campaign to dump Seymour, a proposal that many thought would only make sense if Johnson stepped in to rescue the party.

Election night returns must have convinced Johnson that he could have beaten Grant, winning most of the states of the South, and holding onto New York, Pennsylvania, and perhaps one or two states out West. It would have been a victory he would have relished, not just winning a presidential term in his own right, but defeating the great General.

As it was, Johnson, absorbing the news of Grant's victory, was now consigned to wind down his presidency, preparing for a leave of office in four more months.

During his final weeks in the White House, Johnson threw open the doors of the place, hosting numerous parties, some even attended by Radical Republicans, as well as an unusual children's gathering seeing some three hundred young kids romping through the Executive Mansion while a Marine band played military tunes and a healthy supply of cake and ice cream was devoured by all.

"In numerous ways, a softer side of Johnson's character found appreciation during those final months in Washington," notes historian Lately Thomas. [13]

On December 9, he presented his final Annual Message to Congress, cynically noting of Radical Republican efforts in the South: "The attempt to place the white population under the dominion of persons of color in the South has impaired, if not destroyed, the kindly relations that had previously existed between them."

Those kindly feelings, Johnson contended, had been replaced by a "feeling of animosity which, leading in some instances to collision and bloodshed, has prevented that cooperation between the two races so essential to the success of industrial enterprise in the Southern states." [14]

Determined to complete unfinished business, Johnson on Christmas Day issued a general amnesty for all remaining participants in the Confederate government who had not been subject to his earlier amnesty decrees. This time Jefferson Davis, who had actually been released from Fort Monroe in the spring of 1867 pending a trial on charges of treason, was covered. Johnson, still convinced that Davis could be successfully prosecuted, expected no word of thanks from the former Confederate president for his action and received none.

The strategizing leading up to the amnesty proclamation revealed Johnson and Davis in their characteristic stubbornness. Davis continued to describe Johnson as "My most malignant persecutor," and one whose "vindictive personality and selfish purpose to have me convicted I had no doubt." Johnson, meanwhile, had months earlier not entirely truthfully told Davis' attorney, Charles O'Connor, that there was little he could do in the matter of Davis' prosecution except to grant a pardon, "and that he would *never* grant one." [15]

At the same time, Davis had repeatedly vowed to decline a pardon, should one be offered, on the theory that he had done nothing wrong.

Not once did Johnson show any sympathy for Davis' plight in prison or the possibility that he might be someday tried and executed. Even so, when he learned that a federal district court judge had said he'd get a quick conviction in a Davis trial by populating the jury with black people, Johnson, with some irony, remarked "It used to be fashionable to try a man before they hanged him." [16]

On February 1, Johnson was visited in the Blue Room by a group of more than one hundred cadets from Georgetown College. He lauded their commitment to service and reminded them that they should always revere the Constitution. "Instead of having a sovereign in one man, we have sovereignty in all," Johnson remarked. "The people are the masters, and individuals elevated to places of trust and power are but their servants." [17]

This was the view. Critics could complain that he had done nothing during his time in office to advance the rights of black people, and they'd be correct. The cause of the ex-slaves and the need to provide for their legal protection repeatedly and sadly failed to engage him.

But he would leave office forever convinced that he was perhaps the last man in Washington to protect the Constitution, warring against an expansive and oppressive overreach of government. This was his legacy as he saw it, and one in which he would forever feel an inordinate pride.

Providing a narrative conclusion to the tragic events that had brought him to the presidency, Johnson in early February pardoned Samuel Mudd, the doctor who had been sentenced to a life of hard labor at the Dry Tortugas for mending John Wilkes Booth's leg. He also pardoned Samuel Arnold and Edmund Spangler for their extremely marginal participation in the plot to assassinate Lincoln.

He additionally ordered that the remains of Booth himself be finally turned over to the surviving members of the Booth family, who arranged for his burial in Baltimore.

Just days before Grant's inauguration, Johnson sat down with a reporter for the *New York World* and denied that he had any plans for future political office after leaving the White House. Stories had appeared here and there in the national press that Johnson was thinking about running for the U.S. Senate once he returned to Tennessee. But, said Johnson "I can truly say that I have no further ambitions to realize."

Thoughts of the Senate prompted Johnson to remember the giants he had served with during his many years in Congress: Daniel Webster, Henry Clay, Stephen Douglas. The leadership of the legislative branch had sadly declined since then, thought Johnson, supplanted by "small men" capable of great evils.

Noting that Grant had recently declared that the notorious Tenure of Office Act would make it impossible for him to remove incompetent or corrupt persons from his administration, Johnson, in a rare compliment to the General, said the Grant's announcement "shows that he understands this, and the exertions which his friends make for its repeal show they understand it." [18]

There was no small amount of hypocrisy among Republicans who also now wanted to get rid of a law that they had so vigorously promoted as long as Johnson was president. Nevertheless, he resisted the temptation to call out their mendacity.

As a valediction, Johnson published a lengthy and somewhat philosophical farewell address on March 4. Taking note of the endless conflicts during his presidency, he reflected that "perhaps it was too much" to expect great passions to have cooled in the wake of the Civil War and Lincoln's assassination. But he thought, correctly, that had he agreed to do everything an assertive Congress had demanded of him, "I would have been hailed as all that was true, loyal, and discerning."

He decided instead to follow a different course, said Johnson, one entirely in keeping with his "oath to defeat the Constitution."

He had overseen a significant downsizing of the Civil War military, avoided sending troops to Mexico in an effort to overthrown the French-imposed Maximillian, and did what he could to return the federal government to its proper relationship with the states. He was, he said, "quite content to rest my case with the more deliberate judgment of the people, and, as I have already intimated, with the distant future." [19]

Relations had so soured between Johnson and Grant as to raise the question not only of whether the two men would ride in the same carriage to the inaugural ceremonies, but whether or not Johnson would even attend those ceremonies. Buchanan had done it for Lincoln in 1861, and Pierce had done it for Buchanan in 1857. In fact, every outgoing president going back to 1829 had honored the tradition.

On the morning of the inaugural Johnson was closeted with cabinet members in the White House putting his signature to a pile of bills sent to him in the last day by Congress. As the time grew nearer to depart, Johnson casually but purposefully announced his intention to finish up his bill-signing labors.

He would not watch Grant take the oath of office, applaud his inaugural address, or shake his hand in congratulations. Damn the tradition.

He quietly shook hands instead with his cabinet heads, various aides, and even members of the White House staff, before slipping on an overcoat and hat and walking outside. He left the presidency the same way he came in: on an overcast and rainy day.

A waiting carriage took Johnson to the Missouri Avenue home of John Coyle, publisher of the *Daily National Intelligencer,* where he joined his wife and son Robert, among several other Johnson family members who had moved in several days earlier.

Unlike other presidents who left Washington immediately upon the end of their terms of office, Johnson lingered for several weeks, almost as though he couldn't imagine not being, if not at the center of power, then at least within its orbit.

Exactly one week after his White House departure, Johnson honored a previously offered invitation issued by members of the Baltimore Common Council to visit Maryland's largest city. Baltimore had always been a good city for Johnson with its combination of blue collar Democrats and Southern sympathizers.

Now thousands of people turned out to cheer the former president, who was escorted to the Brown Hotel where a dinner was held in his honor. Perhaps overcome by the visible evidence that he still had supporters, and exhibiting the discipline that he had freely dispensed with during the swing around the circle, Johnson now kept his comments short, polemically proclaiming that he felt "more pride in being an American citizen tonight than I would in being inaugurated President over the ruins of a violated constitution." [20]

To Johnson's delight, the response in Baltimore soon proved to be anything but a singular event. Upon Johnson and his family at last leaving Washington on March 18, he was cheered along a Southern train route from northern Virginia to eastern Tennessee at stop after stop. Supporters beseeched him to think about mounting a return bid for the White House in 1872.

"It is reasonable & natural that you should desire quiet & repose," Augustus Garland, a Democrat activist in Little Rock, would soon tell Johnson. "But great interests are at stake & they demand, in my judgement, your services." [21]

The letter writer touched on an essential contradiction in Johnson's thinking during the months to come. He did, indeed, yearn for "quiet & repose." But Johnson was also possessed of a boundless energy that only a person who is biologically and endlessly ambitious could enjoy. He told family members and friends upon returning to Greeneville on March 20 that he was simply happy to be back home and more than content to look after his business and real estate interests, observing the national scene from afar.

Outwardly, he seemed content. Dropping in on neighbors, working in a yard to the rear of the Johnson family home, and even driving his own horse and buggy about town. "We have a beautiful country here in East Tennessee, but we need a little capital and enterprise," Johnson told a reporter for the *Cincinnati Commercial* who came by to interview him, noticing that on the walls of Johnson's parlor were pictures of Swiss scenery as well as portraits of Washington, Lincoln, and himself.

Johnson, observed the reporter Augustus Ricks, seemed both vital and optimistic. "There never has been such a glorious country on the face of the earth, and if we can only get along and patiently bear with each other, all will come right finally," the ex-president was convinced.

"If the North and South understood each other better there would be no such thing in the way of our being united, prosperous, and happy," Johnson added. [22]

Appearing entirely at peace with himself, Johnson, certainly by the late spring of 1869, was nevertheless soon restless. It was probably too much to expect that a man who had been at the center of national power for a decade, including four of the stormiest years in the history of the presidency, would be happy with life in a town of just over 1,000 people.

Front porch ruminations delivered from the comfort of a rocking chair with neighbors and friends talking about the price of corn and potatoes, weather conditions, and the health of a favored milking cow, could only satisfy Johnson for so long.

Inevitably, variously describing Greeneville as dull, flat, and grey, Johnson yearned for the active life of an active politician in a big city.

But how to get back? In late June, after the tragic death of son Robert, who appears to have drunk himself to death, Johnson travelled to Washington to witness the graduation of his last son, 17 year-old Andrew Johnson, Jr., from Georgetown College.

Checking into the Metropolitan Hotel on Pennsylvania Avenue, Johnson agreed to an interview with the *New York Herald* and almost immediately launched into a sweeping attack on Grant.

"I had ample time to study him when I was President," Johnson said of Grant, "and I am convinced he is the greatest farce that was ever thrust upon a people."

This was strong language, but Johnson was only warming up, additionally calling Grant "mendacious, cunning, and treacherous," and even daring to attack Grant's appearance. Noting that Grant had been repeatedly favorably compared to George Washington, Johnson declared: "Why, he is so small you must put your finger on him. He, a little upstart, a coward, physically and intellectually, to be compared to George Washington! Why, it makes me laugh." [23]

Such remarks could do Johnson no good. Even among those who didn't vote for Grant was a certain reverence for a General who was in all ways regarded as a good man.

But still Johnson pushed on. "Physically and mentally and morally he is a nonentity," the ex-president continued in a bizarre run of words. "Why, sir, his soul is so small you could put it within the periphery of a hazel nut shell and it might float about for a thousand years without knocking against the walls of the shell." [24]

It would have been impossible for Grant, an inveterate reader of the *Herald,* to not have seen Johnson's acidic remarks, which were published on June 28. The meanness of those comments may have stunned the new President, but then again, they were uttered by Johnson, whom Grant had long since concluded was capable of saying anything.

Even so, Grant must have felt at least a little bit happy four months later, in October, upon learning that Johnson had embarrassingly failed in a comeback attempt in Tennessee, losing a legislative race for the U.S. Senate. Historians have since concluded that Johnson failed because he was squeezed out by both Unionists in the state angry over his anti-Reconstruction policies as president, and former secessionists who well remembered his moves against the Confederacy.

But the truth may have been less complicated. It's possible that fewer than eight months after the close of his presidency, Johnson remained too much of an inevitable and even exhausting presence. He had not allowed those who would decide his fate, in this case the members of the Tennessee State Legislature, enough time to miss him.

Worse was to come. He spent the most of 1870 and 1871 attending to business in Greeneville, occasionally involving himself in state politics and now and then commenting upon national affairs. He was, by all reports, irascible. His mood darkened all the more in the late summer of 1872, after dutifully endorsing the candidacy of Horace Greeley, the famous, if irrational publisher of the *New York Tribune*, who had secured the Democratic presidential nomination. Johnson's problem with Greeley wasn't that the publisher had spent most of his career aligned with the Republican party. Johnson was too wary of blind party loyalty for that. Rather, he just wasn't certain that Greeley could ever be organized and disciplined enough to mount a successful effort against Grant. From Johnson's perspective, the whole thing smacked of a lost opportunity.

As Johnson tried to come to grips with the idea of Greeley as president, he announced his own candidacy for an at-large congressional seat from Tennessee. It may have seemed a great comeuppance for a former president to even think about running for the House of Representatives, but Johnson could remember when John Quincy Adams did just that in his retirement years. And besides, Johnson desperately needed the station and position that holding a new political office would give him.

He presented himself, incongruously, as a unifier, someone determined to bring the country back together after the divisiveness of the Civil War and Reconstruction, telling one gathering in Knoxville that "there is no chasm now but what should be filled up. It is human to err, divine to forgive." [25]

As it was, Johnson suffered a punishing defeat in the October 1872 balloting, coming in a very distant third in a three-candidate race.

Now, surely, his hopes for a return to the limelight were finally at an end. He had, in the span of for four years, been rejected as a presidential candidate at the Democratic National Convention in New York, and subsequently defeated for the U.S. Senate and U.S. House in Tennessee.

Could his fortunes possibly be more forlorn? Johnson must have wondered, by late 1872, if there was any public office he could ever again be elected to. Perhaps, before it was all over, he'd be reduced to running, as he had in the 1830s, for the state legislature, or even mounting a triumphant return to the mayor's office in Greeneville.

Johnson must have shuddered, contemplating his bleak fortunes, a foretelling of darkness and angst made all the worse by Grant's landslide election in November 1872 over Greeley.

In the spring and summer of 1873, as a new cholera epidemic swept the nation, Johnson fell ill. Certain that he was about to die, he wrote a note entitled: "All seems gloom and despair," describing his imminent ending: "Approaching death to me is the mere shadow of God's protecting wing. Beneath it I almost feel sacred."

He welcomed his ending. Inevitably casting matters in a political context, Johnson said he imagined traveling to some place where "the influence of envy and jealous enemies, where Treason and Traitors in state, back sliders, and hypocrites in church can have no place." [26]

But, perhaps even to his own surprise, Johnson by the fall of 1873 had endured, and was soon feeling well enough to vigorously take part in the reappearance of a festering controversy regarding new charges levelled against him by Judge Advocate Joseph Holt.

Not for the first time, Holt, this time in a lengthy letter submitted to the *Washington Chronicle,* claimed that Johnson clearly knew about the military commission's reservations in 1865 regarding the execution of Mary Surratt.

Assertions from Johnson to the contrary, declared Holt, only proved that the ex-president was a liar.

Old partisans on both sides of the divide reacted to the re-ignited dispute, with Gideon Welles not only challenging Holt's veracity, but saying of Surratt: "I thought then and think now [that] she was as deserving of punishment as any of those implicated." [27]

Visiting Washington in mid-October, Johnson wrote out a lengthy rebuttal to Holt's charges for publication in the *Chronicle,* roundly castigating the Judge. "I have never attempted, through friends or otherwise, to shrink from my responsibility in connection with the execution of President Lincoln's assassins," Johnson proclaimed, before reasserting that Holt had never given to him any documentation recommending clemency for Surratt. [28]

The controversy would never entirely die out, and neither Holt nor Johnson were the kind of men likely to any time soon give the matter a rest. But judging from press accounts of the dispute, it appeared that Johnson had the better of it, with the *Atlanta Constitution* remarking: "Johnson has one strong advantage over Holt. His temper is perfect. Holt rages like a crazy hyena. We are rather disposed from this to think that

Holt was the worse criminal of the two, and the one most badly hurt and consciously guilty." Said the *Brooklyn Daily Eagle:* "Whatever opinion of the political wisdom or lack of wisdom displayed by Andrew Johnson any man may entertain, there are few, very few, who, on a question of veracity, would not accept his bare word against the most solemn oaths of Holt." [29]

In early 1874 the Tennessee and national press reported rumors that Johnson was considering mounting yet one more campaign, in this case an effort to return to the U.S. Senate. He declined initially to declare his intentions, but after talking with old friends from across the state, began to perceive that this was a race he could win. "I am free to say that if I could be returned to the U.S. Senate in accordance with popular sentiment reflected by the Legislature, it would be appreciated by me as the greatest compliment of my life," he told Tennessee lawyer and supporter Richard Edwards on July 20.

Never one to forget opponents of the past, Johnson was quick to add that a Senate victory would also prove a "deserved rebuke to treachery and ingratitude." [30]

He would make the race, absolutely convinced that in so doing he could also successfully exploit a new issue that had not been available to him in his 1869 and 1872 runs for office: the growing discontent with the Grant Administration.

While Grant himself remained personally popular, a series of scandals involving cabinet and administration figures using their influence to enrich themselves or others greatly damaged his effectiveness. "It is odd that Ulysses S. Grant, a man who was personally honest and a sworn foe of profiteering, should have his times so linked with the darker side of politics," historian Michael Riccards has pondered. [31]

The Credit Mobelier scandal saw backers of the Union Pacific Railway setting up a dummy company that highly inflated the building costs of the Transcontinental Railroad and in the process also distributed blocks of stock at bargain prices to any number of federal office holders, including Grant's first vice-president Schuyler Colfax, who declined to run for re-nomination because of the scandal, as well as his replacement, Massachusetts Senator Henry Wilson.

The administration also came off looking badly by what was known as the Salary Grab, legislation that Grant signed into law doubling his own salary and giving a 50% raise to members of Congress. Meanwhile, Wilbur Richardson, Secretary of the Treasury, was forced to resign after it was disclosed that he had hired an agent who essentially shook down various U.S. businesses, supposedly in an effort to retrieve back taxes.

Johnson thought Grant, or at least his presidency, was on the ropes, telling a gathering in Shelbyville that under Grant's rule "the country has been controlled by rings and cliques." [32]

Johnson was further emboldened by the results of the 1874 mid-term elections seeing the Democrats picking up 9 seats in the Senate, and a historic 94 in the House, winning control of the lower chamber.

Finally, Johnson thought that the post-war struggles that had proven so damaging to his presidency, with Radical Republicans pulling in one direction and Democrats and ex-Confederates in another, had lessened, now more than five years after he had left the White House. This seemed as true for regular voters as it did for the state lawmakers representing them, the same lawmakers who would decide whether or not to send Johnson back to the U.S. Senate.

It was a hunch, and nothing more than that. But Johnson invested much in his instincts. He was thinking more clearly now, not blinded by what appeared to be frantic attempts in 1869 and 1872 to return to office. Instead, he calmly sized up what very much appeared to be a promising political terrain heading into early 1875 when balloting for the Senate race would take place in the state legislature.

By the time the General Assembly convened in mid-January, Johnson had settled into Nashville's Maxwell House hotel, personally coordinating the effort to secure victory, talking with lawmakers, lobbyists, reporters, and regular citizens, anyone who could help in the cause.

Members of his family, worried that he should suffer yet one more defeat, remained in Greeneville, crossing their fingers.

There were at least half a dozen candidates for the seat when voting began on January 20, with the first balloting showing Johnson far ahead of his competitors. This initial show of strength sparked a ripple of excitement, if not a certain giddiness, throughout the capitol. Was it really possible that the dreaded, detested and defeated former president was on the verge of the vindication he had long thought he deserved? Former presidents Martin Van Buren and Millard Fillmore had mounted similar efforts to return to power and prominence, running third party campaigns, and meeting only with defeat.

It seemed an American political maxim that ex-presidents were never, despite the experience of John Quincy Adams, returned to office, any kind of office. But here, observers suddenly realized, was something different: Andrew Johnson, improbably and seemingly out of nowhere, was on the verge of real power, the first office he would win on his own since 1857.

The balloting, with the hallways and galleries of the state capitol packed with partisans, went on for six excruciating days, with an anxious Johnson, pacing in his hotel room, endlessly strategizing.

Finally on January 26 came the break: out of 100 possible votes of the two houses of the General Assembly, he stood at 47, with his nearest opponent more than 20 votes behind. "For the next half hour, member after member, explaining his actions, switched over to him," Johnson biographer Hans Trefousse later noted. At last, Johnson was over the top with 52 votes, and the assembly hall exploded in a tumult of deafening cheers. [33]

It was unprecedented, improbable, and even a little absurd, but Andrew Johnson, at the age of 66, one of the most derided public figures in American history, was back, his victory resulting in a massing estimated at more than 5,000 people who cheered him as he left the Maxwell

House to acknowledge his victory in a brief speech delivered in the city's downtown public square.

"I congratulate you most sincerely on this act of justice, and the opportunity it will give you to correct, in the highest legislative body of the nation, some of the many errors and misrepresentations of yourself and your administration," wired an exultant Gideon Welles. [34]

"The public satisfaction is widespread here, at the triumph of honest, patriotism & public worth recognized to have been vindicated in your election," remarked James O'Beirne from Washington, the police officer who had escorted Johnson to Lincoln's death bed on the night of his assassination, now serving as a reporter for the *New York Herald*. [35]

"It has ever been my wish that you would take the field and enter your solemn protest against the misrule of the present time," wrote F.A. Howe, a Johnson supporter in Belford, Massachusetts. "It has also been my wish that you could once more be brought before the people as a candidate for president." [36]

Stationed at Fort Abraham Lincoln in the Dakota Territory, George Armstrong Custer, whose admiration of Johnson through the years had never lessened, could not have been happier. Referencing the troubles of the Grant administration, Custer pointedly told Johnson: "Your election—in connection with other important recent events of a similar import is a favorable sign on behalf of an unrestrictive constitutional government." [37]

Grant himself, according to a Washington-based dispatch in the *New York Herald,* responded tersely to the Johnson victory. "I am sick again," he was said to have remarked. [38]

A letter writer to Grant thought the Johnson victory was much bigger than his merely being returned to the Senate. "Andrew Johnson," Baltimorean Arthur Rich predicted to the General, was now "likely to be the Democratic candidate for the presidency." [39]

The idea of Johnson as a presidential contender in 1876 also caught the attention of the *Cincinnati Commercial*, observing that should he decide to make the race he would clearly do so with the solid support of "working men, artisans, and farmers," all of whom "recognize in him one of their number." [40]

"The election of Andrew Johnson to the Senate of the United States is the most magnificent personal triumph which the history of American politics can show," marveled the *St. Louis Republican*, additionally questioning: "He has been president once by accident, may he not, perhaps, be president again by popular will?" [41]

Clearly, Johnson's win had captured the imagination of an American public intrigued with the idea of a former president being returned to the White House by a triumphant vote of the people. It had never happened before. But so many other things in his chaotic career had never happened before, leaving the impression that when it came to Andrew Johnson, anything was possible.

It would be a month before the ex-president and junior senator from Tennessee arrived in Washington, his horizons now entirely expanded.

CHAPTER ELEVEN

THE COUNTRY SIDES WITH HIM

The idea of Johnson as a front-runner for the 1876 Democratic presidential nomination wasn't far-fetched. His Tennessee victory showed the world that he remained politically current, but also that he also had more name recognition and cross-regional support than any other major Democrat leader.

Simultaneously, the party leadership had become a hollow vessel. Of the last four Democratic presidential nominees, Stephen Douglas and Horace Greeley were dead, while George McClellan and Horatio Seymour had quietly retired from public life. There was talk that New York Governor Samuel Tilden, Indiana Governor Thomas Hendricks, or Civil War General Winfield Scott Hancock might be interested in being the next nominee, but so far, none of the potential contenders had generated real excitement.

While newspapers and politicians, appraising the upcoming presidential race, certainly saw Johnson as a figure to be contended with, Johnson himself denied any higher aspirations. "I would rather be in the United States Senate fourfold than be president," he told a reporter for the *New York Tribune* who had covered him during his White House years, "and you know me well enough to believe that I speak from the heart."

"I may do more good in the Senate than I could in the White House," Johnson added. [1]

That ambition certainly impressed the likes of Thurlow Weed, the long-time Republican boss in New York. A shrewd appraiser of his fellow politicians, Weed bluntly said he wasn't all that sure that Johnson was actually on his way back to the presidency. But, said Weed, if Johnson provided the kind of leadership in the upper chamber that he had exhibited during his previous service there "the whole country will have reason to rejoice in his political resurrection."

Even so, Weed could not help but be amazed by Johnson's political resurrection, observing that he had entered a retirement "from which no one would suppose he would ever emerge."

"Nor could any common man have dug himself out of a pit so deep and dark as that into which he had fallen," Weed added. [2]

Perhaps a little rattled by the overwhelming crowd that closed in on him on the night of his election in Nashville, Johnson hoped to create as little excitement as possible upon returning to Washington. He published a notice announcing that he would be available to quietly greet and meet old friends, foregoing the pleasures of a large welcoming reception.

Once settled into Washington's Imperial House, Johnson did, in fact, entertain an endless stream of guests: former aides, members of Congress, and reporters, joking that his while his quarters at the Imperial House were not as grand as the White House, "they are more comfortable." [3]

Alone, once the steady stream of visitors had departed, Johnson could reflect upon not just his inspiring change of fortune, but also the changed scene of Washington itself. Perhaps he sighed at least a little thinking of the men who had caused him the most trouble as president: Thaddeus Stevens, Charles Sumner, Edwin Stanton, all now dead.

He looked older, reporters noted, and even to an extent weary. His hair was more gray than when he left office, offset by a face that remained remarkably smooth and unwrinkled. To some he seemed more calm, more at peace with himself.

"My election settled all personal injuries ever afflicted," Johnson disclosed to Melville Stone, a reporter for the *New York Herald*. "I consider that triumph sufficient, and bury all of my grievances behind it." [4]

The moment of his arrival in the Senate brought a tear to the eye of even the most hardened Washington veteran, and was not without the kind of irony frequently seen in a city where fortunes tend to ebb and flow. Hannibal Hamlin, the man Johnson had defeated to win the vice-president nomination in 1864, later bitterly attacking Johnson once he became president, had also just secured a surprising return to prominence, winning election to the Senate from Maine.

Now, Hamlin warmly greeted the former president. Johnson additionally appeared startled when spectators in the gallery broke out in cheers upon seeing him. A Senate page, meanwhile, quietly placed a bouquet of flowers on Johnson's desk, situated in the back row of the chamber.

At some point, Johnson caught sight of an uncomfortable Oliver Morton, the Indiana Republican Senator who had voted in favor of his removal from office in 1868 and was now wondering if he should approach the ex-president. Johnson took the initiative and shook Morton's hand. "There are not many men who could have done that," an impressed Morton later remarked. [5]

"He seemed to feel the solemnity of the occasion as he stood there, a member of the Senate, in the presence of some men, now his fellow Senators, who seven years ago tried to impeach him," observed a reporter. In fact, of the 35 Senators who had voted to convict Johnson in 1868, thirteen remained in the Senate, not counting Vice-President Henry Wilson, who had also voted to convict Johnson and was now serving as President of the Senate.

Upon being sworn in, Johnson took his seat, only to be suddenly surrounded by members of both parties who gathered to shake his hand and offer their congratulations. It was an entirely pleasing feeling as Johnson looked around the handsome stately marble chamber and realized that here was where he had to be, not necessarily in the Senate, but back in Washington, at the center of things.

In the days to come, Johnson tried to unobtrusively take on his Senatorial duties, going through his mail, responding to constituents, following debates on the floor. But mostly he set to work doing research for what everyone assumed would soon prove to be a major address, the kind of classic Johnson effort steeped in legal precedent and literary allusions that would enthrall listeners and take hours to deliver.

He was soon seen leafing through a stack of books ordered from the Library of Congress, making copious notes on so many scraps of paper in his sometimes shaky handwriting.

Johnson had actually known before he even arrived in Washington what the subject of his first speech would be. For weeks and even months he had been amazed by President Grant's response to the ongoing specter of racial violence in New Orleans. A "state of anarchy," as described by Grant biographer Ron Chernow, existed in the South's largest city, seeing thousands of whites, many members of the paramilitary Ku Klux Klan-spirited White League, brutalizing black citizens, particularly those daring to become politically involved. [6]

"The streets of the city were stained with blood," Grant declared in September of 1874 as he issued a proclamation leading to the sending to New Orleans of some 5,000 federal troops. [7]

In January, a determined Grant in a special message to Congress defended the action. "I have deplored the necessity which seemed to make it my duty under the Constitution and laws to direct such interference," the President admitted.

But, not for the first time revealing a steely resolve, Grant continued: "To the extent that Congress has conferred power upon me to prevent it, neither Ku-Klux-Klan, White Leagues, nor any association using arms and violence to execute their unlawful purposes, can be permitted in that way to govern any part of this country." [8]

To Johnson, reading these remarks in the newspapers while he was still in Tennessee, this was all infernal nonsense. Now, returned to prominence in Washington, Johnson sought to provide a clarion refutation of everything Grant had done in New Orleans, a narrative undoubtedly fired by his continuing contempt for the man.

On the early afternoon of March 22, Johnson rose before a hushed Senate to deliver a more than 10,000-word speech that would take more than two and a half hours to deliver.

Thousands of spectators had packed themselves into the halls of the Capitol and the Senate galleries, including ex-slave and abolitionist leader Frederick Douglass and feminist attorney Phoebe Couzins, hoping to hear an address that had been anticipated for days in the press.

Not since his lengthy, comprehensive lacerations of Jefferson Davis and the secession movement, would Johnson deliver an address as all-encompassing and eviscerating, standing next to a desktop loaded with books, a glass of water, and a half a lemon. The lemon, as any great 19th century orator knew, to be sucked on in order to keep his throat lubricated.

He began his speech on a parliamentary note, announcing that he was only rising in response to an earlier resolution proposed by New Jersey Senator Frederick Frelinghuysen approving Grant's actions in New Orleans.

Johnson contended that such a resolution was offensive because Grant had sent troops to New Orleans without first obtaining Congressional approval. To commend the President for what he had done, said Johnson, was tantamount to "reversing the policy and principles on which the Legislature has acted for a number of years."

He then launched into a vigorous discussion regarding events in both New Orleans and Louisiana, events he, not wrongly, likened to a struggle between warring and frequently violent local and state factions in Tennessee in 1866. How strange it was, thought Johnson, that Grant at that time had issued an order stating that it was "the duty of the United States," not to "interfere in any way in the controversy between the political authorities of the State."

This proved, said Johnson, that Grant, at least in 1866, had been "familiar with and understood what was the construction of the government in cases of this kind, as to the interference of the military with the civil power."

"We see the question is not a new one to him," Johnson continued with a slight hint of sarcasm, "and that he has not acted without proper and thorough information upon the subject."

Johnson then sought to explain the thinking of Louisiana residents, although he surely was confining his remarks to the white residents of the state, noting "I know the determination of that people. Their great object is to be restored back into the Union upon equal footing with all the other states, and have a fair participation in the legislation of the country."

This he understood. What he could not wrap his brain around, Johnson continued, was "those who are acting behind the curtain and who are aspiring to retain power."

These were the people, said Johnson in a clear reference to a current movement to nominate Grant for another term of office, who "would inaugurate a system of terrorism, and in the midst of the excitement, in the midst of the war cry, triumphantly ride into the Presidency for a third presidential term, and when that is done, farewell to the liberties of the country."

This last comment elicited a loud round of applause from the gallery, prompting Michigan's Thomas Ferry, the Senate president pro tempore, to gavel for order.

It was clear from that response that Johnson had the galleries with him, regular people who were perhaps equally troubled by Grant's New Orleans actions, concerned about the prospects for an unprecedented presidential third term, or just plain enjoying this latest missive in the continuing Johnson/Grant war.

Johnson then engaged in a long aside regarding the sanctity of the two-term tradition, before returning to his central theme: the virtual invasion of a sovereign entity, as Johnson saw matters in New Orleans, by the federal government.

He castigated the federal presence there was an "act of usurpation and an act of tyranny."

"Where does this power come from?" Johnson, in full outrage, demanded. "And I might ask, where would it go?"

"It is time that the people had begun to consider and weigh well these things," Johnson plodded on.

A president deciding to send in federal troops to one of the states of the Union, a president taking that action without the consent of Congress, a president actively contemplating a third term, suggested Johnson, were all pieces of the same thing.

"We have got a stratocracy," continued Johnson. "We have not got a democracy, and we have not got a republican form of government."

"How far off is empire?" Johnson wondered. "How far off is military despotism? I warn the people of my native country and of my native state of the danger ahead."

Not for the first time equating the excesses of the Confederates under Jefferson Davis with the Radical Republicans under Grant, Johnson reminded his audience that he had once warned against a "contest that would result in the shedding of blood and the sacrifice of property."

Now he warned one and all of a "total disregard of the Constitution of the United States."

This may have been a stretch for many. Grant was no Jefferson Davis, and the federal incursion into New Orleans could in no way be equal to the dozen states of the South 14 years earlier who had formed their own confederacy and declared war on the United States.

But such actions then and now, insisted Johnson, were nothing more or less than variations on a theme: the encroachment of the Constitution. It was an encroachment he would do all in his power to resist, while at the same time calling the "attention of the country to it as well as I can."

Nearing the end of his remarks, Johnson invited his listeners to think about the allegorical figure comprising the massive bronze Statute of Freedom crowning the dome of the U.S. Capitol, a statue only finally in put in place in late 1863 after years of planning and design.

Incorrectly describing the statue as the "Goddess of Liberty," Johnson proclaimed that a failure to preserve and defend the Constitution would see the Goddess "driven from this land staggering over fields of blood and carnage to witness the loss of a representative government."

As was often the case with Johnson's metaphoric flights of fancy, the Goddess reference made no sense at all. If she was driven from the land, how could she still be on hand to "witness the loss of representative government"?

In using the statue as a point of reference, Johnson may have also forgotten that it was Jefferson Davis who, as Secretary of War in 1856, had given the final approval to the impressive statue's original design.

Nevertheless, Johnson's point was made: the republic was in danger, and at risk of losing its freedom that the Statue of Freedom, or the Goddess or Liberty, or whatever one wanted to call it, represented.

Challenging his fellow senators, as well as the country at large, to soundly confront what he regarded as the usurpations of the Grant administration, Johnson at last commanded: "Let us lay aside our party feelings; let us lay aside our personalities, and come up to the Constitution of our country and lay it upon an altar and all stand around resolved that the Constitution shall be preserved." [9]

Returning to his seat, Johnson was hailed with the applause of his fellow senators and cheers from the galleries that this time went unstilled by the President pro tempore.

Johnson was followed in his remarks by Missouri Senator Lewis Bogy, who endorsed his sentiments, modestly remarking: "I fully realize the embarrassed position in which I am placed in speaking immediately after the distinguished and able Senator from Tennessee. I am very well aware that the large crowd now occupying the galleries did not come to listen to me." [10]

The special session of the 44th Congress concluded business two days after Johnson's speech on March 24; with the first full session set to convene on December 6.

As he prepared to return to Greeneville, Johnson continued to hear congratulations from friends and supporters for his exhaustive March 22 address.

Editorial response to Johnson's speech, meanwhile, proved overwhelmingly positive, although the always-critical *Chicago Tribune* described the address as a "bitter, cowardly attack upon the Chief Executive of the Nation." [11]

Far more typical was the reaction of the *New York Herald*, which contended that Johnson had "honestly uttered unwelcome truths and warned the nation of danger it will be wise to heed." Said the *San Francisco Examiner*: "Without any trace of vindictiveness or personal malice, it administers to Grant a most merciless castigation." [12]

More succinctly, the *Brooklyn Daily Eagle* said of the speech and Johnson: "The country sides with him." [13]

It was a thought spiriting the hopes of those who genuinely wanted to see Johnson run for president again. From Shelbyville, Tennessee, supporter Clement Moody asked Johnson for a copy of the speech, and then suggested it might be well for the ex-president to publish the entirety of his remarks in pamphlet form.

"It may be a very important campaign document in '76," Moody helpfully suggested. [14]

CHAPTER TWELVE

THE PEOPLE'S FRIEND

Johnson remained in Washington for several more weeks after the conclusion of the special session, attending to financial matters with the First National Bank. Daughter Martha had earlier updated him on the latest downturn in his wife's health, noting not only the frail condition of Mrs. Johnson, but her feelings of depression.

Perhaps revealing his own new sense of calm, Johnson told Martha: "Tell your mother she must be cheerful and to think and feel for the best. We are all in the hands of destiny and I have long since bowed to my fate, and the rest of you must do the same." [1]

He returned to Greeneville by the end of April, where he caught up with old friends and upbraided a business associate for having allowed an older black woman named Phoebe Wheelock to be evicted from property that he owned.

"Understanding that it was your intention and desire that she would be provided for, I caused her to be moved into one of my houses until some provision was made for her," a displeased Johnson continued. [2]

With a little more time to call his own, Johnson mulled bringing a libel suit against the *New Orleans Times* for a story claiming that he had bribed lawmakers in Tennessee to secure his Senate victory in January. The report was outrageous not just because it was untrue, but also because Johnson had evicted from his hotel room in Nashville an enthusiast who suggested the use of a slush fund for just that purpose. There were many things in his career, he sometimes admitted, that he would change if he could. But one that would remain forever the same was that he had won every election to office honestly and wasn't going to change now.

On June 16, John Roush, a Union Army veteran living in Memphis, reported to the former president of a journey he had recently taken to Indiana during which he had spoken to several civic groups on political affairs. "I mentioned your name as the workingman's friend on several occasions, and it was approved on all sides," exclaimed Roush, who added that he was gratified to observe that Johnson was at last "approved by the populace at large." [3]

Johnson fell into a comfortable schedule once returned to Greeneville, the angst and boredom that had previously been his constant companion now gone, undoubtedly due to a realization that since his Senate election victory his hometown was no longer his destiny, but a pleasant place to rest before traveling back to the hubbub of Washington.

Yet, for all of his new-found enjoyment of Greeneville, Johnson was not entirely at ease during the early summer weeks. He complained to friends of feeling tired and was bothered, in a way he had never been before, by the heat. It seemed like the hottest summer in memory. One day watching a young man walking briskly down one of the town's streets wearing a simple white linen coat, Johnson actually contemplated discarding the heavy black cloth coat, one of many that had always been a daily part of his attire, in favor of something light and airy.

He woke up early on most mornings, did a brief survey of his property, and then spent much of the rest of the day reading and catching up on his correspondence. Gideon Welles had recently sent him a copy of his just-published work, *Lincoln and Seward,* which downplayed the role that the former Secretary of State had played in the Lincoln administration. It was a book that Johnson, whose respect for both Seward and Welles was manifest, gave every appearance of enjoying.

When not at home, Johnson casually talked with townspeople on the street and in public squares, while dropping in on the local Masonic Lodge for its bi-monthly get-togethers.

Finally, in late July, Johnson determined to make a quick 40-mile trip to the east and the farm of daughter Mary Stover Brown near Elizabethon, where his wife had relocated several weeks earlier.

Family members were only too happy for Johnson to spend time with them, but they also worried about a possible campaign trip Johnson was contemplating to several northern states, including Ohio, which was holding state elections in the fall that would result in the victory of future Republican president Rutherford Hayes, running for governor.

Johnson's only conceivable reason for inserting himself into the Ohio contest was a desire to keep intact a Democratic network of public officials and volunteers across the country that might be called upon to work in his behalf in the upcoming 1876 presidential race.

Knowing him better than perhaps anyone else, his daughters in particular noted that their father's usual energy and verve seemed depleted, a condition they chalked up to the excitement of his Senate win and triumphant return to Washington.

"I will be at Carter's Depot on Wednesday morning," Johnson told Mary on July 26, asking for her to arrange for a carriage to pick him up once he arrived. [4]

On the train ride to the depot, Johnson, always interested in the lives of virtually everyone he met, fell into a conversation with several men sitting near him, before providing his fascinated fellow travelers with an uneven narrative of his extraordinary career.

Repeatedly, Johnson claimed, he had pondered the decisions he made in the White House, wondering if the "calm and great historians will say one hundred years from now 'He pursued the right course.'"

Soon Johnson was entertaining his companions with stories of battles long since concluded and men long since gone.

As the late morning summer sun beat down on the train, Johnson, for no reason, summoned up the ghost of Edwin Stanton, describing him, not incorrectly, as a "very bitter, uncompromising, and self-assertive man." [5]

With the pleasant views of trees and hills whizzing past the train's windows, Johnson brought up the controversy of Mary Surratt's execution. But instead of blaming Joseph Holt for withholding information regarding a plea for her clemency, which was the direction that conversations of this nature usually took, Johnson now blamed Stanton for the whole tragedy, contending that the Secretary of War should have never pursued an indictment of Mrs. Surratt in the first place.

As with his description of Stanton, Johnson's criticism of Surratt's prosecution was anything but inaccurate.

Johnson detrained in Elizabethton, eventually climbing into the carriage that would take him to his daughter's farm. There, he enjoyed a mid-day meal with Mary and several grandchildren, catching up on family news in the process. Before long, he mounted the stairs to the house's second floor and the room he would be sleeping in, sitting briefly on an armchair before all of a sudden leaning forward and falling to the wooden floor before him.

Hearing the noise, family members rushed to his assistance, noting that Johnson appeared disoriented, with the left side of his body suddenly paralyzed. He was urged to bed, but resisted calls that a doctor be called.

Not until two days later, after Martha Patterson arrived with two physicians who had long treated the Johnson family, was the former president examined. Although he had intermittingly talked since his fall, Johnson now seemed incapable of speech, and soon was unable to recognize those around him.

He died at 2:30 on Saturday morning, July 31.

News of his death flashed across the country for the next several days, while members of the local Masonic Lodge took charge of Johnson's funeral arrangements once the train bearing the former president's body returned to Greeneville. The town's leaders and residents went all out for Greeneville's most famous citizen, decorating houses and buildings in black cloth and American flags in his memory.

In Washington, Assistant Secretary of State John Cadwallader sent a note to President Grant informing him of Johnson's passing and noting that upon the deaths of Franklin Pierce in 1869 and Millard Fillmore in 1874, "an executive order was issued draping [the] executive mansion & departments in mourning and suspending public business on the day of the funeral." [6]

Several hours later the White House released an official order over Grant's signature noting "It becomes the painful duty of the President to announce to the people of the United States, the death of Andrew Johnson, the last survivor of his honored predecessors, which occurred in Carter County, East Tennessee, at an early hour this morning."

The order continued: "The solemnity of the occasion which called him to the Presidency, with the varied nature and length of his public service, will cause him to be long remembered, and occasion mourning for the death of a distinguished public servant." [7]

The order was written by a White House staffer and approved by the President, but even so was more respectful than anything Johnson would have approved had their positions been reversed.

While Masonic officials and friends worked to plan a funeral that would attract thousands of visitors, including dozens of reporters, from across the country, John R. Brown, a long-time Greeneville merchant given the honorific title of chairman of the funeral arrangements, pondered Johnson's legacy, observing that even his greatest foes would have to admit that, at the very least, Johnson was "a man that could not be bribed." [8]

In one day discussing his funeral arrangements with his Masonic friends, Johnson had asked for two things: He wanted his body to be wrapped in a large American flag, and a copy of the Constitution—the document that was his Bible—placed beneath his head.

A massively large funeral with more than 5,000 people in attendance was officially held on Tuesday, August 3, as Johnson's casket arrived in a hearse led by four horses to Signal Hill, a 23-acre site roughly one mile to the south of Greeneville offering a sweeping view of the tree-lined landscape.

With virtually all of Johnson's extended family in attendance, and a host of local and state officials quietly watching, Johnson's casket was lowered into a zinc and cement-coated grave while a male choir rendered a dirge.

Tennessee Governor James Porter, bowing his head at the gravesite, would later perceptively observe that Johnson's life was "full of encouragement, illustrating that neither humble origin, poverty, or want of sound influences in early life present insuperable barriers to the triumph of an indomitable will and free spirit." [9]

As the somber ceremony neared its conclusion, a townswoman gently placed a bouquet of roses and white lilies on the dirt-covered grave, tied together with a satin ribbon partially bearing the words: "The People's Friend." [10]

FOOTNOTES

Chapter One Footnotes

[1] "Impeachment," *New York Herald,* 26 February 1868, p. 5; "Society in Washington," *Daily National Intelligencer,* 25 February 1868, p. 2; "The National Crisis," *New York Tribune,* 25 February 1868, p. 1.

[2] "Society in Washington," *Daily National Intelligencer,* 25 February 1868, p. 2.

[3] "Impeachment," *New York Herald,* 26 February 1868, p.5.

[4] *Congressional Globe—Senate 40th Congress, 2nd Session,* 1389-93.

[5] Ibid., 1390, 1396.

[6] Hans L. Trefousse, *Andrew Johnson—A Biography* (Newtown: American Political Biography Press, 2009), 191-92; Gene Smith, *High Crimes & Misdemeanors—The Impeachment and Trial of Andrew Johnson* (New York: McGraw Hill Book Company, 1976), 64.

[7] "The Inauguration," *Louisville Daily Courier,* 11 March 1865, p. 1; William E. Gienapp and Erica L. Gienapp, *The Civil War Diary of Gideon Welles, Lincoln's Secretary of the Navy* (Urbana: Knox College Lincoln Studies Center, 2014), 597-98.

[8] John Niven, *The Salmon P. Chase Papers, Volume 5, Correspondence, 1865-1873* (Kent: Kent State University Press, 1998), 13-15.

[9] *Congressional Globe,* 1400.

[10] Ibid., 1386.

[11] Brenda Wineapple, *The Impeachers—The Trial of Andrew Johnson and the Dream of a Just Nation* (New York: Random House, 2019), 262-63.

[12] "The President as an Apostate," *New York Tribune,* 24 February 1868, p.4.

[13] As an illustration of the sort of passions Johnson's struggles aroused, a small group of Navy veterans in Boston had signed a letter to the President on February 2 suggesting that he "seize and imprison all the radical members of the present Congress for disloyalty to the Union and trying to trample on the constitution of the U.S." O.W. Gardner to Andrew Johnson, 24 February 1868; William Lordan, Alexander Smith, Jon White, and Thomas Maxwell to Andrew Johnson, 21 February 1868; both letters in Andrew Johnson Papers, Reel 31.

[14] James McLaughlin to Andrew Johnson, 24 February 1868, Andrew Johnson Papers, Reel 31.

[15] Joseph Leigh to Andrew Johnson, 24 February 1868, Andrew Johnson Papers, Reel 31.

[16] James Hammond to Andrew Johnson, 25 February 1868, Andrew Johnson Papers, Reel 31.

[17] David O. Stewart, *Impeached—The Trial of President Johnson and the Fight for Lincoln's Legacy* (New York: Simon & Schuster, 2009), 140-41.

[18] *Congressional Globe,* 1388.

[19] "State Dinner at the Executive Mansion," *Washington Evening Star,* 22 February 1868, p. 1; "The President's State Dinner," *New York Herald,* 22 February 1868; p. 5; Wineapple, *The Impeachers,* 252.

[20] Trefousse, *Andrew Johnson,* 315.

21 "Impeachment," *New York Herald*, 26 February 1868, p. 5.

22 "Andrew Johnson," *Chicago Tribune*, 2 August 1868, p. 1.

23 John J. Craven, *Private Life of Jefferson Davis* (New York: Carleton Publisher, 1866), 298-302.

24 John Y. Simon, *The Papers of Ulysses S. Grant—Volume 16: 1866* (Carbondale: Southern Illinois University Press, 1988), 394-95.

25 M. A. DeWolfe Howe, *Home Letters of General Sherman* (New York: Charles Scribner's Sons, 1909), 373.

26 William H. Crook, *Through Five Administrations—Reminiscences of Colonel William H. Cook* (New York: Harper & Brothers, 1910), 83-84.

27 Gideon Welles, *Diary of Gideon Welles, Volume III, January 1, 1867-June 6, 1868* (Boston: Houghton Mifflin Company, 1911), 49.

20 "President Andrew Johnson," *Indianapolis Star*, 12 May 1865, p. 2. Reprint of the original *St. Louis Republican* article.

29 George Dolby, *Charles Dickens As I Knew Him—The Story of the Reading Tours in Great Britain and America* (London: T. Fisher Unwin, 1885), 236-37.

30 Beverly Wilson Palmer, *The Selected Letters of Charles Sumner, Volume Two* (Boston: Northeastern University Press, 1990), 380-81.

31 Milton Meltzer, *Lydia Maria Child—Selected Letters, 1817-1880* (Amherst: University of Massachusetts Press, 1982), 463-64.

32 "Who is Responsible?" *Chicago Tribune*, 2 September 1866, p. 2.

Chapter Two Footnotes

[1]   Albert Castel, *The Presidency of Andrew Johnson* (Lawrence: University Press of Kansas, 1979), 2.

[2]   Paul H. Bergeron, *Papers of Andrew Johnson, Volume 12, February-August 1867* (Knoxville: University of Tennessee Press, 1995), 287, 301-04; "The President," *Philadelphia Inquirer,* 5 June 1867, p. 1.

[3]   Leroy P. Graf and Ralph W. Haskins, *Papers of Andrew Johnson, Volume 1, 1822-1851* (Knoxville: University of Tennessee Press, 1967), xii.

[4]   Ibid., 3-4.

[5]   According to author John H. Dewitt, Jr., Johnson received formal lessons from Wolstenholme several times a week during the evening. Other Johnson scholars have suggested that at least two other visitors regularly read aloud in Selby's shop and may have also influenced him. John H. DeWitt, Jr., "Andrew Johnson and the Hermit," *Tennessee Historical Quarterly,* Volume XXVII, Spring-Winter 1968, 60-61; Robert W. Winston, *Andrew Johnson—Plebian and Patriot* (New York: Henry Hold and Company, 1928), 6, 9-10; Hans L. Trefoussee, *Andrew Johnson—A Biography* (Newton: American Political Biography Press, 2009), 384.

[6]   Graf and Haskins, *Papers of Andrew Johnson, Volume 1,* 3-4.

[7]   Castel, *Presidency of Andrew Johnson,* 3.

[8]   Graf and Haskins, *Papers of Andrew Johnson, Volume 1,* 28-29.

[9]   Leroy P. Graf and Ralph W. Haskins, *Papers of Andrew Johnson, Volume 3, 1858-1860)* (Knoxville, University of Tennessee Press, 1972), 404-05; Leroy P. Graf and Ralph W. Haskins, *Papers of Andrew Johnson, Volume 5, 1861-1862* (Knoxville: University of Tennessee Press, 1979), 296-99.

[10] Graf and Haskins, *Papers of Andrew Johnson, Volume 1,* 36-58.

[11] Ibid., 152-54.

[12] Ibid., 187-207.

[13] Ibid., 331-33.

[14] Ibid., 424-27.

[15] Trefousse, *Andrew Johnson—A Biography,* 65-66.

[16] Earl L. McKitrick, *Andrew Johnson: A Profile* (New York, Hill and Wang, 1969), 42-53.

[17] Andrew Johnson to Blackston McDannel, 10 January 1847, Andrew Johnson Papers, Reel 1.

[18] Dr. Sam Arnold's Great Union Pills," *Tennessean,* 20 October 1851, p. 2, "Dr. Arnold's Union Pills," *Nashville Union and American,* 26 April 1853, p.4.

[19] Leroy P. Graf and Ralph W. Haskins, *Papers of Andrew Johnson, Volume 2, 1852-1857* (Knoxville: University of Tennessee Press, 1970), 392-92.

[20] Andrew Johnson to Blackston McDannel, 4 November 1848, Papers of Andrew Johnson, Reel 1; "Amusements," *Baltimore Sun,* 9 November 1848, p. 3; Thomas Bogar, *American Presidents Attend the Theater—The Playgoing Experiences of Each Chief Executive* (Jefferson: McFarland & Company, 2006), 79.

[21] Andrew Johnson to Blackston McDannel, 4 November 1848, Papers of Andrew Johnson, Reel 1.

[22] Roy P. Basler, *Collected Works of Abraham Lincoln, Volume II* (New Brunswick: Rutgers University Press, 1953), 217-18.

23 Graf and Haskins, *Papers of Andrew Johnson, Volume 1*, 590-91.

24 Ibid., 629-31.

25 Ibid.

26 Graf and Haskins, *Papers of Andrew Johnson, Volume 3, 1858-1860*, xxi.

27 Graf and Haskins, *Papers of Andrew Johnson, Volume 2, 1852-1857*, 86-87, 100-04.

28 Graf and Haskins, *Papers of Andrew Johnson, Volume 3, 1858-1860*, xv; Trefousse, *Andew Johnson--A Biogaphy*, 84-86.

29 Graf and Haskins, *Papers of Andrew Johnson, Volume 2, 1852-1857*, 172-84; "Inaugural Address of Andrew Johnson," *Nashville Union & American*, 18 October 1853, p. 2.

30 Graf and Haskins, *Papers of Andrew Johnson, Volume 2, 1852-1857*, 261.

31 Ibid., 387-90, 393-94.

32 Ibid., 393-94.

33 Ibid., 457-58; "Prelude to the Presidency: The Election of Andrew Johnson to the Senate," *Tennessee Historical Quarterly*, Volume XXVI, Spring-Winter, 1967, 150-51.

34 Graf and Haskins, *Papers of Andrew Johnson, Volume 3, 1858-1860*, 6-8.

35 "The Homestead Bill," *New York Herald*, 26 June 1860, p.12.

[36] "Andrew Johnson," *Lincoln Journal,* 1 March 1860, p.4; "The Charleston Convention," *New York Herald,* 24 January 1860, p.6; "Andrew Johnson," *Nashville Union and American,* 28 January 1860, p.2.

[37] "Washington News and Gossip," *Washington Evening Star,* 14 March 1860, p. 2.

[38] Graf and Haskins, *Papers of Andrew Johnson, Volume 3, 1858-1860),* 517-20; Henry Wise to Andrew Johnson, 13 February 1860, and Anthony Van Eyck to Andrew Johnson, 20 February 1860, both Andrew Johnson Papers, Reel 39.

[39] Graf and Haskins, *Papers of Andrew Johnson, Volume 3, 1858-1860,* 652-53.

[40] The division of the Democrat party may have been one of the few times in which Johnson and Jefferson Davis saw things the same way. After Stephen Douglas refused to enter into a fusion ticket with John Breckinridge, Davis, echoing, Johnson's election pessimism, remarked "It must be that we have been doomed to destruction." Jefferson Davis to Franklin Pierce, 23 November 1860, Franklin Pierce Papers, Reel 2; Graf and Haskins, *Papers of Andrew Johnson, Volume 3, 1858-1860,* 656-58.

[41] "Johnson and Nicholson at Memphis," *Republican Banner,* 20 October 1860, p. 2.

[42] Philip S. Klein, *James Buchanan* (Newtown: American Political Biography Press, 2010), 352.

[43] Graf and Haskins, *Papers of Andrew Johnson, Volume 3, 1858-1860,* 623-24.

[44] *Congressional Globe, 36th Congress, 2nd Session,* 117-20, 134-43; "From Washington," *Richmond Dispatch,* 27 December 1860, p.1.

[45] "Another Sensation," *Washington Evening Star,* 20 December 1860, p. 2; "Light Breaking Ahead," *Wheeling Intelligencer,* 22 December 1860, p. 3.

[46] "Andrew Johnson's Speech," *Chicago Tribune,* 24 December 1860, p.2.

[47] "The Crisis of the Union," *New York Times,* 12 December 1860, p.1; Leroy P. Graf, "Andrew Johnson and the Coming of the War," *Tennessee Historical Quarterly,* Volume XIX, March-December 1860, 208-21.

[48] Joshua Bell to Andrew Johnson, 20 December 1860, Papers of Andrew Johnson, Reel 2.

[49] William Crook to Andrew Johnson, 20 December 1860, Papers of Andrew Johnson, Reel 2.

[50] T.W. Linder to Andrew Johnson, 20 December 1860, Papers of Andrew Johnson, Reel 1.

[51] "A Southern Man for Coercion," *Charleston Courier,* 25 December 1860, p. 1.

[52] "Mr. Andrew Johnson's Bid for Black Republican Favor," *Louisville Daily Courier,* 25 December 1860, p.2.

[53] Hiram Smith to Andrew Johnson, 26 December 1860, Papers of Andrew Johnson, Reel 1.

[54] Leroy P. Graf and Ralph W. Haskins, *Papers of Andrew Johnson, Volume 4, 1860-1861* (Knoxville: University of Tennessee Press, 1976), 196.

[55] Blackston McDannel to Andrew Johnson, 29 December 1860, Papers of Andrew Johnson, Reel 1.

[56] "The Coahoma Citizen," *Daily Evening Citizen,* 15 January 1861, p. 2.

[57] Lynda Laswell Crist, *Papers of Jefferson Davis, Volume 7, 1861* (Baton Rouge: Louisiana State University Press, 1992), 3-6; Herman Cox to Andrew Johnson, 11 February 1861, Papers of Andrew Johnson, Reel 1.

[58] Felicity Allen, *Jefferson Davis—Unconquerable Heart* (Columbia: University of Missouri Press, 1999), 98-99.

[59] Graf and Haskins, *Papers of Andrew Johnson, Volume 4, 1860-1861*, 206-61.

[60] "Visiting Delegations," *Washington Evening Star*, 5 March 1861, p. 3.

[61] "A Southern Tour," *New Orleans Daily Crescent*, 19 March 1861, p. 1.

Chapter Three Footnotes

[1] Leroy P. Graf and Ralph W. Haskins, *Papers of Andrew Johnson, Volume 4, 1860-1861* (Knoxville: University of Tennessee Press, 1976), 472.

[2] Kinson McVay to Andrew Johnson, 15 January 1862, Andrew Johnson Papers, Reel 4.

[3] Hans L. Trefousse, *Andrew Johnson—A Biography* (Newtown: American Political Biography Press, 2009), 140; Lately Thomas, *The First President Johnson—The Three Lives of the Seventeenth President of the United States of America* (New York: William Morrow & Company, 1968), 190-92; "Andrew Johnson Returned," *Tennessean*, 24 April 1861, p.3; "Andrew Johnson in Lynchburg," *Alexandria Gazette*, 23 April 1861, p. 3; "The Lynchburg Editorial Tragedy," *Nashville Union and American*, 26 July 1860, p.2.

[4] Graf and Haskins, *Papers of Andrew Johnson, Volume 4, 1860-1861*, 473-74.

[5]   Ibid., Oliver P. Temple, *East Tennessee and the Civil War* (Freeport: Books for Libraries Press, 1971), 182-86.

[6]   Graf and Haskins, *Papers of Andrew Johnson, Volume 4, 1860-1861,* 102-03.

[7]   Temple, *East Tennessee and the Civil War,* 425.

[8]   Leroy P. Graf and Ralph W. Haskins, *Papers of Andrew Johnson, Volume 5, 1861-1862* (Knoxville: University of Tennessee Press, 1979), 13-29.

[9]   Graf and Haskins, *Papers of Andrew Johnson, Volume 4, 1860-1861,* 492-98.

[10]   Ibid., 505-07; "Senator Johnson's Speech," *Weekly Times,* 4 July 1861, p. 1.

[11]   Lynda Lasswell Crist, *Papers of Jefferson Davis, Volume 7, 1861* (Baton Rouge: Louisiana State University Press, 1991), 217-19; *War of the Rebellion—Series I, Volume LII, Part II* (Washington: Government Printing Office, 1898), 115-16; John Niven, *Salmon P. Chase Papers, Volume 3, Correspondence, 1858-March 1863* (Kent: Kent State University Press, 1996), 78-79.

[12]   Crist, *Papers of Jefferson Davis, Volume 7, 1861,* 217-18.

[13]   Graf and Haskins, *Papers of Andrew Johnson, Volume 4, 1860-1861,* 546.

[14]   Ibid., 606-49.

[15]   "Mr. Johnson's Speech," *Chicago Tribune,* 31 July 1861, p.1; "Voice of a True Democrat," *New York Tribune,* 12 August 1861, p. 6.

[16]   Graf and Haskins, *Papers of Andrew Johnson, Volume 4, 1860-1861,* 650.

[17] Ibid., 669-70.

[18] Ibid., 700-05; Noel C. Fisher, *War at Every Door—Partisan Politics and Guerilla Violence in East Tennessee, 1860-1869* (Chapel Hill: University of North Carolina Pres, 1997), 48-49.

[19] Graf and Haskins, *Papers of Andrew Johnson, Volume 4, 1860-1861,* 700-05.

[20] Bruce Catton, *Terrible Swift Sword* (New York, Doubleday & Company, 1963), 60-66.

[21] Crist, *Papers of Jefferson Davis, Volume 7, 1861,* 406, 410, 411, 437, 454; Fisher, *War At Every Door,* 57-58.

[22] Graf and Haskins, *Papers of Andrew Johnson, Volume 5, 1861-1862,* 40-43.

[23] Ibid., 48-50.

[24] *War of the Rebellion—Series I, Volume IV* (Washington, Government Printing Office, 1882), 432-43.

[25] Ibid., 343.

[26] Ibid., 347-48.

[27] Ibid.

[28] Stephen D. Engle, *Don Carlos Buell—Most Promising of All* (Chapel Hill: University of North Carolina Press, 1999), 49.

[29] *War of the Rebellion—Series I, Volume IV,* 342.

[30] *War of the Rebellion—Series I, Volume VII* (Washington: Government Printing Office, 1882), 443-44.

[31] Graf and Haskins, *Papers of Andrew Johnson, Volume 5, 1861-1862*, 43-44.

[32] Ibid.

[33] Ibid., 46.

[34] *War of the Rebellion—Series I, Volume VII*, 520-21.

[35] Roy P. Bassler, *Collected Works of Abraham Lincoln, Volume 5* (New Brunswick: Rutgers University Press, 1953), 90.

[36] *War of the Rebellion—Series I, Volume VII*, 520-31.

[37] *Collected Works of Abraham Lincoln, Volume 5*, 91.

[38] T. Harry Williams, "Andrew Johnson as a Member of the Joint Committee on the Conduct of the War," *East Tennessee Historical Society Publications*, December 1940, 70-83; Bruce Tap, *Over Lincoln's Shoulder—The Committee on the Conduct of the War* (Lawrence: University Press of Kansas, 1998), 24, 30, 48, 54.

[39] Williams, "Andrew Johnson as a Member of the Joint Committee on the Conduct of the War," 70-83.

[40] In his correspondence with Davis, Bright had sought to introduce a man named Thomas Lincoln, a Confederate sympathizer who had developed an new kind of firearm he thought might prove beneficial to the Confederates. Bright was ultimately expelled by the Senate on a 32 to 14 vote. Graf and Haskins, *Papers of Andrew Johnson, Volume 5, 1861-1861*, 114-45.

[41] Ibid., 143.

[42] John Y. Simon, *Papers of Ulysses S. Grant, Volume 4: January 8-March 31, 1862* (Carbondale: Southern Illinois University Press, 1972), 218-19.

[43] Ron Chernow, *Grant* (New York: Penguin Press, 2017), 181-86; Ronald C. White, *American Ulysses—A Life of Ulysses S. Grant* (New York: Random House, 2016), 197-202; "Letter from Donelson," *Chicago Tribune,* 19 February 1862, p.1; "The Great Victory," *New York Times,* 19 February 1862, p.1.

[44] Lynda Lasswell Crist, *Papers of Jefferson Davis, Volume 8, 1862* (Baton Rouge: Louisiana State University Press, 1995), 92-95.

[45] Graf and Haskins, *Papers of Andrew Johnson, Volume 5, 1861-1862,* 177-78.

[46] Thomas, *The First President Johnson,* 227.

Chapter Four Footnotes

[1] Paul H. Bergeron, *Andrew Johnson's Civil War and Reconstruction* (Knoxville: University of Tennessee Press, 2011), 14.

[2] Ibid.

[3] "Our Military Budget," *Washington Evening Star,* 4 March 1862, p.2; "The War for the Union," *New York Tribune,* 5 March 1862, p. 5.

[4] "The Condition of Affairs in East Tennessee," *Charleston Mercury,* 4 April 1862, p.1.

[5] *War of the Rebellion—A Compilation of the Officials Records of the Union and Confederate Armies, Series I—Volume 10, Part II* (Washington: Government Printing Office, 1884), 25.

[6] Leroy P. Graf and Ralph W. Haskin, *The Papers of Andrew Johnson Volume 5, 1861-1862* (Knoxville: University of Tennessee Press, 1979), 181-2, 201.

[7] Ibid., 201.

[8] Ibid., 202-04.

[9] William C. Harris, *With Charity for All—Lincoln and the Restoration of the Union* (Lexington: University Press of Kentucky, 1997), 44.

[10] Graf and Haskins, *Papers of Andrew Johnson, Volume 5*, 209-12; "Andrew Johnson's Appeal to the People of Tennessee," *Louisville Courier*, 24 March 1862, p.2.

[11] Graf and Haskins, *Papers of Andrew Johnson, Volume 5*, 208-09; Harris, *With Charity for All*, 45; "Affairs in Nashville," *New York Times*, 16 March 1862, p. 8; "Bank of Tennessee," *Louisville Courier-Journal*, 1 April 1862, p.4; "Bank of Tennessee," *Memphis Daily Avalanche*, 26 April 1862, p. 2.

[12] Graf and Haskins, *Papers of Andrew Johnson, Volume 5*, 213.

[13] Ibid.

[14] Ibid., 220.

[15] Graf and Haskins, *Papers of Andrew Johnson, Volume 5*, 222; *War of the Rebellion, Series I—Volume 10, Part II*, 57-58.

[16] Graf and Haskins, *Papers of Andrew Johnson, Volume 5*, 268, 290-91.

[17] Graf and Haskins, *Papers of Andrew Johnson, Volume 5*, 247-48; "Free Gift Prizes," *Nashville Union and American*, 24 December 1861, p. 3; "Public Meeting Last Night," *Nashville Union and American*, 16 May 1861, p.2.

[18] Graf and Haskins, *Papers of Andrew Johnson, Volume 5*, 278-80; "Items of Nashville News," *Louisville Courier-Journal*, 3 April 1862, p. 3; "Arrests at Nashville," *Baltimore Sun*, 5 April 1862, p. 1.

[19] "From Tennessee," *Chicago Tribune*, 12 March 1862, p. 3.

[20] Graf and Haskins, *Papers of Andrew Johnson, Volume 5*, 300-02; "Mr. George Barber," *Louisville Courier-Journal*, 27 March 1862, p.3; "From Nashville," *National Republican*, 19 March 1862, p.1; "Our Nashville Correspondent," *New York Times*, 31 March 1862, p. 2.

[21] Graf and Haskins, *Papers of Andrew Johnson, Volume 5*, 314-15.

[22] "Take the Union!" *Nashville Daily Union*, 19 June 1862, p.1.

[23] "Duty of Christians with Regard to the War," *Southern Western Baptist*, 23 January 1862, p. 1.

[24] Graf and Haskins, *Papers of Andrew Johnson, Volume 5*, 287-90, 513-16, 534-40; "Gov. Johnson and the Clergymen of Nashville," *New York Times*, 4 July 1862, p. 2.

[25] *War of the Rebellion—A Compilation of the Officials Records of the Union and Confederate Armies, Series I—Volume III* (Washington: Government Printing Office, 1898), 642-43, 666; Graf and Haskins, *Papers of Andrew Johnson, Volume 5*, 569-70.

[26] Stephen D. Engle, *Don Carlos Buell—Most Promising of All* (Chapel Hill: University of North Carolina, 1999), 217.

[27] Graf and Haskins, *Papers of Andrew Johnson, Volume 5*, 254.

[28] Graf and Haskins, *Papers of Andrew Johnson, Volume 5*, 220, 301; *War of the Rebellion—A Compilation of the Official Records of the Union and Confederate Armies, Series II—Volume 3* (Washington: Government Printing Office, 1898), 435.

[29] Graf and Haskins, *Papers of Andrew Johnson, Volume 5*, 330; *War of the Rebellion, Series I—Volume 10, Part II*, 621.

[30] Graf and Haskins, *Papers of Andrew Johnson, Volume 5*, 331-32.

[31] *War of the Rebellion, Series I—Volume 10*, 128-29.

[32] Ibid., 621.

[33] Ibid., 129.

[34] Ibid., 131.

[35] Ibid.

[36] Ibid., 180-81; Graf and Haskins, *Papers of Andrew Johnson, Volume 5*, 378.

[37] Graf and Haskins, *Papers of Anew Johnson, Volume 5*, 379-87; "Resolutions of the Union Convention," *Nashville Daily Union*, 15 May 1862, p.2.

[38] "Howard's Letter," *Philadelphia Times*, 16 May 1880, p.5; "Current Events," *Brooklyn Daily Eagle*, 14 May 1880, p.2; J. Cutler Andrews, *The North Reports the Civil War* (Pittsburgh: University of Pittsburgh Press, 1955), 61-62.

[39] Graf and Haskins, *Papers of Andrew Johnson, Volume 5*, 416-17; "From Tennessee," *Washington Evening Star*, 27 May 1862, p.1.

[40] Graf and Haskins, *Papers of Andrew Johnson, Volume 5*, 570-71.

[41] *War of the Rebellion, Series I—Volume XVI, Part II* (Washington: Government Printing Office, 1886), 118-19.

[42] Roy P. Basler, *The Collected Works of Abraham Lincoln, Volume V* (New Brunswick: Rutgers University Press, 1953), 313-14.

[43] Ibid.

[44] Ibid., 313.

[45] *War of the Rebellion, Series I—Volume VVI, Part II*, 135.

[46] Two months after this communication, Nelson was murdered in the lobby of the Galt Hotel in Louisville as a result of an argument with Union Brigadier General Jeff C. Davis. Demanding an apology from Nelson, who had loudly criticized his abilities as a soldier, Davis shot Nelson in the chest when the latter refused. *War of the Rebellion, Series I—Volume XVI, Part II*, 815-17; Engle, *Don Carlos Buell*, 297; "Terrible Tragedy," *New York Herald*, 30 September 1862, p. 1.

[47] J. Cutler Andrews, *The North Reports the Civil War*, 287.

[48] Hans L. Trefousse, *Andrew Johnson—A Biography* (Newtown: American Political Biography Press, 1989), 159-60.

[49] Graf and Haskins, *Papers of Andrew Johnson, Volume 5*, 628.

[50] *War of the Rebellion, Series I—Volume XVI, Part II*, 451.

[51] Clifton R. Hall, *Andrew Johnson—Military Governor of Tennessee* (Princeton: Princeton University Press, 1916), 61-62.

[52] Ibid.

[53] Ibid.

[54] Trefousse, *Andrew Johnson—A Biography*, 159-60.

[55] *War of the Rebellion, Series I—Volume 16, Part I* (Washington: Government Printing Office, 1886), 697-98; "Gen. Buell's Department," *New York Times*, 19 September 1862, p.8.

[56] William Montgomery Churchwell, a colonel in the Confederate Army and former Tennessee congressman, had been tasked six months earlier with seeing to Mrs. Johnson's removal from Tennessee. Worried about the state of her health, Churchwell several times extended the deadline for Mrs. Johnson to leave. Churchwell's concern were shared by Deputy Provost Marshall William Springfield, who nevertheless bluntly decided: "I think Mrs. Johnson's health is not likely to improve, so if

she has to go now is as good a time as any." Despite this determination, Mrs. Johnson did not finally pass through Federal lines heading north until September. It seems obvious that far from physically assaulting Mrs. Johnson, as had been reported in the press, Confederate officers were extremely solicitous, reflecting either a South gallantry or fears regarding the public relations disaster of doing anything that might lead to the death of the 52 year-old wife of the Military Governor. *War of the Rebellion: A Compilation of the Official Records of the Union and Confederate Armies, Series II—Volume I* (Washington: Government Printing Office, 1894), 883-89; Graf and Haskins, *Papers of Andrew Johnson, Volume 5,* 352-53, 357-58; "Our New President," *New York Herald,* 24 April 1865, p.8.

[57] "The Very Latest News," *Chicago Tribune,* 13 October 1862, p. 1.

[58] "Our New President," *New York Herald,* 24 April 1865, p.8.

[59] Although Buell appears to have not known that he was being relieved until around October 29, Ulysses S. Grant speculated as early as October 23 that Buell was on his way out, noting sympathetically: "It is a great annoyance to gain rank and command enough to attract public attention. I have found it so and would now really prefer some little command where public attention would not be attracted towards me." *War of the Rebellion, Series I—Volume XVI, Part II,* 650-53; John Y. Simon, *Papers of Ulysses S. Grant, Volume 6: September 1-December 8, 1862* (Carbondale: Southern Illinois University Press, 1977), 182-85.

[60] Engle, *Don Carlos Buell—Most Promising of All,* 318.

[61] Leroy P. Graf and Ralph W. Haskins, *Papers of Andrew Johnson, Volume 6: 1862-1864* (Knoxville: University of Tennessee Press, 1983), 44.

Chapter Five Footnotes

[1] Leroy P. Graf and Ralph W. Haskins, *Papers of Andrew Johnson, Volume 6, 1862-1864* (Knoxville: University of Tennessee Press, 1983), 59-61.

[2] Ibid., 48-50.

[3] Ibid., 59-61.

[4] Forney additionally published the *Washington Chronicle*, a newspaper consistently loyal to Lincoln and utilized by him to advance certain policy proposals. As historian Harold Holzer has observed, Forney's incessantly positive coverage of the President "brought him as close to the leading personality of the day as any editor in the country." That Forney liked Johnson, while publishing stories favorable to the Tennessee Military Governor in a newspaper that Lincoln read and enjoyed, could only have played to Johnson's best interests. Graf and Haskins, *Papers of Andrew Johnson, Volume 6*, 59-61; Harold Holzer, *Lincoln and the Power of the Press* (New York: Simon & Schuster, 2014), 308-11.

[5] Graf and Haskins, *Papers of Andrew Johnson, Volume 6*, 64.

[6] *War of the Rebellion—A Compilation of the Officials Records of the Union and Confederate Armies, Series I—Volume XX, Part II* (Washington: Government Printing Office, 1887), 317.

[7] Graf and Haskins, *Papers of Andrew Johnson, Volume 6*, 76; "Guarantee of Protection," *Nashville Daily Union*, 29 November 1862, p.2.

[8] Graf and Haskins, *Papers of Andrew Johnson, Volume 6*, 235.

[9] Allen Nevins, *The War for the Union—War Becomes Revolution, 1862-1863* (New York: Charles Scribner's Sons, 1960), 408-09; John

Niven, *Salmon P. Chase Papers, Volume 3, Correspondence, 1853-March 1863* (Kent: Kent State University Press, 1996), 382-83.

[10] Niven, *Salmon P. Chase Papers, Volume 3*, 304-05.

[11] Graf and Haskins, *Papers of Andrew Johnson, Volume 6*, 148-59; "Republican Mass Convention," *Indiana Daily Sentinel*, 27 February 1863, p. 2; "From Indianapolis," *Cleveland Daily Leader*, 28 February 1863, p. 3; "The War for the Union," *New York Tribune*, 3 March 1863, p.2.

[12] Graf and Haskins, *Papers of Andrew Johnson, Volume 6*, 173.

[13] "The Loyal League Meeting," *New York Herald*, 15 March 1863, p. 1; "Union Meetings," *Daily National Intelligencer*, 19 March 1863, p. 2.

[14] Graf and Haskins, *Papers of Andrew Johnson, Volume 6*, 175-93; "Union Meeting at Maryland Institute Hall," *Baltimore Sun*, 21 March 1863, p. 1; "Immense Union Meeting in Baltimore," *Washington Evening Star*, 23 March 1863, p. 2.

[15] "Union Mass Meeting in Washington," *New York Herald*, 1 April 1863, p. 5; "Correspondence of the Baltimore Sun," *Baltimore Sun*, 2 April 1863, p. 4; "Great Union Demonstration at the Capitol," *National Republican*, 1 April 1863, p. 1; "The Union Mass Meeting in Washington," *New York Tribune*, 1 April 1863, p. 1.

[16] "The Great Union Demonstration," *Washington Evening Star*, 1 April 1863, p. 3.

[17] Graf and Haskins, *Papers of Andrew Johnson, Volume 6*, 200-04.

[18] "Our Special Washington Dispatches," *New York Times*, 1 April 1863, p.4.

[19] Roy P. Basler, *Collected Works of Abraham Lincoln, Volume VI* (New Brunswick: Rutgers University Press, 1953), 149-50.

20 Graf and Haskins, *Papers of Andrew Johnson, Volume 6*, 82-83.

21 *War of the Rebellion—A Compilation of the Official Records of the Union and Confederate Armies, Series I—Volume XXIII, Part II* (Washington: Government Printing Office, 1889), 191.

22 Ibid., 208.

23 Graf and Haskins, *Papers of Andrew Johnson, Volume 6*, 205-06.

24 Ibid., 209.

25 *War of the Rebellion, Series I—Volume XXIII, Part II*, 380-81.

26 Graf and Haskins, *Papers of Andrew Johnson, Volume 6*, 212-14.

27 Ibid., 233.

28 Basler, *Collected Works of Abraham Lincoln, Volume VI*, 238.

29 Graf and Haskins, *Papers of Andrew Johnson, Volume 6*, 344-45.

30 *War of the Rebellion—A Compilation of the Official Records of the Union and Confederate Armies, Series I—Volume XXX, Part I* (Washington: Government Printing Office, 1890), 182-83.

31 Graf and Haskins, *Papers of Andrew Johnson, Volume 6*, 359; "Bragg and Rosecrans," *New York Times*, 1 September 1863, p. 1; "From Gen. Burnside's Army" *New York Times*, 4 September 1863, p. 1; "Our Flag in Tennessee," *New York Times*, 8 September 1863, p. 4.

32 *War of the Rebellion—A Compilation of the Official Records of the Union and Confederate Armies, Series I—Volume XXX, Part III* (Washington: Government Printing Office, 1890), 440-41.

33 Ron Chernow, *Grant* (New York: Penguin Press, 2017), 309.

[34] Graf and Haskins, *Papers of Andrew Johnson, Volume 6*, 427-28.

[35] Elizabeth D. Samset, *Annotated Memoirs of Ulysses S. Grant* (New York: Liveright Publishing Corporation, 2019), 516-17.

[36] John Y. Simon, *Papers of Ulysses S. Grant, Volume 9: July 7-December 31, 1863* (Carbondale: Southern Illinois University Press, 1982), 303-04.

[37] *War of the Rebellion—A Compilation of the Official Records of the Union and Confederate Armies, Series I—Volume XXXI, Part I* (Washington: Government Printing Office, 1890), 728-29.

[38] Ibid., 728-29, 744.

[39] Graf and Haskins, *Papers of Andrew Johnson, Volume 6*, 488-92.

[40] Ibid., 514.

[41] "For the Presidency," *Chicago Tribune*, 30 December 1863, p.3; "The Presidency," *Washington Evening Star*, 12 January 1864, p.2; "Our Candidate for Vice-President," *Evansville Daily Journal*, 15 January 1864, p. 2; "Vice-President," *Chicago Tribune*, 19 January 1864, p.1.

[42] Graf and Haskins, *Papers of Andrew Johnson, Volume 6*, 559-62.

[43] Ibid., 548-51; Hans L. Trefousse, *Andrew Johnson* (Newtown: American Political Biography Press, 2009), 171-72; "Affairs at Nashville," *New York Times*, 24 January 1862, p. 1.

[44] Weighing the results, Johnson scholar Paul Bergeron argues: "Given the conditions of the day—a war still in progress, the disruption of transportation and communication, and the disputes, if not hostility, engendered by the new oath—perhaps the turnout was not disappointing." Clifton R. Hall, *Andrew Johnson—Military Governor of Tennessee* (Princeton: Princeton University Press, 1916), 122-23; Paul H. Bergeron, *Andrew Johnson's Civil War and Reconstruction* (Knoxville: University of Tennessee Press, 20110, 51.

[45] Graf and Haskins, *Papers of Andrew Johnson, Volume 6*, 669.

[46] Ibid., 669-79.

[47] "Lincoln and Johnson," *Cleveland Daily Leader*, 9 June 1864, p. 1.

[48] Graf and Haskins, *Papers of Andrew Johnson, Volume 6*, 723-28.

[49] The jingle was taken from a popular marching son sung by Union soldiers called "Battle Cry of Freedom." *Songs of the Soldiers and Sailors—U.S.* (Washington: Government Printing Office, 1917), 11.

Chapter Six Footnotes

[1] Hans L. Trefousse, *Andrew Johnson* (Newtown: American Political Biography Press, 1989), 176.

[2] David Herbert Donald, *Lincoln* (New York: Touchstone Book, 1995), 506.

[3] "Our Special Dispatch," *Pittsburgh Gazette*, 6 June 1864, p. 3.

[4] *Presidential Election, 1864, Proceedings of the National Union Convention Held in Baltimore, Maryland, June 7th and June 8th, 1864* (New York: Baker & Godwin, 1864), 69-70.

[5] Charles Eugene Hamlin, *The Life and Times of Hannibal Hamlin* (Cambridge: Riverside Press, 1899), 477-83.

[6] Ibid.

[7] Leroy P. Graf and Ralph W. Haskins, *Papers of Andrew Johnson, Volume 6, 1862-1864* (Knoxville: University of Tennessee Press, 1983), 730-31; Dan E. Fehrenbacher, "The Making of a Myth: Lincoln and the Vice-Presidential Nomination in 1864," *Civil War History*, Volume 41, Number 4, December 1995, 273-90; "The Ticket's Other Half:

How and Why Andrew Johnson Received the 1864 Vice-Presidential Nomination," *Tennessee Historical Quarterly,* Volume LXV, Spring 2006, Number 1, 43-68; John C. Waugh, *Reelecting Lincoln—The Battle for the 1864 Presidency* (Cambridge: Da Capo Press, 1997), 196-201.

8   "The Nominations," *Baltimore American,* 9 June 1864, p. 1; "Andrew Johnson," *Harper's Weekly,* 15 June 1864, p. 402.

9   "Our Candidate for the Vice-Presidency," *New York Times,* 22 June 1864, p. 4.

10   William C. Davis, *With Charity for All—Lincoln and the Restoration of the Union* (Lexington: University Press of Kentucky, 1997), 218.

11   Leroy P. Graf, *Papers of Andrew Johnson, Volume 7, 1864-1865* (Knoxville: University of Tennessee Press, 1986), 37-38.

12   Ibid., 99-100; Roy P. Basler, *Collected Works of Abraham Lincoln, Volume VII* (New Brunswick: Rutgers University Press, 1953), 502-03.

13   Ibid.

14   Graf, *Papers of Andrew Johnson, Volume 7,* 138; Basler, *Collected Works of Abraham Lincoln, Volume VII,* 540.

15   Grad, *Papers of Andrew Johnson, Volume 7,* 98-99.

16   Ibid., 153.

17   Beverly Wilson Palmer, *Selected Letters of Charles Sumner, Volume Two* (Boston: Northeastern University Press, 1990), 252.

18   Graf, *Papers of Andrew Johnson, Volume 7,* 218-31; "Personal Defamation," *Cleveland Daily Leader,* 22 June 1864, p. 2; "The Nomination of Abraham Lincoln," *Brooklyn Daily Eagle,* 9 June 1864, p.2; Waugh, *Reelecting Lincoln,* 201.

[19] Graf, *Papers of Andrew Johnson, Volume 7,* 218-31.

[20] Ibid., 251-53.

[21] "Andrew Johnson's Great Speech to the Colored People," *Liberator,* 11 November 1864, p. 3.

[22] "Andrew Johnson," *Memphis Bulletin,* 7 January 1865, p.1; Palmer, *Selected Letters of Charles Sumner, Volume Two,* 248-49; Milton Meltzer, *Lydia Maria Child, Selected Letters, 1817-1880* (Amherst: University of Massachusetts Press, 1982), 449-50.

[23] Meltzer, *Lydia Maria Child, Selected Letters, 1817-1880,* 449-50.

[24] "Letter from Professor Newman," *Liberator,* 23 December 1864, p.2.

[25] "Andrew Johnson's Great Speech to the Colored People," *Liberator,* 11 November 1864, p.3.

[26] Graf, *Papers of Andrew Johnson, Volume 7,* 269-71.

[27] Ibid., 281-83.

[28] Ibid., 369; John Y. Simon, *Papers of Ulysses S. Grant, Volume 13: November 16, 1864-February 20, 1865* (Carbondale: Southern University Press, 1985), 96, 107, 124-25.

[29] *War of the Rebellion, A Compilation of the Official Records of the Union and Confederate Armies, Series I, Volume XVI,--Part II* (Washington: Government Printing Office, 1894), 471.

[30] Graf, *Papers of Andrew Johnson, Volume 7,* 404; Roy P. Basler, *Collected Works of Abraham Lincoln, Volume VIII* (New Brunswick: Rutgers University Press, 1953), 216-17; "Tennessee State Convention," *Memphis Bulletin,* 15 January 1865, p. 1; "The State Convention," *Memphis Bulletin,* 17 January 1865, p. 2.

[31]   Basler, *Collected Works of Abraham Lincoln, Volume VIII*, 216-17.

[32]   Graf, *Papers of Andrew Johnson, Volume 7*, 420-21.

[33]   Graf, *Papers of Andrew Johnson, Volume 7*, 427; Basler, *Collected Works of Abraham Lincoln, Volume VIII*, 235.

[34]   There was some speculation during this time that President Lincoln might name Forney to his cabinet, most likely as Secretary of the Treasury. It's possible that Forney thought having his old friend Johnson, whom he presumed to be close to Lincoln, back in Washington might improve his chances for the post. Graf, *Papers of Anew Johnson, Volume 7*, 439; "Cabinet Changes," *Pittsburgh Daily Post*, 16 January 1865, p.2; "Col. John W. Forney," *Daily Evening Express*, 19 January 1865, p. 2.

[35]   "The Health of Andrew Johnson," *Philadelphia Inquirer*, 18 February 1865, p. 4.

[36]   Graf, *Papers of Andrew Johnson, Volume 7*, 498.

[37]   Ibid., 498-99.

[38]   "A Serenade," *Cincinnati Enquirer*, 28 February 1865, p. 3.

[39]   Hamlin, *The Life and Times of Hannibal Hamlin*, 497-98.

[40]   In his memoirs published in 1873, Forney made no mention of the party at his residence the evening before the inauguration. But he did remark of the immediate response to Johnson's speech: "Bitter maledictions were immediately hurled against the new Vice-President. I hastened to his defense to the best of my abilities, believing the affair to have been an accident." "Inauguration," *New York Herald*, 6 March 1865, p. 6; John W. Forney, *Anecdotes of Public Men* (New York: Harper & Brothers, 1873), 177.

[41]   Graf, *Papers of Andrew Johnson, Volume 7*, 502-07.

[42] . Ibid.

[43] "Inauguration," *New York Herald*, 6 March 1865, p.6.

[44] "The Extraordinary Address of the Vice President," *Daily Empire*, 9 March 1865, p.2. Reprint of the *New York Tribune* article.

[45] Trefousse, *Andrew Johnson*, 190.

[46] Frederick Douglass, *Life and Times of Frederick Douglass* (Hartford: Park Publishing Company, 1881), 355.

[47] Doris Kearns Goodwin, *Team of Rivals—The Political Genius of Abraham Lincoln* (New York: Simon & Schuster, 2005), 698-99.

[48] Ibid., Basler, *Collected Works of Abraham Lincoln, Volume VIII*, 332-33.

[49] Virginia Jeans Laas, *Wartime Washington—The Civil War Letters of Elizabeth Blair Lee* (Urbana: University of Illinois Press, 1991), 482.

[50] John B. Pickard, *The Letters of John Greenleaf Whittier* (Cambridge: Belknap Press, 1975), 87-88.

[51] "Andrew Johnson," *Fall River Daily News*, 9 March 1865, p.2.

[52] "Mr. Stephens," *Brooklyn Daily Eagle*, 9 March 1865, p.2; "Vice-President Johnson," *Chicago Tribune*, 14 March 1865, p.2.

[53] "Andy Johnson's Exhibition of Himself," *Manchester Guardian*, 21 March 1865, p. 7. Reprint of *London Times* article.

[54] "Inauguration of President Lincoln," *Nottingham Guardian*, 24 March 1865, p. 12.

[55] "The Civil War in America," *London Times*, 25 March 1865, p. 29.

[56] Palmer, *Selected Letters of Charles Sumner, Volume Two*, 272-73.

[57] Donald C. Bacon, *Encyclopedia of the United States Congress, Volume 1* (New York: Simon & Schuster, 1995), 44.

[58] Paul H. Bergeron, *Andrew Johnson's Civil War and Reconstruction* (Knoxville: University of Tennessee Press, 2011), 66; "Vice-President Johnson," *Daily Morning Chronicle*, 24 March 1865, p. 2.

[59] Lass, *Wartime Washington*, 481.

[60] Graf, *Papers of Andrew Johnson, Volume 7*, 511-12; Bergeron, *Andrew Johnson's Civil War and Reconstruction*, 66.

[61] "The President's Advice to Gen. Hooker," *Vermont Journal*, 15 April 1865, p. 2; "Gleanings," *Buffalo Courier*, 11 March 1865, p.2.

[62] Graf, *Papers of Andrew Johnson, Volume 7*, 543.

[63] Basler, *Collected Works of Abraham Lincoln, Volume VIII*, 399-405.

[64] Graf, *Papers of Andrew Johnson, Volume 7*, 543-46.

[65] David Dixon Porter, *Incidents and Anecdotes of the Civil War* (New York: Appleton & Company, 1886), 287.

[66] William H. Crook, *Through Five Administration—Reminiscences of Colonel William H. Crook* (New York: Harper & Brothers Publishers, 1910), 44.

[67] Ibid.

[68] Graf, *Papers of Andrew Johnson, Volume 7*, 546-47; Leroy P. Graf and Ralph W. Haskins, *Papers of Andrew Johnson, Volume 5, 1861-1862* (Knoxville: University of Tennessee Press, 1979), 38, 548-49; James T. Sears, *Rebels, Rubyfruit and Rhinestones—Queering Spaces in the Stonewall South* (New Brunswick: Rutgers University Press, 2001), 341.

[69] Graf, *Papers of Andrew Johnson, Volume 7,* 546-47.

[70] No title, *Washington Evening Star,* 14 April 1865, p. 2.

[71] James L. Swanson, *Manhunt—The 12-Day Chase for Lincoln's Killer* (New York: Harper Perennial, 2007), 18-19.

[72] "The Executions," *Washington Evening Star,* 7 July 1865, p. 2.

[73] Edward Steers, Jr., *The Trial—The Assassination of President Lincoln and the Trial of the Conspirators* (Lexington: University Press of Kentucky, 2003), 300-07.

[74] Michael W. Kaufman, *American Brutus—John Wilkes Booth and the Lincoln Conspiracies* (New York: Random House, 2004), 24.

[75] Ibid., 239. 274.

[76] Ibid, 30.

[77] *War of the Rebellion—A Compilation of the Officials Records of the Union and Confederate Armies, Series I—Volume XLVI, Part III* (Washington: Government Printing Office, 1894), 780-81.

[78] Trefousse, *Andrew Johnson,* 194.

[79] John Niven, *Salmon P. Chase Papers, Volume 5, Correspondence 1865-1873* (Kent: Kent State University Press, 1998), 29-31.

[80] Immediately upon Lincoln's passing, the Cabinet heads, with the exception, of course, of Seward, sent Johnson official note that the "office of President has devolved under the Constitution upon you." Navy Secretary Gideon Welles, who had been with Lincoln until the moment of his passing, later recorded that when Postmaster General William Dennison suggested that Welles present the notice to Johnson, "I saw that it disconcerted Stanton, who had expected and intended to be the man and to have [Attorney General] Speed associated with him."

Ultimately, Stanton did not attend the brief ceremony at the Kirkwood. William E. Gienapp and Erica Gienapp, *The Civil War Diaries of Gideon Welles—Lincoln's Secretary of the Navy* (Urbana: University of Illinois Press, 2014), 628; William Marvel, *Lincoln's Autocrat—The Life of Edwin Stanton* (Chapel Hill: University of North Carolina Press, 2015), 370; Graf, *Papers of Andrew Johnson, Volume 7,* 553; Niven, *Salmon P. Chase Papers, Volume 5,* 29-31.

[81] Hugh McCulloch, *Men and Measures of Half a Century: Sketches and Comments* (London: Sampson, Low, Marston, Searlf & Rivington, 1888), 376.

[82] Stanton, who continued to issue orders throughout the following two days, sent the following announcement to Ulysses S. Grant early on April 16: "you will please announce by General Order to the armies of the United States that on Saturday the 15th day of April 1865, by reason of the death of Abraham Lincoln, the office of President of the United States devolved upon Andrew Johnson, Vice-President, who on the same day took the official oath prescribed for the President and entered upon the duties of that office." Graf, *Papers of Andrew Johnson, Volume 7,* 553-54; John Y. Simon, *Papers of Ulysses S. Grant, Volume 14: February 21-April 1865* (Carbondale: Southern Illinois University Press, 1985), 391.

Chapter Seven Footnotes

[1] William Gienapp and Erica Gienapp, *The Civil War Diary of Gideon Welles, Lincoln's Secretary of the Navy* (Urbana: University of Illinois Press, 2014), 629.

[2] William Marvel, *Lincoln's Autocrat—The Life of Edwin Stanton* (Chapel Hill: University of North Carolina Press, 2015), 370.

[3] William Seale, *The President's House—A History* (Washington: White House Historical Association, 1986), 420-21.

[4] Paul H. Bergeron, *Andrew Johnson's Civil War and Reconstruction* (Knoxville: University of Tennessee Press, 2011), 69-70.

[5] Bruce Tap, *Over Lincoln's Shoulder—The Committee on the Conduct of the War* (Lawrence: University Press of Kansas, 1998), 243.

[6] Beverly Wilson Palmer, *Selected Letters of Charles Sumner, Volume Two* (Boston: Northeastern University Press, 1990), 294-96.

[7] Ibid.

[8] Leroy P. Graf, *Papers of Andrew Johnson, Volume 7, 1864-1865* (Knoxville: University of Tennessee Press, 1986), 560-61.

[9] *War of the Rebellion: A Compilation of the Official Records of the Union and Confederate Armies, Series I—Volume XLVII, Part III* (Washington: Government Printing Office, 1895), 301.

[10] Ibid.

[11] Ibid., 301-02; "Sherman," *New York Herald*, 23 April 1865, p.5.

[12] Gienapp and Gienapp, *Civil War Diary of Gideon Welles*, 634.

[13] *War of the Rebellion, Series I—Volume XLVII, Part III*, 301-02.

[14] Ibid.

[15] Ron Chernow, *Grant* (New York: Penguin Press, 2017), 536-37.

[16] *War of the Rebellion: A Compilation of the Official Records of the Union and Confederate Armies, Series I—Volume XLVI, Part III* (Washington: Government Printing Office, 1894), 989, 847-48.

[17] *War of the Rebellion: A Compilation of the Official Records of the Union and Confederate Armies, Series II—Volume VIII* (Washington: Government Printing Office, 1899), 696-700.

[18] Graf, *Papers of Andrew Johnson, Volume 7*, 544.

[19] John Y. Simon, *Papers of Ulysses S. Grant, Volume 29: November 1, 1876-September 30, 1878* (Carbondale: Southern Illinois University Press, 2005), 421.

[20] "Review of the Armies," *New York Times*, 24 May 1865, p.1; "The Review," *New York Herald*, 24 May 1865, p.1; "The Grand Review," *Washington Evening Star*, 24 May 1865, p. 2.

[21] *War of the Rebellion, Series I—Volume XLVII, Part III*, 530-31.

[22] Paul H. Bergeron, *Papers of Andrew Johnson, Volume 8, May-August 1865* (Knoxville: University of Tennessee Press, 1989), 93.

[23] Marvel, *Lincoln's Autocrat*, 379.

[24] John Y. Simon, *Papers of Ulysses S. Grant, Volume 15: May 1-December 31, 1865* (Carbondale: Southern Illinois University Press, 1988), 92-94.

[25] Ibid., 100.

[26] Author David S. Reynolds quotes Whitman as remarking that there was "something in Johnson which indicated the existence of democratic instincts." Reynolds himself adds that "Johnson had gained his power in a way that had natural appeal for Whitman: by going directly to the people." Edwin Haviland Miller, *Walt Whitman—The Correspondence, Volume I: 1842-1867* (New York: New York University Press, 1961), 260-61; David S. Reynolds, *Walt Whitman's America—A Cultural Biography* (New York: Alfred A. Knopf, 1995), 466-67.

[27] Palmer, *Selected Letters of Charles Sumner, Volume Two*, 299-300.

[28] Bergeron, *Papers of Andrew Johnson, Volume 8*, 128-31; *War of the Rebellion: A Compilation of the Official Records of the Union and Confederate Armies, Series III—Volume V* (Washington: Government Printing Office, 1900), 37-39.

[29] Palmer, *Selected Letters of Charles Sumner, Volume Two,* 311-12; Charles Sumner to Gideon Welles, 4 July 1865, Papers of Gideon Welles, Reel 23.

[30] Thaddeus Stevens to Andrew Johnson, 16 May 1865, Andrew Johnson Papers, Reel 15.

[31] Thaddeus Stevens to Charles Sumner, 3 June 1865; Thaddeus Stevens to Andrew Johnson, 6 July 1865, both Thaddeus Stevens Papers, Roll 4.

[32] Benjamin Brown French, *Witness to the Young Republic—A Yankee's Journal, 1828-1870* (Hanover: University Press of New England, 1989), 483.

[33] Ibid., 384.

[34] Charles H. Coleman, *The Election of 1868—The Democratic Effort to Regain Control* (New York: Octagon Books, 1971), 162.

[36] Ibid., 107-08.

[37] *War of the Rebellion, Series II—Volume VIII,* 563-64.

[38] William J. Cooper, *Jefferson Davis, American* (New York: Vintage Books, 2000), 583-84.

[39] Bergeron, *Papers of Andrew Johnson, Volume 8,* 672-73; Lynda Laswell Crist, *Papers of Jefferson Davis, Volume 12, June 1865-December 1870* (Baton Rouge: Louisiana State University Press, 2008), 21, 24, 27, 43-44.

[40] Virginia Clay-Clopton, *A Belle of the Fifties—Memoirs of Mrs. Clay of Alabama* (Tuscaloosa: University of Alabama Press, 1999), 311-12; Virginia Clay to Andrew Johnson, 11 February 1866, Andrew Johnson Papers, Reel 20; Virginia Clay to Andrew Johnson, 5 May 1866, Andrew Johnson Papers, Reel 22.

[41] Paul H. Bergeron, *Papers of Andrew Johnson, Volume 9, September 1865-January 1866* (Knoxville: University of Tennessee Press, 1991), 85-87.

[42] Bergeron, *Papers of Andrew Johnson, Volume 8*, 536-37.

[43] Bergeron, *Papers of Andrew Johnson, Volume 9*, 89-90.

[44] Palmer, *Selected Letters of Charles Sumner, Volume Two*, 346; "Interview Between the President and Senator Sumner," *Columbus Daily Enquirer*, 21 December 1865, p. 2.

[45] Palmer, *Selected Letters of Charles Sumner, Volume Two*, 346.

[46] Bergeron, *Papers of Andrew Johnson, Volume 9*, 466-85.

[47] Ibid.

[48] Ibid.

[49] Schuyler Colfax to Alfred Wheeler, 8 January 1866, Papers of Schuyler Colfax, Reel 1.

[50] *Congressional Globe, 39th Congress, 1st Session*, 936-42.

[51] Paul H. Bergeron, *Papers of Andrew Johnson, Volume 10, February-July 1866* (Knoxville: University of Tennessee Press, 1992), 120-27.

[52] Gene Smith, *High Crimes & Misdemeanors—The Impeachment and Trial of Andrew Johnson* (New York: McGraw-Hill Book Company, 1976), 145-46; Brenda Wineapple, *The Impeachers—The Trial of Andrew Johnson and the Dream of a Just Nation* (New York: Random House, 2019), 115-16.

[53] Johnson loyalists particularly disliked the three men he singled out in his speech. A Confederate Army veteran, specifically mentioning Sumner, Stevens, and Phillips, warned Johnson several days earlier that

following their ideas would result in the "overthrow of this government and possibly involve us in a worse conflict than we have just passed through." Bergeron, *Papers of Andrew Johnson, Volume 10,* 145-57; Charles Dement to Andrew Johnson, 19 February 1866, Andrew Johnson Papers, Reel 20.

54 "From Washington," *Chicago Tribune,* 24 February 1866, p.1.

55 "The Dead Duck," *Louisville Daily Courier,* 26 February 1866, p.1.

56 "The New York Evening Post," *Fall River Daily News,* 26 February 1866, p.2.

57 Bergeron, *Papers of Andrew Johnson, Volume 10,* 312-20.

58 "The Riot in New Orleans," *New York Times,* 1 August 1866, p.5; "The New Orleans Riot," *New York Herald,* August 1866, p.5; Giles Vandal, "The Origins of the New Orleans Riot of 1866, Revisited," *Louisiana History,* Spring 1982, Volume XXII, Number 2, 135-65; Philip Sheridan to Ulysses S. Grant, 1 August 1866, Ulysses S. Grant Papers, Reel 24; Phillip Sheridan to Andrew Johnson, 6 August 1866, Andrew Johnson Papers, Reel 23.

Chapter Eight Footnotes

1 "White House," *Washington Evening Star,* 13 August 1866; George Armstrong Custer to Andrew Johnson, 13 August 1866, Andrew Johnson Papers, Reel 23; T.J. Stiles, *Custer's trials—A Life on the Frontier of a New America* (New York: Alfred A. Knopf, 2015), 245-46.

2 "Custer on Custer," *Chicago Tribune,* 15 August 1866, p.2; "Affairs in Texas," *New York Times,* 1 April 1866, p.1.

3 Lawrence A. Frost, *General Custer's Libbie* (Seattle: Superior Publishing Company, 1976), 152.

4   Jay Monaghan, *Custer—The Life of General George Armstrong Custer* (Lincoln: University of Nebraska Press, 1959), 189, 213; Custer Battlefield Frames, Reel 4, Monroe County Library System.

5   George Armstrong Custer to Andrew Johnson, 13 August 1866, Andrew Johnson Papers, Reel 1.

6   "Meeting of the United States Offices," *New York Herald*, 19 August 1866, p. 1; "Letter from Major General Custer," *Daily National Intelligencer*, 21 August 1866, p.2.

7   "Restoration," *Daily National Intelligencer*, 27 August 1866, p. 2.

8   Frost, *General Custer's Libbie*, 156.

9   Howard K. Beale, *Diary of Gideon Welles, Volume II, April 1, 1864-December 31, 1866* (New York: W. W. Norton & Compny, 1960), 585.

10   Fanny Seward, the daughter of Secretary Seward, was one of the few who found Stanton an entirely enjoyable presence. Getting the family mansion ready in Auburn, New York for a visit by the presidential party, she wrote to her father: "The papers say that Mr. Stanton will not be one of the party of the excursionists. I hope the papers are wrong." Beale, *Diary of Gideon Welles, Volume II*, 587; Fanny Seward to William H. Seward, 19 August 1866, Papers of William H. Seward, Reel 116.

11   James Doolittle to Andrew Johnson, 16 August 1866, Andrew Johnson Papers, Reel 23.

12   "Entrance of Gen. Grant," *New York Times*, 20 August 1866, p.1.

13   "Gen. Grant at the Executive Mansion and Upon the Presidential Tour," *Daily National Intelligencer*, 30 August 1866, p. 2; Jean Edward Smith, *Grant* (New York: Simon & Schuster, 2001), 679; Ron Chernow, *Grant* (New York: Penguin Press, 2017), 577.

[14] "Reception at Baltimore," *New York Herald*, 29 August 1866, p.1; "The Presidential Tour," *Baltimore Sun*, 30 August 1866, p. 1.

[15] "Associated Press Account," *New York Times*, 29 August 1866, p.1; Charles D. Cashdollar, "Andrew Johnson and the Philadelphia Election of 1866," *Pennsylvania Magazine of History and Biography*, Volume XCII, Number 3, July 1868, 372.

[16] "Grand Ovation at Philadelphia," *New York Herald*, 29 August 1866, p.1; Greg Phiger, "Andrew Johnson Takes a Trip," *Tennessee Historical Quarterly*, Volume XI, March-December 1952, p.

[17] "The Tour," *New York Times*, 29 August 1866, p. 1.

[18] 18. "Andrew Johnson, *New York Times*, 28 August 1866, p. 1.

[19] Ibid.

[20] "The President," *New York World*, 29 August 1866, p. 1.

[21] "The Arrival in New York," *New York World*, 30 August 1866, p. 1.

[22] "President Johnson," *New York Times*, 30 August 1866, p. 1.

[23] "The Reception," *New York Herald*, 30 August 1866, p. 1.

[24] Thomas Schoonover, "The Mexican Minister Describes Andrew Johnson's 'Swing Around the Circle,'" *Civil War History*, June 1973, Volume 19, Number 2, 152.

[25] Paul H. Bergeron, *Papers of Andrew Johnson, Volume 11, August 1866-January 1867* (Knoxville: University of Tennessee Press, 1994), 153-66; "At Delmonico's," *New York World*, 30 August 1866, p. 8.

[26] Ulysses S. Grant to Julia Dent Grant, 31 August 1866, Ulysses S. Grant Papers, Reel 1; Schoonover, "The Mexican Minister Describes Andrew Johnson's 'Swing Around the Circle,'" 153-54.

[27] Beale, *Diary of Gideon Welles, Volume Two,* 589.

[28] In a time when department heads weren't in constant communication with their underlings, staffers in Washington got most of their information about the presidential tour from reading the newspapers. Responding to press accounts of the collapsed platform in Schenectady five days after in actually happened, Assistant Secretary William Faxon wrote to Welles: "I hope, sincerely, that you are suffering no inconvenience from an accident I see reported in the papers," "The Tour," *New York Herald,* 4 September 1866, p. 10; William Faxon to Gideon Welles, 4 September 1866, Papers of Gideon Welles, Reel 24.

[29] Sylvanus Cadwallader, *Three Years with General Grant* (New York: Alfred A. Knopf, 1995), 340; Chernow, *Grant,* 578-79.

[30] John Y. Simon, *Papers of Ulysses S. Grant, Volume 16: 1866* (Carbondale: Southern Illinois University Press, 1988), 307.

[31] *Trial of Andrew Johnson, Volume I* (Washington: Government Printing Office, 1868), 326, 328.

[32] Ibid., 311, 326, 314.

[33] Bergeron, *Papers of Andrew Johnson, Volume 11,* 174-80; *Trial of Andrew Johnson, Volume I,* 327.

[34] Earl L. McKitrick, *Andrew Johnson and Reconstruction* (Chicago: University of Chicago Press, 1960), 438; David Seward Rosenberger, *Ohio Press Reaction to Andrew Johnson's 'Swing Around the Circle,' 1866* (MA thesis, Ohio State University, 1847), 32.

[35] Rosenberger, *Ohio Press Reaction to Andrew Johnson's 'Swing Around the Circle,' 1866,* 30; "Andrew Johnson and Congress During the Past Year," *New York Herald,* 26 September 1866, p. 6.

[36] Despite the negative fallout from Johnson's Cleveland stop, he still continued to receive invitations from municipal leaders across the

country who wanted their cities to be a part of the presidential tour. "The Tour," *New York Herald*, 5 September 1866, p.7; New Orleans Citizens to Andrew Johnson, 8 September 1866; Lexington City Council to Andrew Johnson, 9 September 1866; Citizens of Omaha, Nebraska to Andrew Johnson, all Andrew Johnson Papers, Reel 24.

[37] "The President's Tour," *Washington Evening Star*, 6 September 1866, p.1; "The Detroit Reception," *New York Herald*, 5 September 1866, p. 1; "The President," *Detroit Advertiser and Tribune*, 5 September 1866, p.4.

[38] "The United States," *London Times*, 18 September 1866, p. 7.

[39] "Douglas Monument," *New York Herald*, 7 September 1866, p. 2.

[40] Thirteen years later, Grant, in a visit to Chicago, exclaimed to a well-wisher: "I met you here in 1866 when I was 'swinging around the circle' with Andy Johnson. I remember it well—when he nearly forgot what he came out here for, when he made a political speech. He almost forgot that we came to build a monument." "The President at Chicago," *Washington Evening Star*, 7 September 1866, p.1; "The Douglas Monument," *Daily National Intelligencer*, 7 September 1866, p.3; John Y. Simpson, *Papers of Ulysses S. Grant, Volume 29: October 1, 1878-September 30, 1880* (Carbondale, Southern Illinois University Press, 2008), 298; "Gen. Grant," *Chicago Tribune*, 16 November 1879, p.2.

[41] "A Letter from Gen. Custer," *New York Times*, 16 September 1866, p. 1; Stiles, *Custer's Trials*, 247-48.

[42] Schoonover, "The Mexican Minister Describes Andrew Johnson's 'Swing Around the Circle,'" 156-58.

[43] Noting a lack of enthusiasm on the part of Springfield's political leadership, former Illinois Congressman John McClernand optimistically told Johnson: "It is the people here who will give you a reception." "Mr. Johnson's Reception," *Daily State Journal*, 8 September 1866, p. 1; John McClernand to Andrew Johnson, 5 September 1866, Andrew Johnson Papers, Reel 24.

[44] "The President's Tour," *Washington Evening Star,* 10 September 1866, p.1; "The Tour," *New York Herald,* 8 September 1866, p.5.

[45] Bergeron, *Papers of Andrew Johnson, Volume 11,* 192-201; Brenda Wineapple, *The Impeachers—The Trial of Andrew Johnson and the Dream of a Just Nation* (New York: Random House, 2019), 154-56.

[46] "The United States," *London Times,* 25 September 1866, p. 8.

[47] Simon, *Papers of Ulysses S. Grant, Volume 16,* 308-09.

[48] "The President's Tour," *New York Times,* 11 September 1866, p. 1; "The President at Indianapolis," *Evansville Daily Journal,* 11 September 1866; "The Radical Riot at Indianapolis," *Albany Argus,* 15 September 1866, p. 2.

[49] Brooks D. Simpson, *Let Us Have Peace—Ulysses S. Grant and the Politics of War and Reconstruction* (Chapel Hill: University of North Carolina Press, 1991), 179.

[50] "The Danger to the Life of the President at the Indianapolis Riot," *Daily National Intelligencer,* 13 September 1866, p.3.

[51] "The Tour," *New York Herald,* 12 September 1866, p.1; "The Late Indianapolis Riot," *Daily National Intelligencer,* 14 September 1866, p.2.

[52] "The Tour," *New York Herald,* 14 September 1866, p.1; Stiles, *Custer's Trials,* 251.

[53] Ibid.

[54] Ibid.

[55] "The President's Tour," *New York Times,* 15 September 1866, p.1.

[56] Henry McPike to Andrew Johnson, 15 September 1866, Andrew Johnson Papers, Reel 24.

[57]   Daniel J. Morrell to William G. Moore, 17 September 1866, Andrew Johnson Papers, Reel 24.

[58]   William Seward, Jr. to Jenny Seward, 16 September 1866, Papers of William H. Seward, Reel 118; Walter Stahr, *Seward—Lincoln's Indispensable Man* (New York: Simon & Schuster, 2012), 474.

[59]   John M. Taylor, *William Henry Seward—Lincoln's Right Hand* (New York: HarperCollins Publishers, 1991), 265-66.

[60]   Edwin Stanton to Andrew Johnson, 15 September 1866, Andrew Johnson Papers, Reel 24.

[61]   "The Tour," *New York Herald,* 16 September 1866, p.1.

[62]   "The President's Return," *Washington Evening Star,* 17 September 1866, p.1.

Chapter Nine Footnotes

[1]   William H. Crook, *Through Five Administrations—Reminiscences of Colonel William H. Crook* (New York: Harper and Brothers, 1910), 11.

[2]   Thomas Frederick Wooley, *Great Leveler—The Life of Thaddeus Stevens* (Freeport: Books for Libraries Press, 1969), 225-37.

[3]   "My Policy," *Chicago Tribune,* 29 September 1866, p.4.

[4]   Beverly Wilson Palmer, *The Selected Letters of Charles Sumner—Volume Two* (Boston: Northeastern University Press, 1990), 380-81.

[5]   George Frisbie Hoar, *Charles Sumner—His Complete Works* (Boston: Lee and Sheppard, 1990), 182-219; "From Boston," *Chicago Tribune,* 3 October 1866, p.1.

[6]   "The President's Mistake," *New York Times,* 7 September 1866, p.4.

[7] William B. Phillips to Andrew Johnson, 16 September 1866, Andrew Johnson Papers, Reel 24.

[8] John B. Packard, *The Letters of John Greenleaf Whittier, Volume III* (Cambridge: The Belknap Press, 1982), 77-78.

[9] James Perry Whipple, "The Johnson Party," *Atlantic Monthly*, Volume XVIII, Number CVIL, September 1986, 374-81.

[10] James Russell Lowell, "The Seward-Johnson Reaction," *North American Review*, Volume 103, Number 213, 520-49.

[11] Edward Perry Whipple, "The Johnson Party," *Atlantic Monthly*, Volume XVIII, Number CVIL, September 1866, 374-81.

[12] Edward Perry Whipple, "The President and His Accomplices," *Atlantic Monthly*, Volume XVIII, Number CIX, November 1866, 634-43.

[13] David R. Locke, *Swingin' Around the Cirkle* (Upper Saddle River: Literature House, 1866), 224-26.

[14] "Caricatured Celebrities by Nast," *New York Times*, 14 April 1866; "Grand Masquerade Ball," *Harper's Weekly*, 14 April 1866, p. 235.

[15] "Reconstruction and How It Works," *Harper's Weekly*, 1 September 1866, p. 552.

[16] "Andy's Trip," *Harper's Weekly*, 27 October 1866, p.680.

[17] "King Andy," *Harper's Weekly*, 3 November 1866, p. 696.

[18] Fiona Deans Halloran, *Thomas Nast—The Father of Modern Cartoons* (Chapel Hill: University of North Carolina Press, 2012), 97.

[19] "Shall the President Be Impeached?" *Harper's Weekly*, 3 November 1866, p. 690.

20 "Wendell Phillips Demanding the Impeachment of the President," *Daily Columbus Enquirer,* 2 October 1866, p. 2.

21 "Impeachment of the President," *Daily Columbus Enquirer,* 20 September 1866, p. 2; "The Impeachment of the President," *Daily Columbus Enquirer,* 4 October 1866, p.2; "Impeachment of the President," *Baltimore Sun,* 11 October 1866, p.2.

22 Oscar Sherwin, *Prophet of Liberty—The Life of Wendell Phillips* (New York: Bookman Associates, 1958), 560.

23 "Impeachment," *New York Times,* 4 January 1867, p. 1; "The Impeachment Fiasco," *Daily National Intelligencer,* 8 January 1867, p.2; David O. Stewart, *Impeached—The Trial of President Andrew Johnson and the Fight for Lincoln's Legacy* (New York: Simon & Schuster, 2009), 74-75, 83.

24 No title, *Springfield Daily Republican,* 28 June 1867, p. 2; "Mr. Johnson's Two Pilgrimages," *New York Herald,* 1 July 1867, p 4; "The Presidential Excursion," *Springfield Daily Republican,* 26 June 1867, p. 4.

25 Paul H. Bergeron, *Papers of Andrew Johnson, Volume 12, February-August 1867* (Knoxville: University of Tennessee Press, 1995), 453-56.

26 Andrew Johnson to Edwin Stanton, 5 August 1867, Andrew Johnson, Reel 28; William Marvel, *Lincoln;s Autocrat—The Life of Edwin Stanton* (Chapel Hill: University of North Carolina Press, 2015), 426-28.

27 Edwin Stanton to Andrew Johnson, 5 August 1867, Andrew Johnson Papers, Reel 28; Walter Stahr, *Stanton—Lincoln's War Secretary* (New York: Simon & Schuster, 2017), 494-95.

28 Ulysses S. Grant to Andrew Johnson, 1 August 1867, Ulysses S. Grant Papers, Reel 21.

29 "The Political Situation," *Daily National Intelligencer,* 6 September 1867, p. 1; "Schuyler Colfax's Views on Impeachment and the Duty

of Congress," *Daily National Intelligencer*, 3 October 1867, p.1; "The Conspiracy at Washington," *Atlantic Monthly*, November 1867, 633-38.

[30] "Washington," *New York Herald*, 15 January 1868, p.8; "Interview with the President," *Daily National Intelligencer*, 17 January 1868, p.2; Stewart, *Impeached*, 120.

[31] Ulysses S. Grant to Andrew Johnson, 28 January 1868, Andrew Johnson Papers, Reel 31; Ron Chernow, *Grant* (New York: Penguin Press, 2017), 605-06.

[32] "Washington," *New York Times*, 22 February 1868, p.1; Brenda Wineapple, *The Impeachers—The Trial of Andrew Johnson and the Dream of a Just Nation* (New York: Random House, 2019), 249-52.

[33] Paul H. Bergeron, *Papers of Andrew Johnson, Volume 13, September 1867-March 1868* (Knoxville: University of Tennessee Press, 1996), 629-39.

[34] Ibid.

[35] *Trial of Andrew Johnson, Volume I* (Washington: Government Printing Office, 1868), 6-10; Wineapple, *The Impeachers*, 295-97.

[36] *Trial of Andrew Johnson, Volume I*, 87-90.

[37] Joseph Dear, a reporter for the *Chicago Republican*, under questioning by Attorney General Henry Stanbery, asserted that any journalist could accurately capture up to 30 words of a likely 200 words per minute spoken by a rapid speaker. Acknowledging that Johnson was, indeed, a rapid speaker, Dear said a transcription of his remarks would likely be "about seven times as long" as that of a speaker who spoke less quickly. Asked Stanbery: "Then the long-hand writer who is reporting will get, in the case of a rapid speaker, one word in seven?" Dear admitted it was so. *Trial of Andrew Johnson*, 345-51.

38 "The Impeachment Trial," *Springfield Daily Republican*, 23 April 1868, p.2; "Impeachment," *Baltimore American*, 24 April 1868, p.1; Wineapple, *The Impeachers*, 322-24.

39 *Trial of Andrew Johnson*, 119-20.

40 Ibid., 142.

Chapter Ten Footnotes

1 John Y. Simon, *Papers of Ulysses S. Grant, Volume 18: October 1, 1867-June 30, 1868* (Carbondale: Southern Illinois University Press, 1991), 263-65.

2 Paul H. Bergeron, *Papers of Andrew Johnson, Volume 14, April-August 1868* (Knoxville: University of Tennessee Press, 1997), 7-16; "White House Conversations," *Nashville Union and American*, 8 April 1868, p. 2.

3 Michael P. Riccards, *The Ferocious Engine of Democracy—A History of the American Presidency* (Lanham: Madison Books, 1995), 298; Bergeron, *Papers of Andrew Johnson, Volume 14*, 303-05.

4 Bergeron, *Papers of Andrew Johnson, Volume 14*, 204-05.

5 Ibid., 271-72.

6 Ibid., 303-05.

7 Charles H. Coleman, *The Election of 1868—The Democratic Effort to Regain Control* (New York: Octagon Books, 1971), 166; "By the President of the United States," *National Republican*, 4 July 181, p.2.

8 *Official Proceedings of the National Democratic Convention, Held at New York, July 4-9, 1868* (Boston: Rockwell & Rollins, 1868), 70, 72; Bergeron, *Papers of Andrew Johnson, Volume 13*, 307-08.

[9]   Coleman, *Election of 1868*, 279; "The Campaign," *Monmouth Inquirer*, 23 July 1868, p.2.

[10]   Bergeron, *Papers of Andrew Johnson, Volume 14*, 332-33.

[11]   Paul H. Bergeron, *Papers of Andrew Johnson, Volume 15, September 1868-April 1869* (Knoxville: University of Tennessee Press, 1999), 164; Coleman, *Election of 1868*, 282.

[12]   Bergeron, *Papers of Andrew Johnson, Volume 15*, 185.

[13]   Lately Thomas, *The First President Johnson—The Three Lives of the Seventeenth President of the United States of America* (New York: William Morrow & Company, 1968), 616.

[14]   That opinions on anything Johnson had to say by late 1868 were hardened was seen in an editorial in the *Chicago Tribune*, which remarked: "The effrontery which has characterized all of Andrew Johnson's previous messages and official papers has not deserted him, but is as strongly marked in this, his last annual message, as it is in any of its predecessors." Bergeron, *Papers of Andrew Johnson, Volume 15*, 281-306; "The President's Message," *Chicago Tribune*, 10 December 1868, p.2.

[15]   Lynda Lasswell Crist, *Papers of Jefferson Davis, Volume 12, June 1865-December 1870* (Baton Rouge: Louisiana State University Press, 2008), 325-327, 341-43.

[16]   Ibid., 245.

[17]   Bergeron, *Papers of Andrew Johnson, Volume 15*, 415-16; "Georgetown College Cadets," *Baltimore Sun*, 3 February 1869, p.4.

[18]   Bergeron, *Papers of Andrew Johnson, Volume 15*, 490-95; "General Grant and the Term of Office," *New York Times*, 3 January 1869, p. 3.

[19] Bergeron, *Papers of Andrew Johnson, Volume 15*, 505-15; "Washington," *New York Herald*, 3 March 1869, p.3.

[20] In introducing the ex-president at the dinner, Baltimore Mayor Robert Banks, a long-time Johnson supporter, provided evidence of lingering resentment over the Radical Republican attempt to remove Johnson from office, predicting that "History will vindicate his fame and record an impeachment of his impeachers." Bergeron, *Papers of Andrew Johnson, Volume 15*, 26-27; "Ex-President Johnson," *Baltimore Sun*, 121 March 1869, p.1.

[21] Garland was part of the somewhat disorganized band of Johnson supporters who unsuccessfully argued his cause at the 1868 Democratic convention. Bergeron, *Papers of Andrew Johnson, Volume 15*, 532-34; Bergeron, *Papers of Andrew Johnson, Volume 14*, 342-44.

[22] Bergeron, *Papers of Andrew Johnson, Volume 15*, 538-43.

[23] Paul H. Bergeron, *Papers of Andrew Johnson, Volume 16, May 1868-July 1875* (Knoxville: University of Tennessee Press, 2000), 39-45; "Washington," *New York Herald*, 28 June 1869, p.10.

[24] Ibid.

[25] Bergeron, *Papers of Andrew Johnson, Volume 16*, 331-38.

[26] Ibid., 430-31.

[27] Ibid., 471-75.

[28] Ibid., 475-91; "The National Capital," *Philadelphia Inquirer*, 12 November 1873, p.1; Elizabeth D. Leonard, *Lincoln's Forgotten Ally—Judge Advocate General Joseph Holt of Kentucky* (Chapel Hill: University of North Carolina Press, 2011), 297.

[29] "Johnson vs. Holt," *Atlanta Constitution*, 7 December 1873, p.4; "The Unquiet Ghost," *Brooklyn Daily Eagle*, 14 November 1873, p.2.

[30] Hans L. Trefousse, *Andrew Johnson—A Biography* (Newtown: American Political Biography Press, 1989), 369; Bergeron, *Papers of Andrew Johnson, Volume 6*, 576-77.

[31] Riccards, *Ferocious Engine of Democracy*, 307.

[32] Bergeron, *Papers of Andrew Johnson, Volume 16*, 586-600.

[33] Trefousse, *Andrew Johnson*, 371-72.

[34] Gideon Welles to Andrew Johnson, 27 January 1875, Andrew Johnson Papers, Reel 38.

[35] Bergeron, *Papers of Andrew Johnson, Volume 16*, 565.

[36] F.A. Howe to Andrew Johnson, 28 January 1875, Andrew Johnson Papers, Reel 38.

[37] Bergeron, *Papers of Andrew Johnson, Volume 16*, 695.

[38] "I Am Sick Again!" *New York Herald*, 30 January 1875, p.4.

[39] John Y. Simon, *Papers of Ulysses S. Grant, Volume 26, 1875* (Carbondale: Southern Illinois University Press, 2003), 468-69.

[40] "The Presidential Succession," *Owensboro Monitor*, 17 February 1875, p. 1. Reprint of article that had originally appeared in the *Cincinnati Commercial*.

[41] "Andrew Johnson," *St. Louis Republican*, 27 January 1875, p.4.

Chapter Eleven Footnotes

[1] Paul H. Bergeron, *Papers of Andrew Johnson, Volume 16, May 1869-July 1875* (Knoxville: University of Tennessee Press, 2000), 71-13; "The New Senators," *New York Herald*, 8 March 1875, p.5.

[2]   Referencing Johnson's return to power after his strong of political defeats, Weed also remarked that Jonson had entered a retirement "from which no one would suppose he would emerge. Nor could any common man have dug himself out of a pit so deep and dark as that into which he had fallen." "Thurlow Weed on Andrew Johnson," *New York Tribune,* 30 January 1875, p.6.

[3]   Bergeron, *Papers of Andrew Johnson, Volume 16,* 706-10; "Andrew Johnson's Policy," *New York Tribune,* 8 March 1875, p.1.

[4]   "The New Senators," *New York Herald,* 8 March 1875, p. 1.

[5]   Lately Thomas, *The First President Johnson—The Three Lives of the Seventeenth President of the United States of America* (New York: William Morrow & Company, 1968), 631.

[6]   Ron Chernow, *Grant* (New York: Penguin Press, 2017), 761.

[7]   Chernow, *Grant,* 761; John Y. Simon, *Papers of Ulysses S. Grant, Volume 25: 1874* (Carbondale: Southern Illinois University Press, 2003), 313-14.

[8]   John Y. Simon, *Papers of Ulysses S. Grant, Volume 26: 1875* (Carbondale: Southern Illinois University Press, 2003), 3-16.

[9]   Bergeron, *Papers of Andrew Johnson, Volume 16,* 713-46.

[10]   *Congressional Record—Volume 14, Part I* (Washington: Government Printing Office, 1875), 127-28.

[11]   "Washington," *Chicago Tribune,* 33 March 1875, p. 4.

[12]   "Andrew Johnson's Speech," *New York Herald,* 23 March 1875, p.1; "Andrew Johnson's Speech," *San Francisco Examiner,* 23 March 1875, p.2.

[13]   "Senator Johnson's Speech," *Brooklyn Daily Eagle,* 23 March 1875, p.2.

[14] Bergeron, *Papers of Andrew Johnson, Volume 16,* 750.

Chapter Twelve Footnotes

[1] Andrew Johnson to Martha Patterson, 4 April 1875, Andrew Johnson Papers, Reel 39.

[2] Paul H. Bergeron, *Papers of Andrew Johnson, Volume 16* (Knoxville: University Press of Tennessee, 2000), 753-55.

[3] Ibid., 756.

[4] Bergeron, *Papers of Andrew Johnson, Volume 16,* 760-61; Hans L. Trefousse, *Andrew Johnson—A Biography* (Newtown: American Political Biography Press, 2009), 375.

[5] Trefousse, *Andrew Johnson,* 375-76; Lately Thomas, *The First President Johnson—The Three Lives of the Seventeenth President of the United States of America* (New York: William Morrow & Company, 1968), 633-34; George F. Milton, *The Age of Hate: Andrew Johnson and the Radicals* (New York: Coward, McCann Publishers, 1930), 673.

[6] John Y. Simon, *Papers of Ulysses S. Grant, Volume 26: 1875* (Carbondale: Southern Illinois University Press, 2003), 342.

[7] Ibid.

[8] Bergeron, *Papers of Andrew Johnson, Volume 16,* 773-74.

[9] *Message of Jas. D. Porter, Governor of Tennessee, to the Fortieth General Assembly for the State of Tennessee* (Nashville: Travel, Eastman & Howell Publishers, 1877), 21.

[10] Newspaper accounts of Johnson's life in the days after his death were uneven, with some, such as the *Arkansas Gazette*, praising his efforts to protect the South from the worst excesses of Radical Republican

administration, while the *New York Times,* lauded his very real bravery during the Civil War, standing up to Confederates, many of whom desired nothing less than seeing him dead. But it was the *Macon Weekly Telegraph* that had one of the most unconventional takes on Johnson's life and death, noting: "It was the fierce encounter with personal and political opposition—relentless and unceasing moral and mental warfare—the inflammatory and exhausting toils and struggles of the hustings—the forum—and of an uneasy and belligerent official life, which left their marks on his cerebral and nervous organization and culminated in his sudden death." This observation is obviously not without merit. But taking in the whole of a driven, combative personality, it's possible that Johnson's "fierce encounter with personal and political opposition" is the precise component that sustained him. Those encounters represented life itself, a fire shrouding both his triumphs and defeats. Trefousse, *Andrew Johnson,* 377-78; "Andrew Johnson Dead," *New York Times,* 1 August 1875, p.1; "Death of Andrew Johnson," *Macon Weekly Telegraph,* 3 August 1875, p.6; Bergeron, *Papers of Andrew Johnson, Volume 16,* 779.

INDEX